Digisprudence

Future Law

Series Editors: Burkhard Schafer and Edina Harbinja

Books in the series are critical and topic-led, reflecting the global jurisdiction of technology and culture interacting with law. Each title responds to cutting-edge debates in the field where technology interacts with culture to challenge the ability of law to react to frequently unprecedented scenarios.

Series Editors

Burkhard Schafer is Professor of Computational Legal Theory at the University of Edinburgh
Edina Harbinja is Senior Lecturer in Media/Privacy Law at Aston University

Available or forthcoming titles

Buying Your Self on the Internet: Wrap Contracts and Personal Genomics
Andelka M Phillips

Digisprudence: Code as Law Rebooted
Laurence E Diver

Future Law: Emerging Technology, Regulation and Ethics
Lilian Edwards, Burkhard Schafer and Edina Harbinja (eds)

Technology, Innovation and Access to Justice: Dialogues on the Future of Law
Siddharth Peter de Souza and Maximilian Spohr (eds)

edinburghuniversitypress.com/series/fl

Digisprudence

Code as Law Rebooted

Laurence E Diver

EDINBURGH
University Press

For my late parents,
Beatrix and Brian

Edinburgh University Press is one of the leading university presses in the UK. We publish academic books and journals in our selected subject areas across the humanities and social sciences, combining cutting-edge scholarship with high editorial and production values to produce academic works of lasting importance. For more information visit our website: edinburghuniversitypress.com

We are committed to making research available to a wide audience and are pleased to be publishing an Open Access ebook edition of this title.

Edinburgh University Press Ltd
The Tun – Holyrood Road
12(2f) Jackson's Entry
Edinburgh EH8 8PJ

First published in hardback by Edinburgh University Press 2022

Typeset in 11/13pt Adobe Garamond Pro
by Manila Typesetting Company, and
printed and bound by CPI Group (UK) Ltd,
Croydon, CR0 4YY

A CIP record for this book is available from the British Library

ISBN 978 1 4744 8532 6 (hardback)
ISBN 978 1 4744 8533 3 (paperback)
ISBN 978 1 4744 8534 0 (webready PDF)
ISBN 978 1 4744 8535 7 (epub)

This project has received funding from the European Research Council (ERC) under the European Union's Horizon 2020 research and innovation programme (grant agreement No 788734).

Contents

Expanded Table of Contents

Illustrations

Figures

Tables

Acknowledgements

I would like to thank those who have helped me in many ways, large and small, in the development of this book and the doctoral work on which it is based. I owe a debt to Burkhard Schafer for his support on all matters academic, stretching back to my stint as his research assistant during the LLM programme at Edinburgh, and of course for his supervision of my doctoral work. Discussions with and comments from many people from various quarters have helped develop this text in uncountable ways, for which I am hugely grateful: my thanks in particular to Irina Baraliuc, Roger Brownsword, Tatiana Duarte, Gianmarco Gori, Mireille Hildebrandt, Emilie van den Hoven, Daithí Mac Síthigh, Paulus Meessen, Claudio Michelon, Judith Rauhofer, Manuel Sabin, and Burkhard Schafer. I also want to thank my colleagues – indeed, friends – in and around the project 'Counting as a Human Being in the Era of Computational Law' (COHUBICOL), who over the past couple of years have helped me in lots of ways to get to this point, especially so given the many challenges of the COVID-19 pandemic. A particular thank you must also go to Mireille Hildebrandt, for the opportunity to carry on working in this fascinating and crucially important field. Lastly, but of course not least, thank you to Hannah for your support and kindness, and for your cheerful acceptance of all this.

1

Introduction

The computer programmer, however, is a creator of universes for which he alone is the lawgiver . . . No playwright, no stage director, no emperor, however powerful, has ever exercised such absolute authority to arrange a stage or a field of battle and to command such unswervingly dutiful actors or troops.[1]

The focus of this book is at the under-explored intersection between law and design. The theory I am advancing is about how the behaviour-shaping rules embodied in software code can be designed in a legitimate way. My central claim is this: those who exercise the power to shape the behaviour of citizens in a democracy ought to do so legitimately, which implies both minimal standards for and limits to such exercises of power. We expect this of laws, so why not of code? Software is everywhere, touching and structuring almost every aspect of our lives in ways that are often more effective and direct than what law can, or indeed ought to attempt to, achieve. Despite this, code is subjected to very little scrutiny as to whether or not this is acceptable, both in individual cases and as a whole. This book challenges that status quo, arguing that code-based norms ought to be subject to tests of their legitimacy, and providing concrete ways to achieve this. In a democratic society, the regulation of citizens' behaviour – of whatever kind and from whatever source – ought to meet minimal standards of legitimacy to be acceptable. Code that is not legitimate should not be released – full stop – and we should not be shy about asserting this. This is especially true in a world where myriad troubles are contributed to by code, developed within an economic orthodoxy that is less concerned with curbing abuses of design power than it is with facilitating 'innovation'.[2]

---

[1] J Weizenbaum, *Computer Power and Human Reason: From Judgment to Calculation* (Freeman 1976) 115.

[2] R von Schomberg, 'A vision of responsible research and innovation' in R Owen, J Bessant and M Heintz (eds), *Responsible Innovation* (John Wiley & Sons 2013) 58; K O'Hara and

I

Questioning the legitimacy of code is necessarily an ex ante concern – that is, it must be done at design time, before the code operates in the world. This kind of analysis therefore requires an internal focus on the production of code, rather than just its operation, viewed externally. If lawyers are properly to grapple with the realities of how code regulates, we must embrace an analytical shift that takes into account not just its effects but also the practical realities of its production. This means we must consider the processes and tools that make up the 'legislature' where code is 'enacted', including software development methodologies and the integrated development environments (IDEs) where the text of code is actually written.[3] They are the point at which 'constitutional' protections can be built into the very fabric of the code.

Why 'digisprudence'? As a portmanteau of 'digital' and 'jurisprudence', it mirrors the concept of *legisprudence*, according to which the creation of legislative rules should be seen not as a purely political concern, 'fenced off' from the view of the jurist, but instead as an appropriate subject of both jurisprudential analysis and tests of legitimacy.[4] As with legislative norms, if code regulates behaviour then its behaviour-enabling and behaviour-constraining 'rules' ought also to be subject to such scrutiny. Digisprudence is thus to software rules as legisprudence is to legal rules: it asks how they are created, and whether or not they meet specific formal standards that can render them legitimate, whatever their 'substantive' purpose might be. This raises the practical question: can the standards that make a legal rule legitimate be imported into the realm of design to make a computational rule legitimate? My answer is that they can, and they must. This is a significant challenge that requires novel theoretical and practical translations between domains, but in the face of the ever-greater presence in our lives of potentially illegitimate code, it is one that must be faced sooner or later.

1.1 The Structure of the Argument

To tackle the various elements of this challenge, the book is organised in a roughly dialectical structure. Part I problematises code as a regulator, first conceptualising its regulative characteristics in terms of design theory and the philosophy of technology (Chapter 2) before conceptualising why, from a legal-philosophical perspective, those characteristics are problematic (Chapter 3). From that analysis I posit the notion of *computational legalism*,

---

M Hildebrandt, 'Between the editors' in M Hildebrandt and K O'Hara (eds), *Life and the Law in the Era of Data-Driven Agency* (Edward Elgar Publishing 2020) 37–40.

[3] These will be discussed in more detail in Chapter 7.

[4] L Wintgens, 'Rationality in legislation – legal theory as legisprudence: An introduction' in *Legisprudence: A New Theoretical Approach to Legislation* (Hart 2002) 2.

an extreme species of unreflective rule-following that code can so easily impose upon citizens. Part II sets out existing literature on what constitutes legitimate rule-making, both from a legal perspective (Chapter 4) and in terms of what standards might render code an acceptable form of regulation (Chapter 5). Following that analysis we can appreciate first what formal standards rules ought to exhibit to be deemed legitimate, and second what is absent from the current literature on 'code as law' that deals with this point, the lack of analysis of code production being the primary issue. Finally, the synthesis of the book comes in Part III, where I propose a framework of design standards (the *digisprudential affordances* set out in Chapter 6) that can be used to critique and guide the production of digital artefacts such that they are formally legitimate, whatever their intended use or commercial purpose might be. Throughout that discussion I consider the implications of digisprudence for contemporary technologies, in particular (but not limited to) blockchain applications and the Internet of Things. The framework set out in Chapter 6 is complemented by a discussion in Chapter 7 of various ways in which those standards might be facilitated in a guiding, 'constitutional' manner by the tools and processes of the design environment, from IDEs to development paradigms to programming languages themselves.

In that vein, I take a pragmatic view of code, asking what it in fact does, and how it is in fact made (indeed, the genesis of this study lies in my own experience as a web developer in a small design firm). By looking directly at the processes of code production, they might lose some of their mystique, and we as lawyers might in turn be empowered to ask some difficult but necessary questions.

Speaking of pragmatism and empowerment, I use 'designer' throughout as shorthand for all those involved in the production of code, which will include graphic designers, requirements engineers, programmers, testers, et cetera. I also refer throughout to the citizen as an 'end-user', that being the term often used in technical communities for those who are at the receiving end of the code norms I am concerned with. The term also draws attention to the citizen's position at the *end* of the product design process, and her relative lack of agency in shaping its output.[5] One could interpret this as a somewhat defeatist perspective, but in acknowledging the diminished position of the citizen there is contained a seed of hope: 'end' implies a middle and a beginning – points at which things might be done differently, and better. That is precisely the goal of digisprudence.

---

[5] S Gürses and J van Hoboken, 'Privacy after the agile turn' in E Selinger, J Polonetsky and O Tene (eds), *The Cambridge Handbook of Consumer Privacy* (Cambridge University Press 2018) 581.

1.2 Rebooting 'Code as Law'

Asscher frames the starting point of the enquiry like this:

> Code can present constraints on human behaviour that can be compared
> with constraints by traditional laws. We have argued that even though code
> is not law, in some instances it can be useful to ask the same questions about
> code regulation as we do about traditional regulation. Code as law must be
> assessed by looking at the results of regulation in terms of freedom and indi-
> vidual autonomy and compared to the balance struck by traditional law.[6]

Code is like institutional law in that it possesses normative force, but is also
different from it in fundamental ways. Code is like legislation, in that it is
created to achieve some purposive end; it is 'enacted'. Code is capable of
violating rights, whilst simultaneously resisting the aspirations and oversight
of the rule of law. And finally, there are two pivotal moments at which assessments of code can be made: ex ante at the point of production, or ex post at
the point of operation. Each of these elements plays an important role in the
argument I am presenting, which runs as follows.

When commercial enterprises produce the software code of digital artefacts, they necessarily create alternative normative orders that can replace
institutional law as a primary source of behavioural regulation. Importantly,
the private commercial contexts within which this code is created are not subject to the legitimising formal and procedural standards of law-making found
in constitutional democracies. This means that, in the move from public to
private rule-making, the resulting normative force of that code on behaviour
risks being illegitimate, whether or not this is intended.[7] As the quote above
suggests, the question then arises of whether formal standards of law-making
might be imported into the *sui generis* 'legislature' of the commercial design
environment, in order to ensure that the code produced there is legitimate.

My purpose in framing code in terms of legal legitimacy derives from
the point, made above, that it can so readily augment and even supplant law
as a regulator. Those who create code, whose work is shielded by the private
context of its production, ought to wield the power they hold legitimately.[8]
If notionally sovereign legislatures are bound by constitutions so that they

---

[6] L Asscher, '"Code" as law: Using Fuller to assess code rules' in E Dommering and L Asscher
(eds), *Coding Regulation: Essays on the Normative Role of Information Technology* (TMC Asser
Press 2006) 86.

[7] E Bayamlıoğlu and R Leenes, 'The "rule of law" implications of data-driven decision-
making: A techno-regulatory perspective' (2018) *Law, Innovation and Technology* 1, 12.

[8] K Yeung, 'Why worry about decision-making by machine?' in K Yeung and M Lodge (eds),
Algorithmic Regulation (Oxford University Press 2019) 38 *et seq.*

cannot arbitrarily impose regulations on citizens' behaviour, then neither should this be possible for private enterprise, especially given the characteristics of code that render it more problematic to comprehend and to control than is text-based legislation, both qualitatively and quantitatively. We will see below and in Part I what those characteristics are and what effects they have.

In this context, the term 'code' connects of course to Lessig's seminal work on 'code as law'.[9] His original argument was that individuals, represented by the 'pathetic dot', are regulated not just by law, but also by three further regulatory 'modalities', namely social norms, the market, and architecture. In 'cyberspace', architecture is constituted by software, or code, as opposed to the physical architecture of the 'real' world. The 'architects' of that code therefore have significant power in cyberspace, and because of the greater instrumental potency of code than the other modalities to shape what is and is not possible in that 'place', those architects therefore have disproportionate power within the digital realm. As Lessig puts it, '[a]rchitecture is a kind of law: it determines what people can and cannot do. When commercial interests determine the architecture, they create a kind of privatized law.'[10] Given the power of code to define the rules of behaviour in cyberspace, and given the inherent flexibility of designers to choose those rules, his fear was that they might be captured by state interests mandating backdoors and other measures antagonistic to civil liberties. His general prescription to avoid this was a culture of transparency, including actual transparency, in the form of open source code.[11]

The focus on transparency betrays a dependency on classic-liberal market orthodoxy that seems to obscure both the processes of code production and its ultimate embeddedness within society. The myriad effects of code – possibly good, possibly bad, but certainly never neutral[12] – stretch far beyond the relationship between the classical *homo economicus* and the 'trader' who sells or licenses the code. To fully appreciate this requires consideration of complementary insights deriving from scholarly fields including the philosophy of technology and science and technology studies (STS).[13] The Lessigian

---

[9] L Lessig, *Code: Version 2.0* (Basic Books 2006) *passim*.

[10] Ibid. 77.

[11] Ibid. chapter 5.

[12] M Kranzberg, 'Technology and history: "Kranzberg's Laws"' (1986) 27 *Technology and Culture* 544, 545–6.

[13] As Cohen suggests, without the latter 'one cannot explain how code regulates'. See JE Cohen, *Configuring the Networked Self: Law, Code, and the Play of Everyday Practice* (Yale University Press 2012) 27 *et passim*. See also V Mayer-Schönberger, 'Demystifying Lessig' (2008) *Wisconsin Law Review* 713.

framework does not include such perspectives, nor does it include the intimately connected topic of design practice – how code is actually made.

Lessig's analysis was extremely valuable in opening legal eyes to the potential roles played by technology in regulating individual behaviour, but it was skewed towards a particular view of law and was thus limited in the scope of normative effects and forms of technology it encompassed. By seeking to ensure that code provide market signals through transparency, Lessig's prescriptions can be boiled down to a call for this meta-technology (code) to be adapted to fit a particular market-oriented orthodoxy, driven by an instrumental view of regulation rather than a concern for legal protection and human flourishing. The assumption was that that economic orthodoxy was and is a given, this assumption in turn obscuring the deeper level to which Lessig's own mode of analysis might be extended – the nature of law and the rule of law as the necessary substrate for *any* kind of government and economic system within a constitutional state. Such a view would implicate a broader set of technologies whose mediations in turn affect (and effect) the relationships between the multifarious actors in society.[14]

Lessig's analysis has towered over the 'cyberlaw' landscape for over two decades, and as welcome as it has been in raising important questions about the nature of the relationship between law and code, there is now a need to reframe the topic away from his original assumptions. We are seeing no let-up in the deployment of code-driven systems, both as regulatory tools *per se* and as the building blocks of what is sometimes called the 'onlife'. There is little reason to suppose that this trend will reverse or even decelerate, and so the question is how best to respond. In that vein, in recent years we have seen a number of initiatives aimed at regulating (big) technology, from the European Commission's new proposed Regulations on artificial intelligence and the digital single market,[15] to the United States' proposed Deceptive Experiences To Online Users Reduction (DETOUR) Act, aimed at regulating 'dark patterns'

---

[14] For a pivotal discussion in this vein, see M Hildebrandt, *Smart Technologies and the End(s) of Law: Novel Entanglements of Law and Technology* (Edward Elgar Publishing 2015).

[15] The draft of the former is already creating waves in industry and academia. See European Commission, 'Proposal for a Regulation on a European approach for Artificial Intelligence' (European Commission, 2021) <https://digital-strategy.ec.europa.eu/en/library/proposal-regulation-european-approach-artificial-intelligence> last accessed 23 April 2021. This complements the Commission's two digital single market Regulations – the Digital Services Act and the Digital Markets Act – which are aimed at digital platforms and which will update the E-Commerce Directive (2000/31/EC). See European Commission, 'Shaping Europe's digital future' (European Commission) <https://digital-strategy.ec.europa.eu/en> last accessed 23 April 2021.

in digital product design,[16] to the EU General Data Protection Regulation (GDPR), whose reshaping of the digital landscape is evolving day by day.

Although my interest here is complementary to these sectoral responses, in some crucial respects my focus lies behind or before them. The goal here is to ask a fundamental question about the legitimacy of regulative code in the onlife, which means revisiting the notion of 'code as law' with a fresh willingness to embrace the insights of those other scholarly fields concerned with technology and its effects in the world. Pursuing new intellectual directions can be daunting, especially across disciplinary boundaries, but it can also be hugely valuable and, in this context at least, it is essential.

The nature of code necessarily implies a kind of temporal front-loading: code is designed and implemented before it is out in the world, its effects 'out there' being predetermined, at least in broad structure if not always in every atomic detail. This means we must engage directly with the practices of those who build it, understanding them from an internal perspective insofar as that is necessary to transplant our lawyerly critiques from the anodyne ex post into the incisive ex ante.

Lawyers cannot rely solely on calls for 'greater regulation', especially if the latter is uninformed by knowledge of or appreciation for design practice and the rich philosophical discussions of those things they are arguing ought to be regulated. Bringing all this together will be a crucial challenge for the twenty-first century, and so the time is ripe for a reboot of this twenty-year-old debate, clearing some of the dusty files that have been cluttering our memory so that we can get a renewed appreciation of what the fundamental questions are and how we might start to answer them.

(a) Code and/or Data?

It is true to say that the literature has evolved somewhat since the 'code as law' concepts were first introduced by Reidenberg in his analysis of *lex informatica*.[17] The literature was initially concerned primarily with the regulation of the amorphous cyberspace as a location that is 'out there', that is the Internet as a platform and a 'place'. The discussion has since evolved to consider on the one hand the code of individual and/or networked applications, and on the other code that facilitates data-driven services based on machine learning. Both forms of code are 'algorithmic', but the distinction between the two is

---

[16] See S.1084 – 116th Congress (2019–2020): Deceptive Experiences To Online Users Reduction (DETOUR) Act (4 September 2019) <https://www.congress.gov/bill/116th-congress/senate-bill/1084> last accessed 4 March 2021. I discuss dark patterns in Chapter 2.

[17] JR Reidenberg, 'Lex informatica: The formulation of information policy rules through technology' (1997) 76 *Texas Law Review* 553.

an important one,[18] albeit that they will often now be complementary, with the outputs of data-driven software feeding into the ordering imposed by code-driven architectures.

Broadly speaking, modern data-driven applications are concerned with the use of machine learning algorithms and 'big data' to facilitate automated classification and decision-making. Such systems are based on the processing of vast, often contingent datasets using mathematical models – compressed representations of the so-called 'ground truth' that the model is intended to identify, or 'predict', in any new data that it is provided with. By identifying a sufficiently similar pattern in that new data, such models can assist in classifying unforeseen examples, a function that has been employed across a wide range of applications, from distinguishing pictures of dogs to classifying offenders according to whether or not they are likely to reoffend.[19] Faith in the existence of underlying patterns in data that accurately represent human truths, and the ability of mathematical models to identify those patterns, has led to the use of machine learning in domains, including the law, where one might have thought mathematical reduction was anathema;[20] the unintelligibility of machine learning models, even to experts,[21] has not deterred some of

---

[18] M Hildebrandt, 'Algorithmic regulation and the rule of law' (2018) 376 *Philosophical Transactions of the Royal Society A* 20170355, 2–4.

[19] On the latter, see the influential J Angwin et al., 'Machine bias' *ProPublica* (23 May 2016) <https://www.propublica.org/article/machine-bias-risk-assessments-in-criminal-sentencing> last accessed 4 March 2021. The dog example highlights one of the fundamental problems at the centre of machine learning applications: MT Ribeiro, S Singh and C Guestrin, '"Why should I trust you?": Explaining the predictions of any classifier' (2016) arXiv:1602.04938 [cs, stat] <http://arxiv.org/abs/1602.04938> last accessed 4 March 2021. While the misidentification of a husky as a wolf might at first blush seem a rather insignificant 'mistake', the implications are profound for other contexts where the same or similar machine learning approaches are used, for example credit scoring, facial recognition, and the aforementioned prediction of recidivism (to name only a few examples). The literature on these implications is large and growing all the time; see for example J Buolamwini and T Gebru, 'Gender shades: Intersectional accuracy disparities in commercial gender classification' (2018) 81 *Proceedings of Machine Learning Research* 1; SU Noble, *Algorithms of Oppression: How Search Engines Reinforce Racism* (New York University Press 2018); C O'Neil, *Weapons of Math Destruction: How Big Data Increases Inequality and Threatens Democracy* (Crown 2016).

[20] D McQuillan, 'Data science as machinic neoplatonism' (2018) 31 *Philosophy & Technology* 253. For various examples in the legal domain, see for example MA Livermore and DN Rockmore (eds), *Law as Data: Computation, Text, and the Future of Legal Analysis* (SFI Press 2019).

[21] The literature on algorithmic opacity is significant. See for example E Bayamlıoğlu, 'On the possibility of normative contestation of automated data-driven decisions' in I Baraliuc et al. (eds), *Being Profiled: Cogitas Ergo Sum – 10 Years of Profiling the European Citizen*

a more computationalist bent from pursuing these applications, despite the many risks involved.

A contrast is sometimes drawn between the contingent mathematical algorithms of machine learning applications and the predetermined, logical 'if–then' structure of code-driven software. This may be a false dichotomy, given that data-driven applications are precisely that – applications – operating at a level above code and requiring its foundation for their very existence. The general-purpose computing infrastructure that gathers, transmits, and stores the data that machine learning algorithms process is ultimately based entirely on that general-purpose computing infrastructure, and the algorithms themselves are expressed in code. The issues raised by data-driven applications will in many cases be distinct from those that are purely code-based, but in many cases the implications for the mediated experience of the end-user will be the same, and will raise the same questions of legitimacy, even if the ways of answering those questions will differ in terms of design practice.[22]

As is common in the literature, I use 'code' interchangeably with 'software' and 'architecture', to refer generally to digital systems that have a regulating effect on action and behaviour. This applies whether or not the artefact in question is built around machine learning. Throughout the book, the term 'code' is intended to be contrasted with law as a competing regulator. In the later chapters, however, I do shift to consider code *per se* – its text, rather than the architectures that that text brings into being – as one crucial site of digisprudential enquiry.

(b) Regulation

'Regulation' in this context straddles two of the definitions identified by Black, namely (1) the promulgation of rules by government (posited laws and regulatory instruments), and (2) all mechanisms of social control affecting behaviour, of whatever kind from whatever source, whether intentional or not.[23] The phrase 'social control' in the second of these might be viewed as including 'technical control' or 'commercial control'. This notion of control is connected with the definition of 'normativity' that I adopt, which is to say any mechanism, legal or otherwise, through which action and behaviour are

---

(Amsterdam University Press 2018); J Burrell, 'How the machine "thinks": Understanding opacity in machine learning algorithms' (2016) 3 *Big Data & Society*.

[22] The question of affording transparency, for example, arises whether or not the application is code- or data-driven; the emphasis may change but the requirement does not. I discuss this in more detail in Chapter 6.

[23] J Black, 'Critical reflections on regulation' (2002) 27 *Australian Journal of Legal Philosophy* 1, 11.

enabled or constrained. As Goldoni puts it, 'code as law is normative in the sense that it regulates and guides human behaviour'.[24] Of course, the technological species of normativity is different from legal normativity in crucial ways,[25] which is precisely what makes the present analysis necessary. I set out those mechanisms in greater detail in Part I of the book.

(c) Legitimacy

By 'legitimacy', I refer to the idea that rules that govern behaviour ought to be created according to pre-existing standards that embody values of accountability, transparency, and contestability.[26] Despite a large literature on software as both a target and a conduit of regulation, the question of legitimacy is one that has received only minimal attention with regard to the normative standards to which the designers who create code might be held.[27] Very few scholars have considered the question directly, and the treatment so far has focused more on ex post assessments of code regulation (the effects of its operation in the world) rather than on ex ante normative standards (questioning how it was produced and whether formal standards have been met). Although the former are an important and necessary element of oversight, the characteristics of computational legalism make necessary an additional focus on the application of ex ante standards during the production process. The reasons for this are discussed below and in detail in Chapter 3.

The legal-theoretical analysis of legitimacy that I adopt builds in particular on Fuller's *internal morality of law* and Wintgens's *legisprudence*. The latter is less well-known, but provides us with a serious, historically grounded theoretical inroad into the formal qualities that legislative rules ought to have, a topic so often bracketed by legal theorists concerned mainly with adjudication. I briefly summarise both theories later in this introductory chapter, before returning to them in more detail later in the book. These ideas help in conceptualising the ex ante assessment of other forms of normative rule-making, my contention being that many of the factors that render

---

[24] M Goldoni, 'The politics of code as law: Toward input reasons' in J Reichel and AS Lind (eds), *Freedom of Expression, the Internet and Democracy* (Brill 2015) 119. This meaning is similar to the concept of 'governance' in the regulatory literature. See C Reed and A Murray, *Rethinking the Jurisprudence of Cyberspace* (Edward Elgar Publishing 2018) 140.

[25] See for example N MacCormick, *Institutions of Law: An Essay in Legal Theory* (Oxford University Press 2007) chapter 1. On the essential distinction between orthodox and technological normativity, see M Hildebrandt, 'Legal and technological normativity: More (and less) than twin sisters' (2008) 12 *Techné: Research in Philosophy and Technology* 169, 173–5.

[26] See for example J Waldron, 'Can there be a democratic jurisprudence?' (2009) 58 *Emory Law Journal* 675.

[27] Goldoni (n 24) 123–5.

legislative rules illegitimate according to those theories can also be found in privately ordered code as law. By adapting and importing their principles into the design process, the illegitimacies of computational legalism can thus be mitigated.

(d) Code is both More, and Less, than Law

One of the main criticisms of Lessig was that code is not law, and therefore the perceived attempt to equate them was in some sense fallacious. For my part I agree that they are not the same, but my conviction is that we cannot simply stop there – to dismiss code as being 'not law' is to blind oneself to the central importance of its role in structuring society and our individual interactions, and thus to the fundamental questions of legitimacy, legal and political, that this raises.

To be sure, there are indeed overlaps and 'structural homologies'[28] between code and law, but so too are there significant differences. Code instantiates law, legal effect, and constellations of legally relevant fact, and while code-based artefacts are themselves constituted to some extent by legal reality (contracts, intellectual property rights, etc.), the relationship is lopsided. There exists an inherent 'hermeneutic gap' between the legal norm printed on the page and its instantiation in the physical world via interpretation and behavioural change.[29] In the computational context, law is not nearly as powerful as we might suppose, because it is dependent upon the very medium it is attempting to regulate, and the immediacy and instrumental power of that medium and the 'sovereignty' of the designer in shaping its effects tip the balance against law as the 'apex' regulator. The written law is rendered 'a paper dragon in the age of the "digital tsunami"',[30] with the social and rhetorical power of legal fictions making way for the representationalism of 'digital virtuality', whereby reality is constituted by and through the machine.[31] Adjudication is thus collapsed into obedience,[32] since the rule in the code also represents reality for the end-user.

---

[28] C Vismann and M Krajewski, 'Computer juridisms' (2007) *Grey Room* 90, 92.

[29] A foundational discussion of this temporal gap in hermeneutics can be found in H-G Gadamer, *Truth and Method*, trans. J Weinsheimer and DG Marshall (Bloomsbury 2013) chapter 4. This ultimately translates into the affordance of delay, discussed in Part III.

[30] M Hildebrandt and B-J Koops, 'The challenges of ambient law and legal protection in the profiling era' (2010) 73 *The Modern Law Review* 428, 440.

[31] Vismann and Krajewski (n 28) 92.

[32] Z Bańkowski and B Schafer, 'Double-click justice: Legalism in the computer age' (2007) 1 *Legisprudence* 31, 48.

Fuller defines law widely as 'the enterprise of subjecting human conduct to the governance of rules'.[33] As Chapter 2 will demonstrate, the governing rules that code subjects human conduct to increasingly constitute the very 'terms and conditions of existence and action'.[34] They may not be rules as commonly understood,[35] but they are designed by humans with a purpose in mind, and should therefore be subject to scrutiny as to their legitimacy. The power to decide those purposes is significant:

> The quasi-sovereign power of the computer engineer's code stems from the ease by which posing, implementing, and applying a norm are achieved in technology compared with the cumbersome procedures that legal code must pass through. The swift effectiveness of a technological code, which cannot, when seen through legal eyes, appear as anything other than uncanny, renders any possible competition between law and computer pointless.[36]

Architectural constitutions supplant legal constitutions; code is not just law-like, rather it is both more, and less, than law. As Chapter 2 will demonstrate, it is more than law because of the instrumental power of design to constitute and regulate end-user action and behaviour. But it is simultaneously less than law because, as Chapter 3 explains, it lacks the normative mechanisms designed to keep its textually bound sister in check. This is what Hildebrandt points to when she says that 'technologies that are constitutive for [sic] our interactions may enforce compliance beyond anything that a written law can achieve'.[37] It is precisely because code is not law *per se*, but nevertheless has a power to regulate that is more direct and effective than that of law, that it is necessary to instantiate the sorts of constitutional protections I will be discussing. While code constitutions are not law under any orthodox definition, if we adopt a pluralist perspective[38] we can identify, through a comparison of the regulative aspects of institutional law and code, which of the checks and balances that we expect to be present in the former are absent from the latter.

---

[33] LL Fuller, *The Morality of Law* (Yale University Press 1977) *passim*.
[34] G Longford, 'Pedagogies of digital citizenship and the politics of code' (2005) 9 *Techné: Research in Philosophy and Technology* 68, 71.
[35] I discuss the question of code as rules in more detail later.
[36] Vismann and Krajewski (n 28) 93.
[37] Hildebrandt, 'Legal and technological normativity' (n 25) 178.
[38] MAC Dizon, 'From regulating technologies to governing society: Towards a plural, social and interactive conception of law' in HM Morgan and R Morris (eds), *Moving Forward: Tradition and Transformation* (Cambridge Scholars Publishing 2011). Dizon argues that '[w]hen Lessig uses his four modalities of control to describe the normative orders of cyberspace, he is in fact describing the condition of legal pluralism in the ICT field'.

Whereas traditional regulative norms derive their legitimacy from the institutions and traditions of the rule of law within constitutional democracy, code-based norms have no such necessary democratic provenance or oversight. Whereas legal normativity invites the citizen to comply (she always has the notional option to interpret the norm, contest it, or to ignore it entirely), technological normativity can make compliance a necessity, either in the form of imposing a response to a circumstance or by constituting at the outset all the courses of action that the end-user can possibly take.

The fact that code is not law *per se* is therefore no answer to the problem I am concerned with; as Fuller demonstrates in his discussion of the rules governing a college dormitory, law-systems exist in many contexts that have no explicit or implicit connection with the state[39] – what matters, at least for present purposes, is whether the subjection of human conduct to the governance of rules is legitimate or not. The materiality of that governance is, in the end, what matters: as Le Sueur suggests, 'we should treat "the app" (the computer programs that will produce individual decisions) as "the law" . . . It is this app, not the text of the legislation, that will regulate the legal relationship between citizen and state in automated decision-making.'[40] Precisely because of the supreme efficacy with which code achieves this regulation, it is imperative that the creators of private code are, like public law-makers, constrained by ex ante standards that ensure both legitimacy during operation and the possibility of ex post remediation. Whether or not these are in place is ultimately a question of design, and thus of production.

Design and Regulation

How is behaviour in practice enabled and constrained by code? Numerous concepts from design and the philosophy of technology can help us frame an answer to this question, in particular the notions of inscription, affordance, and technological mediation, each of which is discussed in more detail in Chapter 2. Inscription is the notion of embodying in the design of an artefact a particular 'story' that dictates what the end-user ought and ought not to do.[41] Many of these scripts are so embedded as to become second nature;

---

[39] Fuller (n 33) 125 *et seq.*

[40] A Le Sueur, 'Robot government: Automated decision-making and its implications for Parliament' in A Horne and A Le Sueur (eds), *Parliament: Legislation and Accountability* (Hart 2016) 201. Le Sueur's analysis concerns public administration, but his insight applies to private code too.

[41] M Akrich, 'The de-scription of technical objects' in WE Bijker and J Law (eds), *Shaping Technology/Building Society: Studies in Sociotechnical Change* (MIT Press 1992) 208; B Latour, 'The Berlin key or how to do words with things' in P Graves-Brown (ed.), *Matter, Materiality and Modern Culture* (Routledge 2000).

if you are reading this electronically, for example, consider how easily you 'tapped' or 'double-clicked' the 'icon' to 'open' the 'file'. However natural or 'ready to hand' for us these sorts of scripted concepts and processes might have become, they are none of them given; each has to whatever extent been purposively designed.[42] Of course, this idea of channelling or 'tunnelling'[43] behaviour can be used for different ends, but whatever the choices made by the designer, these invariably mean other possibilities are left out that might otherwise have been built. What is left in will constitute the affordances of the artefact, or the ways in which it can be used by a particular end-user, given her characteristics and those of the code in question.[44] Although many affordances are contingent relationships between user and artefact, they are often consciously designed as features of the system, in which case they will (usually) be signified to the user.[45] A common example is a pad on the surface of a door that signifies the affordance of pushing (but not of pulling).

In contrast to the enablement of behavioural possibilities that designed affordances and their signifiers represent, the concept of *disaffordance* points, in the design context at least, to the conscious and strategic choice to 'enforce or restrict certain user behaviour'.[46] This builds on Lessig's notion of 'architectures of control',[47] and is of course central to the claim made here about the (il)legitimacy of such technological normativity.

Code is designed with a particular class of user in mind, and so its (dis)affordances, inscriptions, and mediations are all fundamentally affected by the directed choices made by the designers who produce it. Although some forms of action are emergent or open to (re)interpretation or resistance on

---

[42] Lessig hints at this truth when he notes that 'there is no choice that does not include some kind of building. Code is never found; it is only ever made.' See Lessig (n 9) 6. For present purposes, Heidegger's notion of 'ready-to-hand' captures an important aspect of the individual's situatedness in-the-world, constituted seamlessly – at least until something breaks – by the environment they inhabit. See M Heidegger, *Being and Time*, trans. J Macquarrie and E Robinson (Blackwell 1962) 95–102.

[43] On the latter, see BJ Fogg, *Persuasive Technology: Using Computers to Change What We Think and Do* (Morgan Kaufmann Publishers 2003) 34 *et seq.*

[44] DA Norman, *The Design of Everyday Things* (MIT Press 2013) 11.

[45] Ibid. 13 *et seq.*

[46] D Lockton, 'Architectures of control in product design' (2006) *Engineering Designer: The Journal of the Institution of Engineering Designers* 28. See also D Lockton, 'Disaffordances and engineering obedience' *Architectures* (22 October 2006) <http://architectures.danlockton.co.uk/2006/10/22/disaffordances-and-engineering-obedience/> last accessed 4 March 2021.

[47] Lessig (n 9) chapter 4.

the part of the end-user,[48] it is nevertheless true to a greater or lesser degree that design choices embed 'programs of action'[49] within the artefact, and so significant normative power inheres in those who make those choices. When a designer embeds (dis)affordances in the design of her artefact, she affects what it is possible to do with that artefact, either expanding or contracting those possibilities.

All of this points to the ways that designers fashion the geography of the artefacts they create, thereby controlling, at least to the extent it plays a role in her experience, that part of the user's mediated reality.[50] The extent to which that control is imposed will differ depending on the artefact and how far it exemplifies the elements of computational legalism.

Computational Legalism

One of the central problematics of code from a legal-theoretical perspective is its 'ruleishness', meaning its application of defined rules in all instances where fixed conditions, specified in the code itself, obtain.[51] In the technical context this is of course a major benefit: even the most complex body of rules can be expected to execute in predetermined ways under precisely defined and controlled conditions, providing a predictability that lies at the centre of the technological advances seen in the silicon age.

In the legal context, however, the rote application of rules is undesirable, at least in a society built around the ideals of democracy and the concept of legality, where the system of rules must have the capacity to interface contingently with its context (that is, the society it serves). Linked with Kant's categorical imperative, *legalism* is the legal equivalent of code's ruleishness. Although it has more than one form in the literature, the relevant conception for my purposes is connected closely with certain forms of legal positivism,[52] and is seen as an ideology under which rules and the strict adherence to them

---

[48] This relates to Ihde's notion of *multistability*. See D Ihde, *Technology and the Lifeworld: From Garden to Earth* (Indiana University Press 1990) 144 *et seq*.

[49] B Latour, 'Where are the missing masses? The sociology of a few mundane artifacts' in WE Bijker and J Law (eds), *Shaping Technology/Building Society: Studies in Sociotechnical Change* (MIT Press 1992).

[50] On the technological mediation of experience, see P-P Verbeek, *What Things Do: Philosophical Reflections on Technology, Agency, and Design* (Penn State Press 2005) chapter 3. See also Ihde (n 48), particularly chapter 5.

[51] J Grimmelmann, 'Regulation by software' (2005) 114 *The Yale Law Journal* 1719.

[52] See Z Bańkowski and N MacCormick, 'Legality without legalism' in W Krawietz et al. (eds), *The Reasonable as Rational? On Legal Argumentation and Justification; Festschrift for Aulis Aarnio* (Duncker & Humblot 2000); JN Shklar, *Legalism* (Harvard University Press 1964) 7.

are the proper fundaments of social ordering. That the state defines what is legal is enough to legitimise the substance of the legal norms it chooses to declare; in constituting the field of play (the legal system), the state legitimises *de facto* that which it consequently promulgates as the rules of the game. Constitutive facts (natural laws, the social contract/constitution, or a mix of these) operate prospectively to legitimise any subsequent act of the sovereign.[53] The citizen is given the imperative to 'not think about it'; the rule is 'just there' and she need only act in accordance with it as written,[54] since by virtue of those constitutive facts the pronouncement of the sovereign is 'imputed to [the people], as if they were its author'.[55] As an outlook, then, legalism tends towards a 'narrow governance of rules, unleavened by the principled approach to interpretation'.[56] This simplicity implies the possibility of abuse: the prioritisation of heteronomy militates against critical reflection and the application of other normative principles of legality that are aspirational characteristics in a democracy. The freedom of the citizen to interpret is seen as a crucial aspect of legality, without which rules become 'implements of tyranny' and legalism a 'vice of narrow governance'.[57]

From this brief summary of legalism (I will expand on the concept in Chapter 3), one can begin to appreciate how code can exemplify these characteristics.[58] In even the most tyrannical state there is space to interpret, and perhaps to disobey, the law – the hermeneutic gap between the text of a norm on the page and its translation into behaviour in the world makes this at least a notional possibility. In the environments where code is designed, however, the elision of that gap is not only easy to do but is entirely standard, not necessarily through malice or intentional obfuscation (though they are of course a problem), but simply by virtue of the ontological characteristics of code, which presents norms to the end-user that 'just are'. Even where the code does allow for choice via configuration, the default settings of code tend to be viewed by end-users as 'a natural and immutable fact'.[59] The hermeneutic gap

---

53 L Wintgens, *Legisprudence: Practical Reason in Legislation* (Routledge 2012) chapters 5–6.

54 Z Bańkowski, 'Don't think about it: Legalism and legality' in MM Karlsson, Ó Páll Jónsson and EM Brynjarsdóttir (eds), *Rechtstheorie: Zeitschrift für Logik, Methodenlehre, Kybernetik und Soziologie des Rechts* (Duncker & Humblot 1993).

55 Wintgens, *Legisprudence: Practical Reason in Legislation* (n 53) 208.

56 Bańkowski and MacCormick (n 52) 194.

57 Ibid.

58 Bańkowski and Schafer (n 32).

59 Goldoni (n 24) 128. Boyle also hinted early on at this 'legalistic' nature of code, noting that '[t]he technology appears to be "just the way things are"; its origins are concealed, whether those origins lie in state-sponsored scheme or market-structured order, and its effects are obscured because it is hard to imagine the alternative.' See J Boyle, 'Foucault in

is thus closed, or at least significantly narrowed, because the 'text' of the 'rule' (the source code) constitutes directly the geography of the artefact: they are not just isomorphic, they are one and the same. Unlike traditional law, whose 'carrier' has hitherto been the inherently passive medium of text, software code allows us to 'conceive of a text (a programming language) that is at once words and actions'.[60] This represents the apex of legalism: the normative collapses into the descriptive (what was once requested becomes simply what is), and there is no choice but to obey the rule as it is expressed by the designer, much less to view and contest it, since it by definition constitutes empirical as well as legal and technological reality.[61] The characteristics of computational legalism – ruleishness, opacity, immediacy, immutability, and pervasiveness, all compounded by privatised production – mean that in many cases code is simultaneously more powerful and less adaptable than a law-system that is built around the characteristics of delay, flexible interpretation, and ex post remediation. Code is thus simultaneously more, and less, than law.

Digital Rights Management
Consider for a moment digital rights management (DRM), a well-studied form of regulative code and a staple of technology law analysis. As I discussed above, it is important to distinguish between compliance with substantive law (generally but not necessarily copyright, in the case of DRM[62]), and broader and more fundamental questions of legitimacy. The computational legalism of DRM is exemplified by the Sony BMG scandal of the mid-2000s,[63] where the record company included DRM software on its CD releases that was designed to limit the scope of playback and the ability to 'rip' the music as digital files or copy it to a blank CD. The software installed itself surreptitiously on end-users' Windows PCs: upon insertion of the CD, if the code detected existing CD copying software installed on the computer, it would

---

cyberspace: Surveillance, sovereignty, and hardwired censors' (1997) 66 *University of Cincinnati Law Review* 177, 205.

[60] Latour, 'Where are the missing masses?' (n 49) n 1. The nature of programming languages as a source of rules is something I consider in Part III.

[61] Bańkowski (n 54); Bańkowski and Schafer (n 32). Representationalism is a key element of the legalistic outlook. See L Wintgens, 'Legisprudence as a new theory of legislation' (2006) 19 *Ratio Juris* 1, 5. I consider the contrast between regulative and constitutive normativity in Part I.

[62] MJ Radin, 'Regulation by contract, regulation by machine' (2004) 160 *Journal of Institutional and Theoretical Economics (JITE)* 142, 152. See also Lockton, 'Architectures of control in product design' (n 46).

[63] See for example BBC News, 'Sony slated over anti-piracy CD' *BBC News* (3 November 2005) <http://news.bbc.co.uk/1/hi/technology/4400148.stm> last accessed 4 March 2021.

cease playback and eject the disc.[64] Any copies made using the system were themselves protected by the same restrictions.[65] Playback was also limited to the included software.

Of course, Sony BMG was a commercial enterprise, a fact that frames the other 'legalistic' characteristics of the system. Self-evidently, the system's code regulated what the end-user could do with her purchased CD. Legitimate playback and copying on a PC were severely constrained. The system was opaque in its operation: those limits on playback and copying were not made clear from the outset, nor did the system notify the end-user that it would install the DRM prior to her consenting (and, incredibly, even if she withheld consent[66]). The license agreement failed to narrate these limitations accurately,[67] and in any event there could be no reasonable expectation in that context that the system would seriously undermine both the security of the end-user's PC and her individual privacy.[68] The system's immediacy was demonstrated by the nature of its installation – those without deeper technical knowledge had no opportunity to refuse its installation, despite the hermeneutic gap implied by the need to accept the license agreement. The cumulative normativity of the system was felt most by those least likely to attempt to circumvent it: infringers were more likely to be technically adept and therefore capable of side-stepping the DRM, while lawful but less technically literate end-users had their rights and convenience circumscribed despite not wishing to engage in unlawful copying.

As mentioned, the system was imposed upon the end-user without consent or choice. It was included on a medium whose contents cannot be changed once produced, leaving problematic code dormant on unchangeable media for a potentially unlimited time.[69] The design of the system had no anticipated means of altering the software after-the-fact; as the scandal gained prominence Sony BMG rushed to release patches that purported to

---

[64] JA Halderman and EW Felten, 'Lessons from the Sony CD DRM episode' in *15th USENIX Security Symposium* (USENIX Association 2006) 80.

[65] Ibid. n 8.

[66] Ibid. 81.

[67] DK Mulligan and A Perzanowski, 'The magnificence of the disaster: Reconstructing the Sony BMG rootkit incident' (2007) 22 *Berkeley Technology Law Journal* 1157, 1162.

[68] Ibid. 1211. On the privacy implications, see Mark Russinovich, 'More on Sony: Dangerous decloaking patch, EULAs and phoning home' <https://techcommunity.microsoft.com/t5/windows-blog-archive/more-on-sony-dangerous-decloaking-patch-eulas-and-phoning-home/ba-p/723452> last accessed 4 March 2021.

[69] As Halderman and Felten note, '[i]f a particular version of DRM software is shipped on a new CD, that software version may well try to install and run decades after it was developed.' See Halderman and Felten (n 64) 89.

uninstall the software, but in fact these caused further serious security prob-lems.[70] Lastly, the system achieved significant distribution, if not pervasive-ness: up to two million users were affected,[71] and in the fallout of the crisis around 7.3 million CDs were recalled.[72]

As I have argued, these characteristics of the code's normativity can be critiqued separately from its implementation of the substantive norms of copyright law.[73] Precisely because of the formal illegitimacies identified above, the ability of the end-user to be aware of and contest the mis-implementation of substantive copyright law was severely limited. By the standards of dig-isprudential legitimacy, the characteristics of the Sony BMG system were illegitimate regardless of the requirements of substantive legal doctrine, and should not have been designed as they were, particularly given that if the issues with the code's design – its computational legalism – had not been stumbled upon, they may well have continued to operate for some consider-able period without being detected and remedied.

1.3 Aspiring to Legitimacy in Code

If the rote heteronomy of legalism is at one end of a spectrum, at the other is the aspirational concept of *legality*, which seeks to maintain a connec-tion between the normative construct of law as a system of governance and the legitimising principles that underlie the exercise of sovereign power in constitutional democracies. Although an unsettled concept, legality has a theoretical pedigree that includes influential analyses that fit well with the normative approach I am adopting. As an aspiration, it is considered to be of fundamental importance in constitutional democracies; Bańkowski goes so far as to say it is 'something worth living for; something worth dying for'.[74] Hildebrandt defines legality by what for her it is not: legal certainty, 'justice', and expediency on their own are insufficient; the characteristic of legality also encompasses the rule of law and the binding of the sovereign's legisla-tive power within constitutional limits.[75] For Brownsword, legality is about human dignity and the creation and maintenance of conditions that 'make moral community possible'. Legality, then, is not just about the substance of

---

[70] See Russinovich (n 68); Halderman and Felten (n 64) 88 *et seq.*
[71] Mulligan and Perzanowski (n 67) 1158.
[72] Ibid. 1169.
[73] I discuss this in more detail in L Diver, 'Law as a user: Design, affordance, and the techno-logical mediation of norms' (2018) 15 *SCRIPTed* 4. See also Halderman and Felten (n 64) 91, stating that 'the [DRM] systems make no pretense of enforcing copyright law as written, but instead seek to enforce rules dictated by the label's and vendor's business models'.
[74] Bańkowski (n 54) 45.
[75] Hildebrandt, *Smart Technologies* (n 14) 157–8.

legal regulations, but also their form.[76] This idea of purpose binding speaks to the ex ante, 'constitutional' nature of the present analysis. Through the guidance of designers' production of technological normativity, we can help ensure that the negative outcomes towards which computational legalism tends are minimised as far as possible.

(a) From Operation to Production

I have already mentioned the importance of widening our focus to include the production of code, in addition to the orthodox ex post assessment of its operation. This relates to the notions of legality just mentioned – one can appreciate the relevance of the 'design' of a rule to the question of whether it meets those ideals. Whereas legalism looks only to sources to discern validity, legality is something altogether more reflexive and rational,[77] seeking evidence of certain requirements in the rule-making process. There is a clear alignment here between this view of legality and the shift in the literature towards design thinking that I mentioned above.

Fuller's *Internal Morality of Law*

This idea of rule production connects with Fuller's influential theory of the *internal morality of law*, whose eight principles of legality provide an underlying quasi-formal substrate necessary for making good legal rules, regardless of any reasonable disagreement there might be about their substantive content (that is, their 'external morality').[78] What several of the principles point towards is how best to design a legal norm, regardless of what its external morality is or ought to be. Indeed, Fuller uses the language of design on various occasions, referring to law-making as a 'craft'[79] and to the eight principles as 'those laws respected by a carpenter who wants the house he builds to remain standing and serve the purpose of those living in it'.[80] We will see later how the internal and external moralities of law relate to input and output reasons for decision-making[81] and, perhaps surprisingly, even to Hart's theory of primary and secondary rules, separating substantive ordinances from the rules which set out how they can be validly created, modified, and extinguished.[82]

---

[76] R Brownsword, 'Lost in translation: Legality, regulatory margins, and technological management' (2011) 26 *Berkeley Technology Law Journal* 1321.

[77] Bańkowski and Schafer (n 32) 31–2.

[78] Fuller (n 33) chapter 2.

[79] Ibid. 43, 156.

[80] Ibid. 96.

[81] Goldoni (n 24) 127, citing J Waldron, 'The core of the case against judicial review' (2006) 115 *Yale Law Journal* 1346.

[82] HLA Hart, *The Concept of Law* (2nd edn, Clarendon Press 1994) chapter V.

Wintgens's *Legisprudence*

The second primary theoretical source I draw upon for the formal qualities that normative orders ought to reflect is Wintgens's *legisprudence*. Although less well-known than Fuller, it can play an important role here as an aspirational framework that challenges legislators to achieve formal legitimacy in the process of developing new legal norms.[83] Wintgens argues that legal theory has in general been preoccupied more with adjudication than with legislative rule-making;[84] legisprudence, by contrast, is specifically aimed at the process of legislating, placing emphasis on the formal characteristics that a legal norm ought to have to be deemed a legitimate incursion on individual freedom. Upholding individuals' subjective notions of freedom ought to be a guiding principle of both politics and law, and any limitation on that freedom by law is legitimate only if it is justified according to the four legisprudential principles.[85] Fidelity to rules remains a necessary part of legal order, but this is via a 'weak' legalism which, unlike the stronger form introduced above (and described in detail in Chapter 3), requires those rules to be formulated in accordance with ex ante standards and not simply on the whim of the sovereign. Expecting citizens to follow rules thus becomes acceptable because those rules, legitimated by application of the legisprudential principles, cannot be arbitrary exercises of power. Briefly, the principles concern whether or not a binary rule is desirable, whether the proposed norm is proportionate to the issue the legislator seeks to address, whether its design enables ongoing assessment of its efficacy, and finally whether it is coherent at the semantic, temporal, intra-systemic, and extra-systemic levels.[86]

As suggested above, computational legalism represents the strongest of legalisms. The impetus to legitimate the exercise of power by designers whose code vies with law to regulate behaviour is therefore all the greater. Designers limit individual and collective freedom in ways that have not been sanctioned by the democratic polity, via mechanisms that are technically and socially opaque and which are not straightforwardly susceptible to public contest, redress, and (judicial) review. They are therefore potentially illegitimate exercises of power whose effects are difficult to arrest or ameliorate, particularly when diffused across millions of devices, often with little or no technical means of applying retrospective fixes.

---

[83] Wintgens, 'Legisprudence as a new theory of legislation' (n 61). For an explanation and history of the term 'legisprudence', see Wintgens, *Legisprudence: Practical Reason in Legislation* (n 53) 231–5.

[84] Wintgens, 'Legisprudence as a new theory of legislation' (n 61) 1.

[85] Wintgens, *Legisprudence: Practical Reason in Legislation* (n 53) 220.

[86] Chapter 4 discusses the principles in greater detail.

(b) Towards Digisprudence: *Legitimate 'Code as Law'*

As Koops suggests, 'a good place to start looking for criteria for acceptability of normative technology is to study criteria for law'.[87] The Fullerian and legisprudential principles are an excellent starting point, concerned as they are with providing criteria for acceptable law-making. Undoubtedly, they do not map directly onto the digital context, and so in Chapter 6 I translate them into the language of affordance, discussed above, in order ultimately to set out a framework for ensuring legitimate rule-making in the commercial design environment.

As Chapter 6 sets out, the proposed framework consists of a set of digisprudential affordances that translate the principled goals that I distil from the literature into concrete suggestions for the design of code. In brief, these cover contestability (with individual and institutional dimensions), transparency (covering provenance, purpose, and operation), choice, delay, and oversight.[88] The affordances are simultaneously general and concrete: they provide a design goal that should be reflected in all legitimate citizen-facing code, regardless of the form of technology, its substantive functionality, or the underlying business model. (A corollary of this is that certain functionalities or business models will therefore be illegitimate by definition.)

There may be edge cases where the affordances are less easy to envisage or implement. However, like the legal-theoretical foundations upon which it builds, digisprudence is aspirational: both legisprudence and the Fullerian principles are intended to encourage better (if not perfect) rule-making, and so similarly it is not expected that the digisprudential framework will cover every conceivable scenario where normative code is being produced. As Fuller suggests, perfect legality is 'utopian';[89] Wintgens notes in a similar vein that respect for the legisprudential principles is about 'the aspiration to do the job as well as possible'.[90] The same can be said of its technological counterpart that I am here proposing.

1.4 'Code as Law', Code *versus* Law, or Something Else?

This book is published in a series called 'Future Law' and has been adapted from a doctoral thesis written in a law school. One might reasonably therefore

---

[87] B-J Koops, 'Criteria for normative technology: The acceptability of "code as law" in light of democratic and constitutional values' in R Brownsword and K Yeung (eds), *Regulating Technologies: Legal Futures, Regulatory Frames and Technological Fixes* (Hart 2008) 162. I discuss Koops's analysis, along with the other literature on criteria for code, in Chapter 5.

[88] See Section 6.3.

[89] Fuller (n 33) 41, 43.

[90] Wintgens, *Legisprudence: Practical Reason in Legislation* (n 53) 280.

expect it to make an argument about, say, the need for better laws, that is legal norms that reflect technological developments or that can more effectively bridge the regulatory gap. Hopefully, it is clear that that is not my focus. Instead, I am interested in the body of normativity that operates separately from and in parallel with institutional law.[91] My argument is first that it exists, and second that it ought to be subject to scrutiny by those whose theoretical expertise in the paradigmatic normative order – the law – can bring something new to bear, particularly when combined with practical knowledge of how the rules of code are made.

(a) Cyberlibertarianism

In acknowledging the existence of this parallel ordering, my aim is not to follow the 'cyberlibertarian' position that welcomes and seeks to validate the usurping of the state by private producers of code.[92] It is in fact precisely the opposite. We are at risk of finding ourselves in a 'Collingridge dilemma', such that by the time consensus has been reached (if it ever is) on the need to directly regulate specific technologies and the questionable business models from which they spring, conditions have become such that implementing any change is expensive, difficult, and time-consuming.[93]

My goal therefore is first to acknowledge the reality of this predicament and then to adopt a precautionary approach, suggesting ways we might guide the practice of design towards outcomes that are more legitimate, as defined according to the existing legal-theoretical frames that I will later adopt. Therefore, while I agree with some of the cyberlibertarians' descriptive characterisations of code, I expressly disagree with their normative positions on what should flow from those characteristics.

One of the traditional counterarguments to the cyberlibertarian position is that code is readily susceptible to regulation by law. Arguments about the regulability of code are valid as far as they go, but they do not adequately encompass the technical characteristics of recent technologies (for example blockchain applications) nor address the question of how code is produced.

---

[91] R Brownsword, 'In the year 2061: From law to technological management' (2015) 7 *Law, Innovation and Technology* 1, 10–14; R Mohr and F Contini, 'Reassembling the legal: "The wonders of modern science" in court-related proceedings' (2011) 20 *Griffith Law Review* 994, 998.

[92] The classic expression of this perspective is JP Barlow, 'A declaration of the independence of cyberspace' (1996) <https://www.eff.org/cyberspace-independence> last accessed 4 March 2021. For another argument in this vein, see DR Johnson and DG Post, 'Law and borders – the rise of law in cyberspace' (1995) 48 *Stanford Law Review* 1367.

[93] MT Young, 'Artifacts as rules: Wittgenstein and the sociology of technology' (2018) 22 *Techné: Research in Philosophy and Technology* 377.

Furthermore, those scholars who have argued against the idea that code is hegemonic have tended to focus on the infrastructure of the Internet and the large platforms that own and operate it,[94] rather than on the individual digital artefacts that constitute our daily lives online. This code is often produced by smaller enterprises[95] who are less easy targets for traditional regulation and who may view the benefits of compliance as being outweighed by its cost,[96] particularly when they lack dedicated legal departments or expertise. (Indeed, a great deal of code is produced by individuals or microbusinesses.[97])

Such scholarship has not engaged in depth with the role and practices of the designer as the creator of the code-based norms that constrain and enable behaviour. Again, though, another counterargument to the thesis I am advancing might be that designers, just like any other legal person, should be the subjects of traditional regulative processes and, therefore, any illegality in the code they produce should be dealt with using traditional ex post legal processes. In the computational context this is necessary, but insufficient: as we shall see below and in subsequent chapters, the ex ante legitimation of code in addition to ex post legal remedial measures is crucial because of its *sui generis* nature as a regulator. The threat of computational legalism means that the stakes are both qualitatively and quantitatively higher than with other instances of problematic regulation that can be ameliorated by traditional legal processes. The statute that is improperly enacted or the contract that is voidably concluded are defeasible, that is they are presumed valid but are nevertheless always open to challenge in, and reduction by, a court with the relevant authority.[98] The characteristics of code as a regulator admit of no such possibility: once its rules are 'promulgated', any 'illegality' has no bearing on its ability to execute and impose any latent normativity that it harbours. From

---

[94] Goldsmith and Wu, for example, focus on the physical networks that underpin the Internet, noting that they are owned by 'some of the most regulated companies on earth'. See JL Goldsmith and T Wu, *Who Controls the Internet?: Illusions of a Borderless World* (Oxford University Press 2006) 73. As discussed above, we also saw this focus in the 'code as law' literature.

[95] G Papadopoulos et al., 'Statistics on small and medium-sized enterprises' (European Commission 2018) <https://ec.europa.eu/eurostat/statistics-explained/index.php/Statistics_on_small_and_medium-sized_enterprises> last accessed 4 March 2021.

[96] See for example London Economics, *Study on the Economic Benefits of Privacy-Enhancing Technologies (PETs)* (London Economics 2010).

[97] See Stack Overflow, 'Developer survey 2020' *Stack Overflow* <https://insights.stackoverflow.com/survey/2020/> last accessed 4 March 2021 (purportedly the largest survey of developers in the world, demonstrating that a quarter work in companies with fewer than twenty employees).

[98] N MacCormick, *Rhetoric and the Rule of Law: A Theory of Legal Reasoning* (Oxford University Press 2005) chapter 12.

the moment of 'shipping', the code will operate as though it was legitimately 'enacted', even where this is manifestly not the case. There is, therefore, a crucial difference between invalid laws and 'invalid' code: with the former, the hermeneutic gap that exists between text and action allows for a space in which validity can be considered, whereas with the latter there is no such opportunity, either to arrest execution or (in many cases) even to observe the invalidity. This in turn connects with the question of ex post contest. If the nature and extent of the code's invalidity cannot be observed, traditional mechanisms of legal redress cannot meaningfully be invoked. Ultimately, we fall into a trap if we assume that institutional law is capable of operating with its usual force where code is the subject of regulation, at least without some form of acquiescence from the other side.

Any attempt to grapple with this difficult reality will require a shift in discourse 'from distribution to production and [thus a] focus on how the digital environment is created'.[99] Thankfully, an emerging turn in the legal literature – so far mostly in the sphere of privacy – demonstrates a shift in focus towards design and the production of code.[100] As Gürses and van Hoboken note, 'the ideological markers, pools of desirable knowledge and practices of technology *production* that bring these sets of [ex post] conditions forth and not others tend to go unquestioned'.[101] The effects of computational legalism make code resistant to the modulating effects of interpretation and ex post remedial measures that are more readily effective in the realm of traditional text-based law. It is clear, therefore, that in addition to those traditional ex post methods of redress, we should aim for ex ante code legitimacy. Digisprudence contributes to that emerging debate with a focus on legitimacy,[102] and the expectations we should have of designers and enterprise in their anticipation of the effects of the code that they produce.

(b) Why Not 'Compliance by Design'?

The goal of 'compliance by design' ('CbD') concerns meeting the requirements of a specific field of substantive doctrinal law within the design of the

---

[99] Goldoni (n 24) 129.

[100] See for example W Hartzog, *Privacy's Blueprint: The Battle to Control the Design of New Technologies* (Harvard University Press 2018); Gürses and van Hoboken (n 5). See also P Nemitz, 'Constitutional democracy and technology in the age of artificial intelligence' (2018) 376 *Philosophical Transactions of the Royal Society A* 20180089, arguing for a design perspective on the effects that artificial intelligence is having on constitutional democracy.

[101] Gürses and van Hoboken (n 5) 580 (emphasis supplied).

[102] Cf. A Murray, 'Looking back at the law of the horse: Why cyberlaw and the rule of law are important' (2013) 10 *SCRIPTed* 310. Murray retains the orthodox position of viewing code as the subject of law.

code, insofar as that field targets its norms at digital artefacts. This interpretation of CbD is in line with the terminological usage of initiatives like 'privacy by design' and the GDPR's 'data protection by design'.[103] These are examples of orthodox technology regulation, where the focus is the regulation of software by substantive doctrinal law.

This is centrally important of course insofar as compliance with the law is important in all contexts. From the perspective of digisprudence, however, it is a limited and inherently legalistic view, one that looks upon the law as a set of rules that is 'just there', to be passively observed and obeyed by the designer of the code. It also narrows our focus away from the broader range of 'techno-effects' that play as important (and indeed larger) a part in regulating behaviour as compared with legally sanctioned code.[104] A perspective of code based solely on this understanding of 'compliance by design' is unsatisfactory, or at the very least incomplete, because it elides the very active role that designers play in the creation of such normative 'reality' in and through the code that they produce.

As a general aim, CbD overlooks (1) the *sui generis* nature of code as a regulator of behaviour (that is, it overlooks computational legalism), and (2) how the translation from textual norms to code-based norms invariably involves some level of modification of the former.[105] The precise nature of the reality envisioned by legal text is not reflected in the reality constructed by code, partly because law itself is (and arguably should be) vague,[106] and partly because the two modes of representing meaning (text and software code) are by nature very different, both because language is vague where code is precise and because words require translation into behaviour whereas code is simultaneously documentary and performative. The point is not just to improve the methods of transferring norms between domains, but also to ensure there are mechanisms in place – safety valves – that allow for mis-translations properly to be dealt with according to the rule of law.

The lack of one-to-one mapping of meaning not only is true of attempts to interpret and instantiate substantive (textual) legal norms in code, but is

---

[103] Regulation on the protection of natural persons with regard to the processing of personal data and on the free movement of such data, and repealing Directive 85/46/EC (General Data Protection Regulation) 2016, Recital 78 and art. 25.

[104] B van den Berg and RE Leenes, 'Abort, retry, fail: Scoping techno-regulation and other techno-effects' in M Hildebrandt and J Gaakeer (eds), *Human Law and Computer Law: Comparative Perspectives* (Springer 2013).

[105] Goldoni (n 24) 129; Hildebrandt and Koops (n 30) 452 *et seq.*

[106] T Endicott, 'Law is necessarily vague' (2001) 7 *Legal Theory* 379; C Reed, 'How to make bad law: Lessons from cyberspace' (2010) 73 *The Modern Law Review* 903, 904 *et seq.*

also demonstrated in the unintended constellations of legal and non-legal effect that are continually being reified by digital artefacts.[107] This is what van den Berg and Leenes refer to as 'techno-effects',[108] or the aggregate normativity of a technology considered regardless of the designer's intent or any legal impetus behind its design. While much of the literature focuses on 'techno-regulation', or the use of technology as a tool to effect legal norms, there has been insufficient consideration of the wider spectrum of techno-effects, including a-legal regulation. This gap is an important one, particularly given that '[t]he "regulatory" potential of technologies – in the broadest sense – is tremendous, and daunting, indeed.'[109] Not only can it be difficult to discern the intention of the designer, but so too is the line between intentional and unintentional normativity difficult to detect – '[t]he affected individual cannot discern which part of the normativity (as could be inferred from the output) is intentional and which part is merely spin-off in the form [of] unforeseen or secondary effects.'[110]

Whereas law benefits from delay and processes of interpretation that permit application across heterogeneous circumstances,[111] code tends by nature towards fixed (or inflexible) configurations of normativity, rather than interpretable standards. These are imposed with unqualified force in every case where the necessary computational conditions arise, regardless of any other relevant considerations. The challenge therefore is to ensure that the fixity of code is as legitimate as it can be *ab initio*. As Goldoni puts it, 'on the one side, code can be a norm-enforcing technology, as has been outlined several times in the debate; on the other side, code can also be a norm-establishing technology as well'.[112] If both law and code create norms, and we as a society have expectations about the legitimacy of the former, then we ought to expect similar standards from the latter. Code, however, is not law, it is only law-like; but it is precisely because of the ways in which it is not law that this kind of analysis is necessary: code can control behaviour more directly than can 'true' law, but simultaneously it lacks the latter's mechanisms of ex ante legitimation, defeasibility, and ex post remediation.

---

[107] Van den Berg and Leenes (n 104).
[108] Ibid. 81.
[109] Ibid. 83.
[110] Bayamlıoğlu and Leenes (n 7) 12. They refer to this phenomenon as 'normative opaqueness'.
[111] Endicott (n 106) 382–3; Gadamer (n 29) 334 *et seq.*; R Dworkin, *Law's Empire* (Belknap Press 1986) *passim*.
[112] Goldoni (n 24) 118.

The need is therefore all the greater for it to be legitimated from the out-set, within the design process, and not only in the aftermath of a high-profile data breach or other scandal. As Goldoni points out,

> [g]iven that code is not exactly like law, it is difficult in the realm of code to adopt a kind of rule of law (or 'rule of code') approach. Yet, we have also seen that when a particular code is 'enacted', it may be too late to remedy the violation of certain rights. This is why the accent should be put on the moment of production, rather than on the moment of distribution.[113]

The opacity of code means that only the most conspicuous illegitimacies are ever likely to be exposed; this highlights the problem of a retrospective, ex post focus centred on the operation of code rather than on its production.

Consider, for example, the controversy surrounding Facebook and the sharing of its users' personal data with third-party application developers, who subsequently used it to micro-target election advertisements online. The case is a complex (and evolving) mix of business ethics, democratic politics, and doctrinal law, but at its heart lie decisions made by designers that are concretised in code: a now-deprecated version of Facebook's application pro-gramming interface (API)[114] allowed developers to access the data of 'friends' of the primary end-user, which enabled the large-scale data harvesting that facilitated the voter profiling at the centre of the controversy.[115] This is a high-profile, high-public interest case, and has thus been subject to relatively inten-sive scrutiny from experts and regulators. Despite this, the challenges of such an ex post remedial approach are precipitous, given the complexity of both the systems involved and of Facebook as an organisation.[116]

---

[113] Ibid. 128.

[114] APIs allow unconnected software systems to communicate with one another, enabling the combination of systems with different specialities, for example mapping, payment process-ing, and biometric authentication.

[115] For a technical overview, see Information Commissioner's Office, 'Investigation into the use of data analytics in political campaigns – investigation update' (Information Commissioner's Office 2018) s. 4.3.1. On the broader political implications, see P Geoghegan, *Democracy for Sale: Dark Money and Dirty Politics* (Head of Zeus 2020) chapter 8.

[116] As Pasquale notes, '[i]t could take weeks to fully map the flow of data from something as simple as commenting on Facebook.' See F Pasquale, *The Black Box Society: The Secret Algorithms that Control Money and Information* (Harvard University Press 2015) 144. Indeed, it took the UK Information Commissioner several months to investigate the nature of Facebook's systems. For a set of fascinating visualisations demonstrating the complexity involved, see Share Lab, 'Immaterial labour and data harvesting' *Share Lab* (21 August 2016) <https://labs.rs/en/facebook-algorithmic-factory-immaterial-labour-and-data-harvesting/> last accessed 4 March 2021.

Facebook is clearly a prominent target for regulators, and its potential role in election tampering means the case is of the greatest public interest. The question remains, however, of the extent to which less significant code infelicities might be operating all around us, never detected or remedied, because the scrutiny and impetus to investigate ex post are relatively minimal or simply absent.

Other Notions of 'by Design'

Broader, more nuanced notions of 'by design' that accord with the perspective I am adopting do exist. For example, Nemitz refers to 'the principles of democracy, rule of law and human rights by design'.[117] Similarly, Hildebrandt defines her concept of 'Legal Protection by Design' as 'a way to ensure that the technological normativity that regulates our lives: first, is compatible with enacted law, or even initiated by the democratic legislator; second, can be resisted; and third, may be contested in a court of law'.[118] One can see how Nemitz's and Hildebrandt's concepts include more fundamental issues than compliance with substantive doctrine. Hildebrandt's and Koops's earlier formulation of 'ambient law' is also close to the idea at hand, where what matters is not (just) compliance with the substantive law, but the kinds of constitutional safeguards that law as a normative enterprise is expected to provide, regardless of the substantive content of its rules.[119]

While the authors are concerned with the reflection of state-sourced law in code, it can equally be said that code which embodies normativity that is not state-sourced ought also to embody 'safeguards' in order for it to be legitimate. In this context, where commercial enterprise is the source of the normativity, the requirement of democratic participation in the design of code is unlikely to be achievable by smaller enterprises with limited resources to invest in the necessary processes.[120] Initiatives connected with this goal include participatory design,[121] constructive technology assessment,[122] value

---

[117] Nemitz (n 100) *passim*.

[118] Hildebrandt, *Smart Technologies* (n 14) 218.

[119] Hildebrandt and Koops (n 30) 445. See also M Hildebrandt, 'A vision of ambient law' in R Brownsword and K Yeung (eds), *Regulating Technologies: Legal Futures, Regulatory Frames and Technological Fixes* (Hart 2008).

[120] Papadopoulos et al. (n 95).

[121] S Costanza-Chock, *Design Justice: Community-Led Practices to Build the Worlds We Need* (MIT Press 2020).

[122] P-P Verbeek, 'Materializing morality: Design ethics and technological mediation' (2006) 31 *Science, Technology, & Human Values* 361, 375 *et seq.*

sensitive design,[123] and ideation.[124] These are valuable initiatives, but their focus tends to individualise the idea of 'constitutional' standards that I am concerned with, through the focus on the practices of a particular designer/ team/enterprise and how these impact on a particular design project. Such initiatives seek to legitimise a design by dint of having involved those with a stake in the outcome in decisions as to the artefact's substantive characteristics. By contrast, the 'constitutional' view of digisprudence comes before such questions, advocating for universal formal standards to be present regardless of the application or the participation of affected groups. Design for all need not require design with all;[125] the characteristics of legitimacy I propose are primarily formal and ought to be present in all citizen-facing technologies, regardless of their substantive purpose. As with legal rules, while we can disagree about the desirability of their substantive content we would, I think, agree generally that the process of their creation ought to meet certain standards, and that they ought to reflect formal qualities such as intelligibility and non-retroactivity. In that vein, then, we can say that digisprudence is to participatory design approaches as legisprudence is to the democratic process; they are separate but complementary aspects of the norm-creation process.

(c) Normative Relationships in Code and Law

To further clarify the location of the enquiry, we can visualise the normative relationships in the digital sphere as shown in Figure 1.1. Relationship (b) represents the classic compact between the citizen end-user and the state – the latter being bound by a constitution in relationship (a) – through which democratic participation results in the state's promulgation of legal norms through both that relationship and relationship (c). The latter represents the traditional understanding of 'compliance by design', discussed above.

Digisprudence focuses on relationships (d) and (e). In relationship (d), the product designer imposes behavioural constraint through a mix of legal and architectural normativity. The legal normativity in this relationship can flow from public-order norms (legislation of various forms) on the one hand, or private-order contractual norms on the other. These are operationalised by

---

[123] B Friedman, 'Value-sensitive design' (1996) 3 *interactions* 16.

[124] E Luger and M Golembewski, 'Towards fostering compliance by design; drawing designers into the regulatory frame' in M Taddeo and L Floridi (eds), *The Responsibilities of Online Service Providers* (Springer 2017); B Friedman and D Hendry, 'The envisioning cards: A toolkit for catalyzing humanistic and technical imaginations' in *Proceedings of the SIGCHI Conference on Human Factors in Computing Systems* (ACM 2012).

[125] A Pols and A Spahn, 'Designing for the values of democracy and justice' in J van den Hoven, PE Vermaas and I van de Poel (eds), *Handbook of Ethics, Values, and Technological Design: Sources, Theory, Values and Application Domains* (Springer 2015) 351.

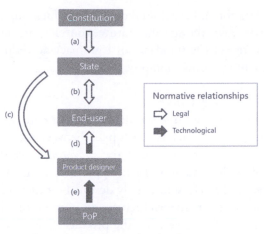

Figure 1.1 Normative relationships in law and technology

(1) the traditional force of law, (2) the norms' implementation in and through the code, or (3) a mixture of the two. In the second and third scenarios, code complements law.[126] Examples include encryption used to implement data protection requirements flowing from a public-order norm in relationship (c), or a firewall preventing an employee's computer from accessing social media, thus implementing a private contractual norm.

Whether or not these code rules aim explicitly to instrumentalise legal norms, they by definition exist separately from the law's corpus of rules.[127] Viewed traditionally, the legal effect of the data protection statute or the employment contract applies regardless of either instrument's implementation in or through code. But a corollary arises from this: it is precisely in the separateness of the two mechanisms of regulation that the architectural force of code, which implements some form of normativity, is able to 'supplant the legal infrastructure of the state'.[128] Whereas the data protection statute or employment contract awaits ex post enforcement following detection of some kind of breach or failure to act, code simply goes ahead and imposes some

---

[126] Leenes calls this 'state endorsed techno-regulation'. See R Leenes, 'Framing techno-regulation: An exploration of state and non-state regulation by technology' (2011) 5 *Legisprudence* 143, 160.

[127] Both Schmidt and Reed discuss the concept of 'law-system quality' in relation to public norms fitting technology (this is top-down, relationship (c) normativity). See A Schmidt, 'Radbruch in cyberspace: About law-system quality and ICT innovation' (2009) 3 *Masaryk University Journal of Law and Technology* 195; Reed (n 106). By contrast, I am concerned with bottom-up instantiation of normativity in relationships (d) and (e).

[128] Radin (n 62) 143.

alternative configuration of behavioural constraint which might not comport with the substantive law (the specific statute, contract, or the whole corpus of legal rules) nor reflect the standards of legitimacy according to which all behaviour-constraining norms should be made.

The Programmer of the Programmer

The notion of underlying, ex ante standards is at the core of digisprudence, and is reflected pragmatically in relationship (e), between the product designer and what Vismann and Krajewski call the *programmer of the programmer* ('PoP').[129] The PoP designs the tools that the product designer in turn uses to create the products and services ultimately destined for the end-user. Situated at a 'constitutional' level of the product design process, the decisions made by the PoP fundamentally frame what the product designer can and cannot do. The PoP thus has a crucial power to define the rules of the design game before it even begins. This idea of 'technological constitutionalism', which I link with Hart's concept of secondary rules,[130] suggests one locus for the operationalisation of formal principles that can constrain the substantive design of code to encourage legitimacy. I will discuss this concept in greater detail in Chapter 2, and then again in Chapter 7 in relation to the operationalisation of digisprudence.[131]

1.5 In the Real World

Above I discussed DRM in terms of computational legalism. Later in Chapters 6 and 7, when setting out the digisprudential framework of affordances and their operationalisation, I ground the theory in real-world code through a discussion of its application to two important contemporary classes of technology, namely blockchain applications and the Internet of Things (IoT). At this point it makes sense to lay some brief groundwork as to how the theory will apply to them.

(a) Blockchain Applications

The first case study focuses on so-called 'smart contracts' built upon the foundation of blockchain technology (later I shift from the term 'smart contract' to 'blockchain application', for reasons I will explain below). Like DRM, smart contracts represent another very explicit example of the embodiment of rules that have normative significance within the fabric of a digital artefact.

---

[129] Vismann and Krajewski (n 28). For an earlier discussion alluding to a similar concept see Weizenbaum (n 1) 100 *et seq.*

[130] Hart (n 82) 91 *et seq.*

[131] See Section 7.1.

Although blockchain technology is still maturing – the Bitcoin paper that proposed its initial design was published anonymously in 2008,[132] and the first blockchain went live in January the next year[133] – the implications and the publicity surrounding it[134] are the subject of increasing scrutiny from the legal academy. While hype on its own does not justify academic attention, the peculiarly normative characteristics of smart contracts and their design raise questions of explicit interest in this context.[135] While there is increasing scepticism about the practical value of blockchains,[136] those characteristics mean they will remain problematic even if they turn out not to be the revolutionary technology some suggest they are.

Blockchain Design
To fully appreciate the relevance of blockchain applications from a digisprudential perspective, some knowledge of their architectural characteristics is necessary.[137] Blockchains are public[138] databases (or 'ledgers' – hence the alternative term 'distributed ledger technology', or 'DLT') which are stored on a number of computers ('miners') which together constitute a peer-to-peer network. To add to the chain requires consensus among the network's

---

[132] S Nakamoto, 'Bitcoin: A peer-to-peer electronic cash system' (2008) <https://bitcoin.org/bitcoin.pdf> last accessed 15 April 2021.

[133] P De Filippi and A Wright, *Blockchain and the Law: The Rule of Code* (Harvard University Press 2018) 205.

[134] By 2016, blockchain had almost reached the 'peak of inflated expectations' in Gartner's Hype Cycle for Emerging Technologies. See Gartner, 'Gartner's 2016 Hype Cycle for Emerging Technologies identifies three key trends that organizations must track to gain competitive advantage' *Gartner* (16 August 2016) <https://www.gartner.com/en/newsroom/press-releases/2016-08-16-gartners-2016-hype-cycle-for-emerging-technologies-identifies-three-key-trends-that-organizations-must-track-to-gain-competitive-advantage> last accessed 4 March 2021.

[135] RH Weber, '"Rose is a rose is a rose is a rose" – what about code and law?' (2018) 34 *Computer Law & Security Review* 701, 705.

[136] I Kaminska, 'Growing scepticism challenges the blockchain hype' *Financial Times* (20 June 2017) <https://www.ft.com/content/b5b1a5f2-5030-11e7-bfb8-997009366969> last accessed 4 March 2021.

[137] For a more in-depth primer on blockchains, see M Pilkington, 'Blockchain technology: Principles and applications' in FX Olleros and M Zhegu (eds), *Research Handbook on Digital Transformations* (Edward Elgar Publishing 2016).

[138] Private ('permissioned') blockchains also exist, but because these are generally used internally within an organisation they mostly lack the focus on end-user behavioural regulation represented in relationship (d) in Figure 1.1 above, and so I do not include them in this analysis. For more on private blockchains, see V Buterin, 'On public and private blockchains' *Ethereum Foundation Blog* (7 August 2015) <https://blog.ethereum.org/2015/08/07/on-public-and-private-blockchains/> last accessed 4 March 2021.

nodes, and so a new 'block' of data will only be added if a majority of miners agree that its addition meets the requirements governing that particular blockchain.[139] These rules are known as the blockchain's 'protocol', and they define how the blockchain operates and what the incentives and costs are for participants, including the miners who provide the network's infrastructure and the end-users who transact with/through it. Two prominent examples of different blockchain protocols are Bitcoin,[140] the cryptocurrency and original application of a blockchain protocol, and Ethereum,[141] the first blockchain to support sophisticated automation through the provision of a decentralised computing platform (the Ethereum Virtual Machine).

The protocol will include some mechanism for the miners to reach consensus on what should be stored, including both metadata about transactions and new smart contracts to be executed. The question of how to reach consensus among anonymous computers is connected with what is known as the 'Byzantine fault problem', where the networked nodes each have a different understanding of the state of the chain but consensus must be reached for the system to be workable. Blockchain protocols overcome this using a combination of public key cryptography and *hashing*.[142] The former is a mechanism for uniquely and conclusively identifying each node within the network by a public signature (key), while the latter is a method for generating a unique signature (a hash) from any given volume of data (in this case, the existing prior state of the blockchain). Each block is assigned a unique hash, generated from a combination of that block's data and the hashes of all the blocks that are already on the chain. This means that if the last block in two copies of the chain have the same hash, one can be completely confident that the copies of the chain are identical all the way back to the first block, and therefore that neither copy has been tampered with.

When a miner solves the mathematical challenge specified in the chain's protocol (this is how new blocks are added, for which the miner receives a reward), the proposed solution is broadcast to the network for the other miners to verify. They independently generate a new hash from the existing state of the chain and the proposed solution broadcasted by the 'winning' miner, and if the solution meets the requirements of the protocol, each miner adds the block to their local copy of the chain. In this way the copies of the chain are kept identical and up to date across the many miners that store them.

---

[139] De Filippi and Wright (n 133) 2.
[140] Nakamoto (n 132).
[141] Ethereum Foundation, 'Ethereum white paper' (Ethereum Foundation, 22 August 2018) <https://ethereum.org/whitepaper> last accessed 4 March 2021.
[142] Pilkington (n 137) 228.

An important corollary of this proposal mechanism, particularly its use of hashes that represent the historical state of the chain, is that once a block has been added its contents are both immutable[143] and verifiable by observers.[144]

Copies of the blockchain, including both its protocol and the data that it stores (for example transaction metadata, account balances, smart contract code) are replicated across the network, providing resilience through decentralisation.[145] Disabling (even physically) one of the network's computers will not delete the blockchain or prevent the code it stores from executing.[146] The lack of centralised (state) authority controlling what gets added to the chain is part of the ideology driving the technology:[147] provided participants follow the rules contained in the protocol, they get the benefits of a tamper-resistant, 'trustless' database with no overseeing entity.

'Smart Contracts'?

At present blockchains are probably best-known as the foundation of cryptocurrencies, but another related application that is potentially more disruptive from a legal perspective are so-called 'smart contracts' ('SCs'). SC platforms provide varying levels of sophistication. The Bitcoin protocol provides some very basic programming capabilities which can allow very limited SCs to be written. Other platforms provide a more sophisticated programming foundation for SCs, of which the most prominent is Ethereum.[148]

Ethereum's creators describe it as a 'next-generation smart contract and decentralized application platform'.[149] It complements the architectural characteristics of blockchains with a fully-fledged programming execution environment, meaning computationally rich functionality can be combined with the immutability, decentralisation, and 'trustless trust' of blockchains. The

---

[143] Ibid. 233–4.

[144] Ibid. 227.

[145] De Filippi and Wright (n 133) 2.

[146] This emulates the ethos of ARPANET, precursor to the modern Internet, designed during the Cold War to be resistant to physical attacks on infrastructure. See BM Leiner et al., 'Brief history of the Internet' (Internet Society 1997) 3 <https://www.internetsociety.org/internet/history-internet/brief-history-internet/> last accessed 4 March 2021.

[147] On which, see D Golumbia, *The Politics of Bitcoin: Software as Right-Wing Extremism* (University of Minnesota Press 2016).

[148] For an empirical overview of the current major SC platforms, see M Bartoletti and L Pompianu, 'An empirical analysis of smart contracts: Platforms, applications, and design patterns' (2017) arXiv preprint arXiv:1703.06322 <https://arxiv.org/abs/1703.06322> last accessed 4 March 2021.

[149] Ethereum Foundation (n 141).

innovative possibilities of software's plasticity can thus be undergirded with the stability inherent in the 'anti-plasticity' of blockchains.

'Smart contracts' combine 'Turing-completeness, value-awareness, blockchain-awareness and state',[150] meaning they can define complex conditions, execute arbitrary behaviours when certain conditions are met, maintain and monitor states over time, and record the outcomes in the immutable blockchain. All of this is potentially automated; conditions defined in the 'contract' are 'live', awaiting whatever change(s) are necessary to trigger the rules it contains. In this sense smart contracts are not passive instructions on what the contracting parties should do, rather they are 'more like "autonomous agents" that live inside of the Ethereum execution environment, always executing a specific piece of code when "poked" by a message or transaction'.[151]

Multiple SCs can be bundled together by a central business logic (itself written in code and stored on the blockchain) to create a 'distributed organisation' ('DO')[152] and even a 'distributed autonomous organisation' ('DAO'), which can operate without any human input.[153] These artefacts' logic enables, disables, and manages individual SCs, using them as tools to effect external changes according to the rules predefined in the code. A DO could, for example, require a majority vote from its (human) members as a condition of a given smart contract being triggered. Again, the decentralised and 'trustless' nature of blockchain design obviates the need for a trusted centralised authority (a traditional board or committee), and so notional governance of the organisation can be achieved even where the membership is geographically dispersed, or even unknown.[154] SCs consult external sources of data, known as 'oracles',[155] to check for particular conditions in the world outside the code, executing predetermined logics when necessary conditions are met. By interacting with a cryptocurrency and the APIs of other services, real-world transactions can be effected, involving human actors (themselves

---

[150] Ibid.

[151] Ibid.

[152] V Buterin, 'DAOs, DACs, DAs and more: An incomplete terminology guide' *Ethereum Foundation Blog* (6 May 2014) <https://blog.ethereum.org/2014/05/06/daos-dacs-das-and-more-an-incomplete-terminology-guide/> last accessed 4 March 2021.

[153] Ibid.

[154] A Wright and P De Filippi, 'Decentralized blockchain technology and the rise of lex cryptographia' (Social Science Research Network 2015) SSRN Scholarly Paper ID 2580664, 15–16 <https://papers.ssrn.com/abstract=2580664> last accessed 4 March 2021.

[155] Cardozo Blockchain Project, '"Smart contracts" & legal enforceability' (Benjamin N Cardozo School of Law 2018) 6.

mediated by code infrastructures, as in the 'gig economy'[156]) and even other artefacts such as drones.[157]

The power of such code is intuitively appreciable. When specific conditions that are computationally representable are met, the code self-executes according to its internal logic, whatever that might be, and the outcomes are enforced regardless of any relevant real-world considerations. With the outcomes of the code's execution being stored in the underlying blockchain alongside the code itself, this means both its logic and its results are immutable once they are 'enacted', executed, and stored. Thus code, in a very real (and legally significant) sense, becomes 'law', through the 'collapsing [of] contract formation and enforcement into a single instrument'.[158] The coincidence of form and substance means that when executed, the material effects of the smart contract are governed by the dictates of pure code, regardless of any ambiguity or subjective understanding that might exist in the minds of the humans involved. One can appreciate the parallel with the discussion of computational legalism above, noting that code is at once rule and reality; the normative collapsed into the descriptive.

(b) The Internet of Things

Compared with blockchain applications, the Internet of Things (IoT) is perhaps a simpler (but no less important) area to conceptualise and analyse. In the early 1990s Mark Weiser, a pioneer of what has variously been termed 'ambient intelligence'[159] and 'ubiquitous computing', spoke of the profundity of technologies that 'weave themselves into the fabric of everyday life until they are indistinguishable from it'.[160] The US Federal Trade Commission has defined the IoT as 'devices or sensors – other than computers, smartphones, or tablets – that connect, communicate or transmit information with or between each other through the Internet'.[161] This focus on sensors

---

[156] Buterin describes a DAO as 'an entity that lives on the internet and exists autonomously, but also heavily relies on hiring individuals to perform certain tasks that the automaton itself cannot do'. See Buterin, 'DAOs, DACs, DAs and more' (n 152).

[157] De Filippi and Wright (n 133) 156. For an example of the latter, see J Perez, 'XYO game-changer: We've executed a smart contract with a drone!' *Medium* (21 November 2018) <https://medium.com/xyonetwork/xyo-game-changer-weve-executed-a-smart-contract-with-a-drone-4deb414af67b> last accessed 4 March 2021.

[158] KEC Levy, 'Book-smart, not street-smart: Blockchain-based smart contracts and the social workings of law' (2017) 3 *Engaging Science, Technology, and Society* 1, 3.

[159] Hildebrandt and Koops (n 30) 430–1.

[160] M Weiser, 'The computer for the 21st century' (1991) *Scientific American* 94.

[161] Federal Trade Commission, 'Internet of Things: Privacy and security in a connected world' (Federal Trade Commission 2015) 6.

and devices other than traditional platforms (computers and smartphones/tablets) implies the 'weaving into daily life' to which Weiser referred. Indeed, IoT devices are designed to do precisely this, both ubiquitously and invisibly, and as such are becoming an increasingly significant proportion of the total number of devices connected to the Internet. This is in part due to a 'chip-centric mentality', where manufacturers have bought into commercial hype suggesting that a connected device is better than an unconnected one.[162] The results of this are occasionally absurd.[163]

IoT devices both illustrate the design theories mentioned above and exemplify numerous aspects of computational legalism, especially opacity, immutability, and pervasiveness. Because they are intended to be embedded and pervasive, they by nature tend towards both minimal affordances and very strictly defined inscriptions. The Amazon Dash Button, for example, consists of just a single button and an LED indicator. Its inscription is thus a simple one of 'press the button', and its design affords that and little more ('adhesion' and 'throwing' are perhaps the only alternative action possibilities). As I describe in more detail in Chapter 6, behind this apparent simplicity and minimal interface lies a complex series of technical events that are kept hidden from the device's end-user but which are potentially of great importance to her (imagine the device being mis-used by a young child or pet).[164] As with other computing systems, the extent to which complex logic should be hidden from the user is one which will vary depending on the system in question. Nevertheless, the central issue of transparency about what lies beneath the physical device's 'tip of the iceberg' is a crucially important one. IoT devices, particularly those that have a single function like the Dash Button, generally combine simple physicality on the part of the object with complex and opaque computation on the 'back-end'. There is therefore significant scope for dissonance between the end-user's understanding of the device's affordances and what it in fact does.[165]

In terms of immutability, the poor infrastructural provision made for updates, coupled with a lack of commitment to long-term oversight, have resulted in many examples of IoT devices being used as nodes in bot-nets,

---

[162] W Hartzog and E Selinger, 'The Internet of Heirlooms and Disposable Things' (2016) 17 *North Carolina Journal of Law & Technology* 581.

[163] For an amusing selection of examples that demonstrate this, see the Twitter account 'Internet of Shit (@internetofshit)' *Twitter* <https://twitter.com/internetofshit> last accessed 4 March 2021.

[164] Federal Trade Commission (n 161) 22.

[165] A Matassa and R Simeoni, 'Eliciting affordances for smart objects in IoT era' in *Internet of Things: User-Centric IoT* (Springer 2015).

being left open to external hacking, and other forms of unintended breach.[166] This lack of flexibility, when coupled with the devices' intended pervasiveness, is potentially deeply problematic.

These problems can even combine with those of blockchain applications – as I mentioned above, the latter are capable of effecting changes in the physical world via IoT devices, such as drones and 'smart' devices. The combination implies the concept of 'smart property', where the hybrid IoT–blockchain artefact is autonomous, such that the IoT device's physical functionality is controlled by the logic contained in the blockchain application (for example a smart door lock might refuse to open after a code-based 'lease' expires[167]).

1.6 Conclusion

The goal of this introductory chapter has been to lay out the main contours of digisprudence, why it matters, and how it differs from existing literature, particularly that on 'code as law' and 'compliance by design'. It has also started to consider contemporary technologies through this novel analytical lens, an applied analysis that will be picked up again in Chapter 6. As mentioned above, the rest of the book follows the dialectical structure of the theory, exploring each element in greater depth: Part I problematises code from both design and legal theory standpoints; Part II considers the existing literature on standards that make both legal and technological normativity legitimate, and identifies the production gap that digisprudence aims to fill; finally, Part III synthesises the analysis, setting out the framework of digisprudential affordances before exploring some options for practical implementation and for future research.

I suggested above that there is real scope for reinvigoration of the debate that Lessig brought to prominence in the late 1990s, to take better account of the conceptual overlaps between legal theory, philosophy of technology, STS, and design studies. In the past two decades, academic lawyers have perhaps relied too heavily on Lessig's framework and the many assumptions that came along with it. My hope in the rest of this book is to reboot this conversation, renewing it through a combination of some of the rich theoretical insights that these fields have to offer with a pragmatic view of how code is actually made. I will only be able to scratch the surface of all of this of course, but in doing so I hope at the very least to raise some interesting new questions and to highlight some useful directions in which this fascinating and hugely important topic might be taken.

---

166 Hartzog and Selinger (n 162).
167 Levy (n 158) 3.

Part I

Computational Legalism
and the Rule(s) of Code

2

A Design Perspective:
Code is *More* than Law

The swift effectiveness of a technological code, which cannot, when seen through legal eyes, appear as anything other than uncanny, renders any possible competition between law and computer pointless.[1]

This chapter sets out how code has a direct, concrete effect on the behaviour of end-users, viewed from the perspective of design theory and the philosophy of technology. I pick up this contribution later in Chapter 6 where I use these same concepts to set out the framework of digisprudential affordances. Engagement with these theories in the legal literature is minimal; the tendency so far has been to treat design only in the abstract, without a concerted engagement with the theory on what things actually do, and how they do it. Without that, the legal view of technology is limited to that of an outside observer, rather than one that can engage with the material processes of production from which the effects of code ultimately flow. As I suggested in Chapter 1, and will consider again in Chapter 5, a focus on production is critical if the aspiration of computational legitimacy is to be realised.

Throughout the book I refer to the concept of 'technological normativity'. Borrowed from Hildebrandt,[2] the term usefully implies a contrast between code's normativity and the legal normativity that lawyers are more familiar with.[3] Her definition of it is also closely linked to the theory of affordance, which I explore in detail below. Technological normativity is 'the way a particular technological device or infrastructure actually constrains human actions, inviting or enforcing, inhibiting or prohibiting types of behaviour'.[4]

---

[1] C Vismann and M Krajewski, 'Computer juridisms' (2007) *Grey Room* 90, 93.

[2] M Hildebrandt, 'Legal and technological normativity: more (and less) than twin sisters' (2008) 12 *Techné: Research in Philosophy and Technology* 169.

[3] On the latter, see N MacCormick, *Institutions of Law: An Essay in Legal Theory* (Oxford University Press 2007) part 1.

[4] Hildebrandt, 'Legal and technological normativity' (n 2) 173.

These effects can be intentionally or unintentionally imposed by the designer, and can be an immediate or emerging characteristic of the code she creates.

The bulk of this chapter sets out three primary and interconnected theories: affordance, inscription, and the theory of technological mediation. Taken together, they provide us with the conceptual tools to consider the ways in which an artefact's design constitutes and delimits its user's possibilities for action. We can then appreciate the same issue from a normative standpoint, considering how, in the process of producing code, one might consciously embody those possibilities, aiming towards the goal of producing legitimate normative architectures. That will be the topic of Part III of the book.

2.1 Affordance

The facilitation by an artefact's design of a particular action or behaviour for a particular individual is known as an 'affordance'. The concept was originally developed in the late 1960s by Gibson, a perceptual psychologist, who defined affordances collectively as what an artefact '*offers* the animal, what it *provides* or *furnishes*, either for good or ill'.[5] The theory of affordance was developed and introduced into the design sphere by Norman, who defines the concept as 'a relationship between the properties of an object and the capabilities of the agent that determine just how the object could possibly be used'.[6] A common representation of the concept of affordance compares two doors, one with a panel for pushing, and another with a handle that can be pulled (Figure 2.1).[7]

All things being equal, the door on the left can only be pushed – that is, it only affords pushing – because there is no part of it that affords pulling (unless one manages to grip the edges of the panel). The handle on the door on the right affords both pulling and pushing – the ability to grasp it readily enables the individual to pull the door towards her (assuming of course that the door's hinges themselves afford pulling in that direction). The door on the right has at least two affordances for a non-disabled person: one of pulling, and another of pushing. (For a disabled person, it might be that neither door affords pulling or pushing, highlighting the contingent relationality of affordance, discussed next.)

---

[5] JJ Gibson, *The Ecological Approach to Visual Perception* (classic edn, Psychology Press 2015) 119 (emphasis supplied). For a valuable discussion of the ecological foundations of affordance theory, see M Heras-Escribano, *The Philosophy of Affordances* (Springer 2019) chapter 2.

[6] DA Norman, *The Design of Everyday Things* (MIT Press 2013) 11.

[7] Norman discusses this ibid. 15. See also W Hartzog, *Privacy's Blueprint: The Battle to Control the Design of New Technologies* (Harvard University Press 2018) 13.

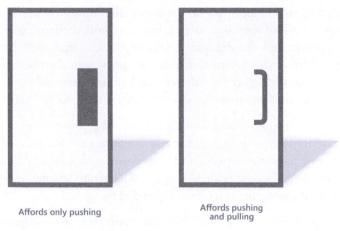

Affords only pushing

Affords pushing and pulling

Figure 2.1 Affordances of pushing and pulling

Individual affordances can be both positive and negative, which is to say beneficial and injurious to the individual, each to varying degrees. Gibson seeks to avoid the value judgements suggested by the terms 'positive' and 'negative', stating instead that such descriptions can be applied objectively if their meanings are 'pinned down to biological and behavioral facts'.[8] So, for example, a fire can afford the warmth that is necessary to life, but it can also afford burning, which can mean injury, and potentially death.[9] The extent of the benefit or injury will depend on the organism in question. Crucially, then, affordances are not objective physical properties of the artefact, but rather they arise through the relationship between it and a particular individual, as governed by those properties. Gibson illustrates this relationship through the examination of a hypothetical walking surface:

> Note that the four properties listed – horizontal, flat, extended, and rigid – would be *physical* properties of a surface if they were measured with the scales and standard units used in physics. As an affordance of support for a species of animal, however, they have to be measured *relative to the animal*. They are unique for that animal. They are not just abstract physical properties. They have unity relative to the posture and behavior of the animal being considered. So an affordance cannot be measured as we measure in physics.[10]

---

[8] Gibson (n 5) 129.
[9] Ibid. 128–9.
[10] Ibid. 120 (emphasis supplied).

A surface that affords support to a domestic cat (that is, it is 'stand-on-able'[11]) may or may not afford the same to an adult elephant; the particular mix of physical properties and the size and weight of both animals will determine which use-possibilities are afforded to each. It can be seen then how the concept of affordance highlights the inherent and simultaneous objectivity and subjectivity of an artefact's potential effects in the world. As Norman puts it,

> [t]he presence of an affordance is jointly determined by the qualities of the object and the abilities of the agent that is interacting . . . We are used to thinking that properties are associated with objects. But affordance is not a property. An affordance is a relationship. Whether an affordance exists depends on the properties of both the object and the agent.[12]

With these definitions in mind, one can appreciate that designers must include the necessary properties in the artefact in order for the desired relationship between it and the intended end-user to arise. This is inevitably a contingent exercise: the designer cannot anticipate the properties of every conceivable end-user. Nevertheless, a central aspect of the design enterprise is imagining certain classes of end-user to whom the process will be oriented, the properties of those proxies implying the properties that the code must have in order to bring about the affordance relationships the designer wishes there to be.[13] The interfaces of products are built around this central notion, translating the state of the underlying code that the designer wishes the end-user to see into some form that is likely to make sense to her.

(a) Real and Perceived Affordance

Importantly, an affordance need not be perceived to exist; it is a fact about how the properties of the artefact and the organism relate to one another.[14] Affordances are potentials that may not be within the organism's awareness and may never be realised, but nevertheless the relationship is always present and ready to be acted upon for as long as the properties necessary for it are extant in both the artefact and the organism.[15]

---

[11] Ibid. 119.

[12] Norman, *The Design of Everyday Things* (n 6) 11.

[13] JR Maier and GM Fadel, 'Affordance-based methods for design' in *Proceedings of DETC* (The American Society of Mechanical Engineers 2003) 4. See also LA Suchman, *Human–Machine Reconfigurations: Plans and Situated Actions* (2nd edn, Cambridge University Press 2007) chapter 11.

[14] Norman, *The Design of Everyday Things* (n 6) 13.

[15] See P Nagy and G Neff, 'Imagined affordance: Reconstructing a keyword for communication theory' (2015) 1 *Social Media + Society* 3; S Faraj and B Azad, 'The materiality of technology: An affordance perspective' in PM Leonardi, BA Nardi and J Kallinikos (eds),

This is what Norman refers to in later work as 'real', as opposed to 'perceived', affordance.[16] For example, a particular fruit may afford nutrition to a particular species of animal, but if the animal is unaware of this the relationship will never be acted on, despite its extant potentiality. Perceived affordances are those which the organism 'picks up on', which, as the example just given demonstrates, do not necessarily represent the full range of relationships that exist between it and the thing in question. The distinction is crucially important in the digital context because, as Norman puts it, 'in graphical, screen-based interfaces, the designer primarily can control only perceived affordances [because] the computer system already comes with built-in physical [i.e. real] affordances'.[17] The potential discrepancy between real and perceived affordances is especially marked in code artefacts, such as the Internet of Things, that have no interface at all (the form of opacity this creates will be discussed in more detail in Chapter 6).

Norman's comment hints at an important truth about the power of the designer to shape end-users' perceptions through the choices they make in designing the interface, or boundary, between the interior of the artefact and those who might use or otherwise be affected by its operation. A corollary of this is that in shaping the end-user's perceptions of what actions the artefact makes possible, other underlying (real) affordances can be hidden from sight. Consider, for example, the ability to view and alter the source code of a webpage via the developer tools built into modern web browsers, or the ability to submit false details to an email registration system to preserve anonymity. More abstractly, but no less powerfully, the 'stickiness' of an artefact's default configuration might suppress any tendency the individual has to question and to imagine whether there might be some configuration that better reflects her interests or preferences. This relates closely to the issue of 'dark patterns' in design, discussed below. I will say more about the normative role of default configurations later,[18] but one can appreciate the importance of the relationship between an artefact's real affordances and how these are communicated to the end-user. That communication might be anywhere between clear, unambiguous, and isomorphic with the system's true state on the one hand, and deceiving, obfuscatory, abstract, and concealing of the real affordance on the other. The crucial point is that in most cases the extent and quality of that communication is defined at the outset by the designer.

Materiality and Organizing: Social Interaction in a Technological World (Oxford University Press 2012) 250–1.

[16] DA Norman, 'Affordance, conventions, and design' (1999) 6 _interactions_ 38.

[17] Ibid. 39.

[18] See 'Default Configurations' in Section 3.2.

Signifiers

The design of the artefact can incorporate signifiers which communicate to the end-user what affordances are present and thus how the artefact 'should' be used (this is an important part of the artefact's normativity and is connected to technological intentionality, discussed below).[19] For example, if we return to Figure 2.1 above, the panel on the door on the left signifies where to push, while the handle on the door on the right signifies where to grasp (which in turn signifies pulling). Another common example on the web is the use of underlining to signify hyperlinks, in contrast to the plain surrounding text.[20] Of course, in order to act as a signifier, that element of the artefact must be perceived by the end-user (it can, however, be ambiguous – the hinges of the door might afford pushing, despite the handle only signifying the affordance of pulling). The presence of signifiers is an important element of communicating to the end-user how the artefact works, but a signifier's utility is also contingent on its accuracy, honesty, and completeness.[21]

The fact that function or capability x is signified to the end-user of course does not entail that function or capability y is also signified – the appropriate functions and capabilities must be signified at the appropriate moment. The question of what to signify, and when, is therefore extremely important in helping the end-user form an accurate mental model of the system;[22] designs often afford functionalities without signifying them, perhaps to hide complex functionality from end-users, or to provide the functionality required by some external force (for example a regulatory or ethical norm) without advertising it because its use is at odds with the commercial interests of the supplier. Consider, for example, the complex cookie preference notices that appeared following the coming into force of the General Data Protection Regulation (GDPR) in 2018. While these often provide an interface for choosing which cookies are set on the end-user's computer (that is, they afford a means of control), the mechanism of accessing this interface, usually a textual link, is often much less clearly signified than the option to accept all cookies. The latter is of course perceived to be more profitable for the website operator, since

---

[19] Norman, *The Design of Everyday Things* (n 6) 13 *et seq.*

[20] For a fascinating discussion of hypertext and the 'signifying strategies' of text, see NK Hayles, 'Print is flat, code is deep: The importance of media-specific analysis' (2004) 25 *Poetics Today* 67.

[21] The efficacy of a signifier also relies on tacit cultural knowledge; a panel on a door is unlikely to signify 'push' uniformly across all cultures (or even age groups). This highlights the role of the designer's assumptions in targeting a given class of end-user. See F Flores et al., 'Computer systems and the design of organizational interaction' (1988) 6 *ACM Transactions on Information Systems (TOIS)* 153, 156–8.

[22] Hartzog (n 7) 27.

it enables targeted behavioural advertising.[23] This type of adversarial design is an example of a 'dark pattern', which will be discussed in the next section.[24] In summary, then, one can appreciate how important signifiers are in assisting the end-user to develop an appropriate mental model of the system she is interacting with.[25]

2.2 Infusing Code with Normativity

Affordances are relationships that arise as a result of the particular characteristics of an individual and an artefact. In many cases they exist simply by virtue of those properties, as in the example of the surface that can bear the weight of – afford support to – an elephant. If that surface is, say, a rocky outcrop, then the affordance does not arise through any conscious decision-making on the part of a 'designer'; it just is. When it comes to code-based artefacts, however, affordances can of course be designed consciously, in order to make them 'usable' and create new behavioural possibilities for a certain class of end-user: 'technology is not the design of physical things . . . It is the design of practices and possibilities to be realized through artifacts.'[26] From the perspective of regulating what end-users can do, the conscious choices about how to make an artefact useful can develop into mechanisms that actively constitute, constrain, or suggest particular courses of action, thus infusing the design not just with usefulness but also with normative effect. These 'grammars of action' inevitably reflect the assumptions of the designer around who will use the system and what it should, will, and ought to be used for.[27] Those assumptions can of course be problematic; in the next chapter I relate this to code's limited representation of the world.[28] These assumptions are what a legitimately designed artefact will allow to be challenged by the end-user, whoever she may be, and with whatever particular characteristics she may have.

---

[23] Whether or not such advertising is effective is a separate (and open) question.

[24] For a study of dark patterns in cookie notice design, see P Grassl et al., 'Dark and bright patterns in cookie consent requests' (PsyArXiv 2020) preprint <https://osf.io/gqs5h> last accessed 4 March 2021.

[25] The role of signifiers in achieving digisprudential legitimacy is discussed further in 'Opacity' in Section 6.3.

[26] Flores et al. (n 21) 153. See also Norman, *The Design of Everyday Things* (n 6) chapter 6. The notion of 'usability' in design has developed into a significant field in its own right, particularly in relation to 'user experience' ('UX') on the web.

[27] PE Agre, 'From high tech to human tech: Empowerment, measurement, and social studies of computing' (1994) 3 *Computer Supported Cooperative Work (CSCW)* 167, 184–5.

[28] See 'Limited Ontology' in Section 3.2.

(a) Disaffordance

Gibson's notion of the positivity or negativity of affordances is concerned with their outcome (for example a fire warming an organism versus burning it). This must be distinguished from both (1) the fact that interaction is prevented and the affordance relationship does not exist (what Norman terms an 'anti-affordance'[29]), and (2) the subjective misapprehension of the end-user as to the existence of the affordance, where she misinterprets the information she is receiving and believes there to be a particular relationship between herself and the artefact when in fact there is no such relationship (or not the one she thinks there is). Both Gibson and Norman discuss the example of a glass pane covering an opening, giving an erroneous impression of the affordance of passage. Norman's notion of an anti-affordance points simply to the objective fact that there is no such affordance, whether or not the end-user is aware of this (a blind person, for example, is simply not afforded passage, regardless of the fact she cannot see the glass to perceive its affordances).[30]

Lockton draws on Lessig's discussion of 'architectures of control'[31] to take the notion of 'anti-affordance' further, adding the element of intention that is less evident in Norman's analysis. Architectures of control are 'features, structures or methods of operation designed into any planned system with which a user interacts, which are intended to enforce or restrict certain user behaviour'.[32] His discussion centres on DRM, including the Sony BMG scandal discussed in Chapter 1. Lockton's notion of positivity refers to what is ex ante permitted by the designer, versus what is not – there is, in other words, the intended, positive affording of a particular action by the designer (cf. Gibson's notion of 'positive'). The corollary for Lockton is that 'negative' affordance is about the 'engineering of obedience'.[33] He is concerned with the intent of the designer, which of course chimes with my central theme of code's production. Lockton suggests the term *disaffordance* to describe designs that have 'functionality deliberately removed . . . or with the functionality deliberately hidden or obscured to reduce users' ability to use the product in certain ways, or a combination of the two'.[34] Disaffordances are thus

---

[29] Norman, *The Design of Everyday Things* (n 6) 11.
[30] Gibson (n 5) 133–4; Norman, *The Design of Everyday Things* (n 6) 11–12.
[31] L Lessig, *Code: Version 2.0* (Basic Books 2006) chapter 4.
[32] D Lockton, 'Architectures of control in product design' (2006) *Engineering Designer: The Journal of the Institution of Engineering Designers* 28.
[33] D Lockton, 'Disaffordances and engineering obedience' *Architectures* (22 October 2006) <http://architectures.danlockton.co.uk/2006/10/22/disaffordances-and-engineering-obedience/> last accessed 4 March 2021.
[34] Ibid.

'deliberate, intentional, and strategic', as opposed to inadvertent or the result of incompetent design. They therefore embody a conscious value in a way which Gibson explicitly, and Norman implicitly, avoid. The term disaffordance has gained only modest traction,[35] but it is instructive in encapsulating the idea of how an artefact can conceal, discourage, or forbid the possibility of certain behaviours as a result of conscious design decisions. In aggregate, one can appreciate the role played by disaffordances in constraining end-users in their interactions with an artefact. As Longford puts it,

> [t]he reconfiguration of the terms of cybercitizenship which these technologies effect is achieved via a gradual process in which new habits, expectations and practices on the part of web users are cultivated and/or inculcated through subtle mechanisms of inducement, coercion, and reward designed into the very experience of cyberspace.[36]

When disaffordances are designed that are contrary to the end-user's interests, they are sometimes termed 'abusive design', and examples that exploit commonly used design conventions against the end-user have come to be known as 'dark patterns'.[37] Such practices demonstrate the power of the designer to exploit the end-user for purposes which may not be in her interests; Conti and Sobiesk describe the 'intent on the part of the designer to deliberately sacrifice the user experience in an attempt to achieve the designer's goals ahead of those of the user'.[38] They set out a taxonomy of approaches used in malicious web interfaces, and provide representative examples that most end-users will be familiar with. These include making form fields mandatory (coercion), use of double or triple negatives in questions (confusion), advertising (distraction), delaying access until an advert is watched (forced work), covering desired text with popups (interruption), hiding access to the free version of an application deep within a website's navigation (manipulating

---

[35] See DE Wittkower, 'Principles of anti-discriminatory design' *2016 IEEE International Symposium on Ethics in Engineering, Science and Technology (ETHICS)* (IEEE 2016) 2 (acknowledging this fact in a discussion on how to avoid unethical discrimination in design).

[36] G Longford, 'Pedagogies of digital citizenship and the politics of code' (2005) 9 *Techné: Research in Philosophy and Technology* 68, 77.

[37] A Narayanan et al., 'Dark patterns: Past, present, and future' (2020) 18 *ACM Queue* 25; Consumer Council of Norway (Forbrukerrådet), 'Deceived by design: How tech companies use dark patterns to discourage us from exercising our rights to privacy' (Consumer Council of Norway (Forbrukerrådet) 2018) <https://fil.forbrukerradet.no/wp-content/uploads/2018/06/2018-06-27-deceived-by-design-final.pdf> last accessed 4 March 2021.

[38] G Conti and E Sobiesk, 'Malicious interface design: Exploiting the user' in *Proceedings of the 19th International Conference on the World Wide Web* (ACM Press 2010) 271.

navigation), reducing the contrast of closure buttons on adverts (obfuscation), and designing adverts to appear to be news content (trickery).[39] These approaches will often be data-driven, which is to say different versions of the same dark pattern will be served to different users in what are known as 'A/B tests', with the resulting data analytics being used to determine the most effective design (as determined from the perspective of the commercial enterprise's business model, of course).[40]

A recent example that exhibited some of these characteristics was the popup GDPR acceptance screen shown to Facebook users following the Regulation's coming into power in May 2018. The interface misleadingly displayed red notification circles behind the acceptance screen, including to users who in reality had no notifications waiting for them. This was a clear attempt to manipulate the end-user into accepting the new terms as quickly as possible, in order to gain access to the awaiting 'notifications'.[41] As Conti and Sobiesk note, such design practices can increase frustration and even render parts of the web inaccessible for certain classes of end-user, and their primary aim is generally to increase revenue for website operators.[42]

(b) Postphenomenology and Code's Mediation of Reality[43]

Postphenomenology explores the relationships between individuals and artefacts, with an emphasis on the material qualities of particular artefacts *per se*.[44] Verbeek describes postphenomenology as the analysis of the 'role played by specific technologies in specific contexts',[45] which asks what the normative effects are of their materiality on the mediation of the relationship between

---

[39] Ibid. 273.

[40] Narayanan et al. (n 37) 75–6, 80–1.

[41] Consumer Council of Norway (Forbrukerrådet) (n 37) 29. This report gives a detailed account of the interfaces Facebook used to communicate their GDPR update, including numerous examples of dark patterns and manipulative design.

[42] Conti and Sobiesk (n 38) 278–9. Interestingly, around a year after the GDPR came into force the Deceptive Experiences to Online Users Reduction Act was introduced to the US Senate, although it has not progressed from there. See <https://www.congress.gov/bill/116th-congress/senate-bill/1084/text> last accessed 4 March 2021.

[43] For a useful survey of the various overlapping terms in this field, see P-P Verbeek, 'Materializing morality: Design ethics and technological mediation' (2006) 31 *Science, Technology, & Human Values* 361, particularly at 368.

[44] P-P Verbeek, *What Things Do: Philosophical Reflections on Technology, Agency, and Design* (Penn State Press 2005) 3. Ihde, the 'father' of postphenomenology, discusses how the theory seeks to draw together classical phenomenology (Husserl, Heidegger, and Merleau-Ponty) and pragmatism (Peirce, James, and Dewey) in his *Postphenomenology and Technoscience: The Peking University Lectures* (SUNY Press 2009).

[45] Verbeek, *What Things Do* (n 44) 7.

humans and reality. A central claim is that technologies are neither wholly neutral nor wholly deterministic, and the ways in which their designs mediate reality are fundamentally more complex and ambiguous than either a simple socially or technologically deterministic view would suggest.[46] The relationships between humans and artefacts are grouped into those of perception – what the individual thinks she can do with the artefact – and those of action – what she can actually do with it (there is a parallel here with the distinction between real and perceived affordances). Technological mediation is the ongoing construction and manipulation of these two relationships by and through artefacts, the result of which is the co-constitution of reality for the end-user. The end-user and the artefact, in bringing together their particular characteristics, constitute a new reality through their relationship. We can conceptualise the relationship as in Figure 2.2.

One can appreciate the parallels with affordance theory; indeed, affordances are the individual building blocks that in aggregate make up the totality of technological mediation between a particular artefact and a particular end-user.[47] As discussed above, designers play a central role in defining what a given artefact affords, and thus the reality that the artefact's mediation of perception and action contributes to is to a significant degree determined by choices made by the designer, for better or worse.[48] This connects with the idea of constitutive normativity built into the architecture of an artefact, a topic I will discuss below.

(c) Code Mediating Perception

Perception is mediated by technology through the amplification or reduction of aspects of the world.[49] This relates to the signifiers discussed above: their design can draw the end-user's attention to the possibility of a particular use, or perhaps ward her off or distract her from perceiving it. Signifying by itself has no direct coercive effect on the end-user, but by mediating her perception it does play an important role in shaping her comprehension of an artefact and her ability to form an accurate mental picture of how it works and what

---

[46] D Ihde, *Technology and the Lifeworld: From Garden to Earth* (Indiana University Press 1990); Verbeek, 'Materializing morality' (n 43). On the latter point see Verbeek, *What Things Do* (n 44) 11.

[47] AH Kiran and P-P Verbeek, 'Trusting our selves to technology' (2010) 23 *Knowledge, Technology & Policy* 409.

[48] As Robertson notes, designers can 'privilege the agency of their users by providing resources for awareness in their systems'. See T Robertson, 'The public availability of actions and artefacts' (2002) 11 *Computer Supported Cooperative Work (CSCW)* 299, 311.

[49] For an in-depth discussion of the forms of perceptual mediation, see Ihde, *Technology and the Lifeworld* (n 46) 72 *et seq.*

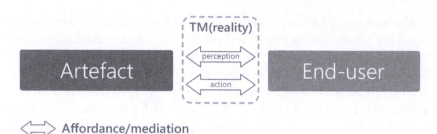

Figure 2.2 Artefact ↔ end-user relationships of technological mediation

she can and ought to do with it.[50] This ability to affect (and effect) reality as it is experienced by the end-user is one aspect of the power of design, particularly when it goes beyond what she can perceive of reality to include how she can and cannot act, at least within the bounds of the artefact's geography.[51] The manipulation of how reality is constructed, both perceptually and in terms of behavioural agency, demonstrates 'an important aspect of the non-neutrality of technology',[52] and points to the significant power that inheres in the designer who determines those mediations.

(d) Code Mediating Action

Whereas the technological mediation of perception amplifies or reduces what can be comprehended of reality, the technological mediation of action invites or inhibits specific behaviours. This form of mediation exerts a physically or logically compelling force on the agency of the end-user, rather than merely a signal that requests a particular type of action. It is here, then, that the regulative nature of code is most apparent: the coercion of action by code (its 'moreness') can be contrasted with the mere signal provided by a textually bound legal norm. The important distinction between constitutive and regulative rules, and their respective instantiations in code and in text, will be discussed later.

Code embodies a particular idea of how the designer intends the artefact to be used. This is what Latour calls a 'program of action',[53] which, like the

---

[50] Norman, *The Design of Everyday Things* (n 6) 26, 31. See also Hartzog (n 7) 278.

[51] For a rich account, building on Merleau-Ponty's phenomenology, of the role of perception in the design of such 'geography', see Robertson (n 48).

[52] Verbeek, *What Things Do* (n 44) 131. Verbeek speaks of perception being 'transformed', while Latour talks of action being 'translated'. See B Latour, 'Where are the missing masses? The sociology of a few mundane artifacts' in WE Bijker and J Law (eds), *Shaping Technology/Building Society: Studies in Sociotechnical Change* (MIT Press 1992) 174 *et passim*.

[53] Latour, 'Where are the missing masses?' (n 52). See also M Akrich, 'The de-scription of technical objects' in WE Bijker and J Law (eds), *Shaping Technology/Building Society: Studies in Sociotechnical Change* (MIT Press 1992).

script of a film or play, describes how the designer intends the artefact to be used or what its envisaged effect in the world ought to be. Akrich makes explicit use of this metaphor in her analysis of 'inscription': 'like a film script, technical objects define a framework of action together with the actors and the space in which they are supposed to act'.[54] Designers envisage these elements of the 'script' when they design the artefact's (dis)affordances: the framework for behaviour, the actors involved (both human and non-human[55]), and the space for action.[56] The various constituents of the script will be determined according to the envisaged uses of the artefact and the business model the designer seeks to follow.[57]

To give an example, a speed bump in a road has the inscription of 'slow down when you approach me',[58] and its physical properties invite in the strongest terms a particular action – slowing down – on pain of serious damage otherwise being done to the vehicle.[59] Latour might also say that the enforcement of that action is 'delegated' to the speed bump (indeed, the description of the latter in the UK as 'sleeping policemen' implies this reassignment of the task from a human to a non-human agent).[60] This coercion of action by the speed bump can be contrasted with the merely signifying effect of a speed limit sign, whose inscription only describes, rather than physically mandates, the desired action.[61]

In other work, Latour describes the example of the Berliner lock, whose design means that once its user is inside the room, if she wishes to close the

[54] Akrich (n 53) 208. See also Verbeek, 'Materializing morality' (n 43) 362.

[55] Actor network theory, to whose literature Akrich and Latour are central contributors, explicitly avoids the creation of a hierarchy between humans and non-humans, instead using the model of a flat web to describe the influences operating between disparate 'actants'. See generally Latour, 'Where are the missing masses?' (n 52).

[56] Akrich (n 53) 208. Latour terms this anticipation 'preinscription'. See Latour, 'Where are the missing masses?' (n 52) 172.

[57] B van den Berg and RE Leenes, 'Abort, retry, fail: Scoping techno-regulation and other techno-effects' in M Hildebrandt and J Gaakeer (eds), *Human Law and Computer Law: Comparative Perspectives* (Springer 2013) 76.

[58] Verbeek, 'Materializing morality' (n 43) 366.

[59] Latour, 'Where are the missing masses?' (n 52) 166. See also Lessig (n 31) 128, 135–6.

[60] Latour, 'Where are the missing masses?' (n 52) 157–8 *et passim*. See also Verbeek, *What Things Do* (n 44) 159–60. For a salient legal analysis, see K de Vries and N van Dijk, 'A bump in the road. Ruling out law from technology' in M Hildebrandt and J Gaakeer (eds), *Human Law and Computer Law: Comparative Perspectives* (Springer 2013) 114 *et seq*.

[61] See C Gavaghan, 'Lex machina: Techno-regulatory mechanisms and rules by design' (2017) 15 *Otago Law Review* 123, 130–1. The connection of these concepts to the legal notions of constitutive and regulative norms and the jurisprudential concept of the internal and external perspective of norms is discussed below.

door she is forced also to lock it.[62] The inscription in the lock's design thus limits the possible states that the user can leave the door in to one of either (1) open, or (2) closed and locked. There is no in-between state permitted by the design of the lock (namely closed and unlocked). This is a physical example of the binary 'ruleishness' of code, a core element of computational legalism discussed in the next chapter.[63]

These concepts of inscription, programs of action, and delegation are closely related to the postphenomenological idea of 'technological intentionality', where technologies encourage (if not necessarily mandate) some form of use distinct from all the contingent possibilities there might be. Ihde contrasts, for example, the technological mediations of a fountain pen and a word processor.[64] The pen implies a slower pace of action that inclines the writer towards taking time and considering her sentences before putting pen to paper, while the word processor permits writing at something closer to the speed of the spoken word, with added facilities (affordances) allowing for easy and fast text editing and recomposition. Neither the pen nor the word processor conclusively predetermines the mode of writing, but their respective designs do nevertheless '*promote* or *evoke* a distinct way of writing'.[65]

More overtly political, Verbeek describes the shortening of municipal gardeners' rake handles in the city of Cluj, intended to prevent them from leaning and thus to discourage laziness: '[t]he rake *mediates* the relation between the workers and the public gardens; it is not merely a means but plays an active role in the way this relation takes shape.'[66]

Similarly, Winner's classic discussion of the bridges on Long Island suggests the politicisation of artefacts. The bridges were reportedly designed to be too low for public buses to pass beneath them, thus preventing those reliant on public transport, which meant to a disproportionate degree the poor and racial minorities, from accessing the public beaches to which the roads led.[67]

The examples above demonstrate the first postphenomenological sense of 'intention', where through the provision of 'a framework for action, [artefacts] do form intentionalities and inclinations within which use-patterns take dominant shape':[68] the speed bump 'intends' to slow drivers down, the

---

[62] B Latour, 'The Berlin key or how to do words with things' in P Graves-Brown (ed.), *Matter, Materiality and Modern Culture* (Routledge 2000). See also Latour, 'Where are the missing masses?' (n 52) 172 *et seq.*

[63] See 'Ruleishness' in Section 3.2.

[64] Ihde, *Technology and the Lifeworld* (n 46) 141–2.

[65] Verbeek, *What Things Do* (n 44) 114–15 (emphasis supplied).

[66] Ibid. 115 (emphasis supplied).

[67] L Winner, 'Do artifacts have politics?' (1980) *Daedalus* 121.

[68] Ihde, *Technology and the Lifeworld* (n 46) 141.

Long Island bridges 'intend' to prevent access by the poor and minorities to public beaches, et cetera. This first sense refers to 'a certain directionality, inclination or trajectory that shapes the ways in which [artefacts] are used',[69] and is of course intimately connected with what (dis)affordances the designer embodies in the design.

The second sense of intentionality refers not to a property of the artefact but rather to the end-user's intention, and how the artefact mediates her relationship with the world by shaping what she can and cannot do.[70] The end-user's sense of her own agency, and of the possibilities in the world which that agency can interact with, are mediated by the artefact, thus blurring the line between subjectivity and objectivity.[71] When she sets about to achieve something, her perception of what she can do and what the world permits is mediated by the artefact, and thus so too is her understanding of her self and her world co-constituted through the lens of that mediation.[72] The operation is mutual and bi-directional – she makes her world and her world makes her, and that 'making' is pushed this way or that by the artefact's technological mediation, as comprised by its (dis)affordances.

Contextual changes result in different configurations of mediation, of both perception and action. This is what Ihde terms the 'multistability' of an artefact: it can facilitate different acts depending on the context of use, the individual using it, and the configuration of the artefact itself. A designed artefact exists for a purpose, but that purpose is not determined entirely by the artefact itself but also by how a particular end-user approaches it at a particular time and within a particular context.[73] The Long Island bridges demonstrate this contextual dependency: over time their normative effect has lessened as those who were intended to be excluded have become wealthier

---

[69] Verbeek, *What Things Do* (n 44) 114.

[70] Ibid. 116; Ihde, *Technology and the Lifeworld* (n 46) 25.

[71] Shedding the post-Enlightenment, 'Modern' dichotomy of subject and object is a central goal of postphenomenology (and indeed much other philosophy inspired by Continental traditions). See Ihde, *Postphenomenology and Technoscience* (n 44) 9 *et seq*.; Verbeek, *What Things Do* (n 44) 161 *et seq*.; Faraj and Azad (n 15) 237–8. More generally, see B Latour, *An Inquiry into Modes of Existence: An Anthropology of the Moderns* (Harvard University Press 2013).

[72] Verbeek, *What Things Do* (n 44) 116. This echoes Cohen's suggestion that 'as we struggle to shape our technologies and configure our artifacts, they also quite literally configure us'. See JE Cohen, *Configuring the Networked Self: Law, Code, and the Play of Everyday Practice* (Yale University Press 2012) 27.

[73] Verbeek, 'Materializing morality' (n 43) 371.

and less reliant on public transport.[74] Multistability refers to how differing contexts can result in different concrete uses of an artefact, the sum of which implies the absence of an 'essential' purpose. Akrich makes a similar argument in relation to inscription: while the designer will envisage some kind of role for the end-users of the artefact she creates, and it is from this image of the end-user that the inscription of the design is ultimately derived, in practice the domain of action is not absolutely predetermined and will to some extent be adapted 'in the wild'.[75]

Although the absence of an essential purpose implied by the notion of multistability means that the mediating effect of an artefact is not entirely within the ex ante control of the designer, she will nevertheless 'inscribe scripts and delegate responsibilities' in and to the artefacts she designs – if she did not, the artefact could sensibly be envisaged and then brought into existence. There is also the logical necessity that in creating one particular configuration of normativity – even one that is multistable – the designer is making a decision that *a priori* excludes at least some others.[76] To a greater or lesser degree, the design of an artefact will '"groom" the user',[77] shaping her perception and her scope for action in ways that may not be legitimate according to any external standard. As Akrich notes, 'the designer not only fixes the distribution of actors, he or she also provides a "key" that can be used to interpret all subsequent events. Obviously, this key can be called into question – consumer organizations specialize in such skepticism.'[78] This 'key' is the inscription embodied in the design, one that I am arguing ought always to be complemented by affordances that facilitate the kind of scepticism Akrich refers to.

---

[74] D Ihde, 'The designer fallacy and technological imagination' in *Ironic Technics* (Automatic Press/VIP 2008) 21. Ihde argues that the interstate initiative, which mandated higher bridges under which vehicles carrying ballistic missiles could pass, was a 'counter-strategy [that] defeated whatever politics were first employed' (ibid.). This may be historically true, but it points only to the evolution of political context, rather than any diminution in the role of the designer's intent in the initial exercise of designing the bridges (something Ihde concedes: ibid. 22 n 1).

[75] Akrich (n 53) 208. Cf. Suchman (n 13) 192 *et seq.*, arguing that scripts are inherently vague. For a contrasting argument that designers ought to take prospective responsibility for the moral role their technologies will come to play, see T Swierstra and K Waelbers, 'Designing a good life: A matrix for the technological mediation of morality' (2012) 18 *Science and Engineering Ethics* 157.

[76] I return to this theme below in the discussion of defaults and the spectrum of normativity.

[77] Akrich (n 53) 218.

[78] Ibid. 216.

This means that an implicit and unavoidable part of the designer's job when defining the artefact's spaces for action is the determining of the threshold between what is strictly inscribed and what can be (re)interpreted by the end-user. The very existence of a designed artefact means that these choices have been made and those thresholds set, whether done intentionally or otherwise. I return to this theme shortly, but first it is worth summarising the relevance of the relationship between affordance theory and technological mediation.

Affordance and Technological Mediation

Following the analysis above, we can conceptualise affordances as the underlying building blocks of inscription and technological mediation.[79] They are a powerful unit of analysis for identifying and critiquing the inscriptions of code which come together in aggregate to mediate the co-constitutive relationship between the end-user and the world.

Both real and perceived affordances are evidence of the second form of technological intentionality, where the artefact mediates the individual's understanding of what she can do in the world as she perceives it.[80] This connects closely with multistability, where a congruence between the artefact's perceived and real affordances provides a margin of opportunity within which the end-user might adapt her response to the predetermined script of the artefact. Unless the artefact embodies 'real' affordances that lie outside the designer's intended inscription, the end-user will by definition be unable to do anything with the artefact that the designer did not intend. In such a case her behaviour vis-à-vis the artefact will be constituted entirely according to the decisions made by the designer. The corollary is that where the designer leaves 'space' for creative interpretation and action – through the conscious (or unconscious) provision of real affordances and their signifiers – the end-user will be able to express her autonomy (within the wider constraints of the artefact's mediation).

Real (dis)affordances are the bread and butter of the first form of technological intentionality: to inscribe a particular programme of action in the artefact, its design must afford that course of action for a particular (class of) end-user; similarly, to proscribe a particular course of action, the designer must either elide the affordances that it would require or, if that elision is not possible, actively disafford it for a particular class of end-user, as in the cases of the Long Island bridges, the Berliner lock, or the shortened rake handles.

---

[79] See Kiran and Verbeek (n 47).
[80] Ibid. 415 *et seq.*

The existence of an affordance is an objective fact about the relationship between a particular artefact and individual in a particular context, which when taken in aggregate with any other (dis)affordance results in a particular assemblage of technological mediation. And, as discussed above, affordances are not fixed attributes of an artefact, rather they come about as relations between particular artefacts and particular individuals in particular contexts, albeit that (as we saw above) designers will anticipate what these are likely to be when they are considering the 'program of action', 'script', or 'use-pattern' they want the end-user to follow.

(e) A Spectrum of Technological Normativity

We have seen how inscriptions and affordances as their building blocks exist on a spectrum, from 'harder' implementations that admit of no choice to softer ones whose normativity is suggestive rather than coercive.[81] The former conception of normativity sees the artefact's 'scripts' as 'wired in', where the end-user has no choice but to follow a succession of code norms as they are presented to her.[82] This is the most 'ruleish' and immediate aspect of technological normativity: the rule is clearly defined (in code for the machine to follow, if not necessarily for the attention of the end-user) and it is applied immediately at runtime with no opportunity for further consideration. These characteristics of code (ruleishness, opacity, and immediacy) are central elements of the concept of computational legalism that I develop in the next chapter.

Less strict are code-based suggestions which 'nudge' the end-user towards a particular course of action, whilst permitting her to express choice or to 'disobey' the default configuration by choosing between two or more options. Despite this notional scope for exercising autonomy, various biasing effects have been shown to operate which render the default setting very 'sticky', implicitly discouraging the end-user from exercising her autonomy and making any change.[83] One approach to minimising this effect is to force a choice at the moment of installation or setup, without any preferred option being suggested.[84] As we have seen in the section on disaffordance, however,

---

[81] Van den Berg and Leenes (n 57) 74–5.

[82] J Kesan and R Shah, 'Setting software defaults: Perspectives from law, computer science and behavioral economics' (2006) 82 *Notre Dame Law Review* 583. See also Fogg's discussion of 'tunnelling' users in *Persuasive Technology: Using Computers to Change What We Think and Do* (Morgan Kaufmann Publishers 2003) 34 *et seq*.

[83] See the discussion in 'Default Configurations' in Section 3.2.

[84] Microsoft were forced to do this when the European Court of Justice found in *Microsoft Corp. v Commission of the European Communities* (2007) T-201/04 that the company's inclusion of its web browser Internet Explorer as the default in the Windows operating

enterprise will often interpret even strict regulations requiring the protection of end-user autonomy in ways that subtly (or not so subtly) favour its interests over those of the end-user – the ubiquitous post-implementation GDPR privacy notices are an example of this.[85] This connects with the contemporary evolution of design practices, such as the adversarial interfaces mentioned above, which may provide notional choice but which are in reality targeted at capturing end-users' attention (often using psychological research to refine the interface's affordances in a behaviourist attempt to maximise attention capture through 'operant conditioning'[86]). The extent to which such approaches have moved beyond the 'libertarian paternalism' of so-called 'nudging' (intended as it was to strike a balance in the civic sphere between the individual's freedom to choose and 'better' societal outcomes[87]) and into the realm of manipulation and even the cultivation of 'tech addiction'[88] is an emerging topic in both the academy and civil society.[89] Whether the analyses that emerge from these new, more critical explorations will break from the behaviourist underpinnings of nudge theory remains to be seen.

Towards the more open end of the spectrum of normativity, code's inscriptions can provide space for interpretation, reinvention, and 'resistance' by the end-user – albeit that once she is using an artefact, such resistance will always be limited reflexively to what the space left for it makes possible within the inherent boundaries of its geography.[90] In many cases the distinctions here will be on the level of the user interface (UI) that guides to varying

---

system was an abuse of its dominant market position. The agreed solution was to provide end-users with a 'ballot' screen asking them to choose from a randomly ordered range of browsers. See J Brodkin, 'EU fines Microsoft €561 million for not giving users a browser choice' *Ars Technica* (6 March 2013) <https://arstechnica.com/tech-policy/2013/03/eu-fines-microsoft-e561-million-for-not-giving-users-a-browser-choice/> last accessed 4 March 2021.

[85] C Utz et al., '(Un)Informed consent: Studying GDPR consent notices in the field' in *Proceedings of the 2019 ACM SIGSAC Conference on Computer and Communications Security* (ACM 2019).

[86] Fogg (n 82) chapter 3 *et passim*. See also van den Berg and Leenes (n 57) 71–2.

[87] CR Sunstein and RH Thaler, 'Libertarian paternalism is not an oxymoron' (2003) 70 *University of Chicago Law Review* 1159; van den Berg and Leenes (n 57) 72–3.

[88] See for example S Parkin, 'Has dopamine got us hooked on tech?' *The Observer* (4 March 2018) <https://www.theguardian.com/technology/2018/mar/04/has-dopamine-got-us-hooked-on-tech-facebook-apps-addiction> last accessed 4 March 2021.

[89] For examples see, respectively, J Williams, *Stand Out of Our Light: Freedom and Resistance in the Attention Economy* (Cambridge University Press 2018); Center for Humane Technology, 'The problem' (Center for Humane Technology) <http://humanetech.com/problem/> last accessed 4 March 2021.

[90] Van den Berg and Leenes (n 57) 77.

degrees the end-user's interactions with the system. There, the role of signifiers is particularly relevant: the end-user cannot avail herself of an affordance
if she does not know it is there. The business model underlying the design
of the artefact will determine the extent to which it is multistable. Take, for
example, the smartphone application Instagram, whose inscription might be
framed as one of 'upload photos and videos to be viewed by other end-users',
which in turn is made possible by a set of affordances for selecting a file,
perhaps making some basic edits, transferring it to a remote server, providing
a title, description, and tags, and then publishing it. Within the geography
of that application, no amount of 'resistance' by the end-user can rewrite
that inscription to enable the calculation of a tax return or the mapping of
her route to work. That being said, there nonetheless might lie within that
inscription some scope for reinterpretation, for example using the layout of
galleries within the application to imagine new expressive possibilities unintended by the application's designers. This can often be observed on Twitter,
for example, when images are manipulated such that when displayed in its
grid gallery layout they relate to one another like stills from a film. In that case
the gallery feature is multistable, having been repurposed beyond its original
function of displaying arbitrary images alongside one another in a simple
grid.

This is a frivolous example, but it does demonstrate the scope of action
possibilities that a given code artefact can provide. We can see how the spectrum of normativity moves from the most 'ruleish' of code norms to the
least, with the overall 'density' of the constraints on the behaviour of the
end-user lessening from one point to the next.[91] The placing of the thresholds between these represents a crucial choice in the process of designing an
artefact. Affordances can thus be distinguished according to their normative
effect.[92] Davis and Chouinard, for example, suggest that affordances exist
on a spectrum, from 'request' to 'refuse'. They give the example of a set of
stairs that might afford easy or difficult climbing depending on the angle of
their construction. For them, affordances can be characterised under one
of six mechanisms: request, demand, allow, encourage, discourage, and refuse.
Adding one of these modifiers adds useful depth to the bare concept of affordance, enabling a more intuitive understanding of a given individual–artefact
relationship. For the example of the stairs above, then, they might allow the

---

[91] The concept of 'normative density' is one of the intersections between legal and design
theory explored later.

[92] JL Davis and JB Chouinard, 'Theorizing affordances: From request to refuse' (2017) *Bulletin
of Science, Technology & Society* 241. See also JL Davis, *How Artifacts Afford: The Power and
Politics of Everyday Things* (MIT Press 2020) *passim*.

non-disabled to climb, discourage careless or fast climbing (if they are particularly steep), and refuse climbing to those who require a wheelchair. Here we get an immediate sense of three normative affordance relationships that exist between the artefact and three hypothetical classes of end-user.

Considered through these affordance mechanisms, it becomes easier to discern the particular makeup of a given artefact's normativity, and from the preceding discussion we can see how wired-in functions tend towards the 'harder' mechanisms of request, demand, allow, and refuse, while the mechanisms of encouragement and discouragement are more likely to be found where the artefact's affordances are designed around nudging and, implicitly, multistability. As previously mentioned, it is important to note that the design of an artefact will always embody some mix of these characteristics, because as soon as code is laid down choices have been made and some configuration of normativity – be it open or closed, strictly ruleish or multistable – has come into existence. As Lessig puts it, 'there is no choice that does not include some kind of building. Code is never found; it is only ever made.'[93]

Constitutive and Regulative Normativity

This spectrum of normativity connects with the theoretical distinction between constitutive and regulative rules.[94] Whereas constitutive rules define how a construct or 'thought-object'[95] may be brought into being (for example a valid game of chess, or a marriage), regulative rules merely request action or inaction on the part of an individual or class of individuals (for example a speed limit on a road, or a rule that bottlebanks should not be used at night). If the requirements of a constitutive rule are not met, then the relevant construct does not and cannot come into being; the mere assertion that a couple is married is insufficient to make it so in the eyes of the relevant order from which the concept derives, which is to say the legal system. At the same time, although a regulative rule can seek some (in)action from the individual (for example not to drive above 70 miles per hour on the motorway), it has no ability directly to impose that requirement – the individual must acquiesce and alter her behaviour accordingly (recall the discussion above of a speed limit sign as a signifier, as compared with the speed bump).

A similar distinction applies in the design sphere; code can initiate both constitutive and regulative normativity, and the decision of where to draw the

---

[93] Lessig (n 31) 6.

[94] I discuss the relevance of this distinction from a legal-theoretical perspective in 'Constitutive and Regulative Rules' in Section 3.2.

[95] O Weinberger, 'The norm as thought and as reality' in N MacCormick and O Weinberger, *An Institutional Theory of Law: New Approaches to Legal Positivism* (Springer 1986).

line between the two is within the gift of the designer. As Hildebrandt notes, 'it makes sense to discriminate between socio-technical arrangements that are constitutive and those that are regulative of our interactions, if only to make clear that technology does not necessarily rule out choice in comparison to law'.[96]

As we have seen, the (dis)affordances and inscriptions embodied in the artefact's design can be constitutive or regulative of the end-user's behaviour.[97] Of course, the very existence of the artefact and its functions are the subject of a set of basic constitutive affordances, for example that it can be seen, that it can be touched, opened, executed, et cetera. The boundaries of the artefact represent a set of foundational 'rules' which define its very nature from the outset – the form of its interface, the platforms it can run on, its physical dimensions, et cetera. Operating above this low-level sense of constitutive affordance, however, are the specific (dis)affordances and scripts that constitute the behavioural possibilities open to the end-user when she is interacting with the artefact.[98] As with the example above, she may wish very much to find her way to work using Instagram, but the code's constitutive norms do not permit such a use. The possibility is simply not within the 'constitution' of the code. Although the designers of Instagram (presumably) did not consciously decide not to include mapping or tax calculation functionality in their code, the example underlines the point that design always involves the privileging of one configuration of normativity – one 'technical constitution' – over the near-infinite alternative possibilities that code would otherwise have allowed them to build.[99] This speaks to code's plasticity – 'programmers can implement almost any system they can imagine and describe precisely',[100] but of course that very precision will necessarily exclude a huge range of other possibilities.

From the perspective of regulative normativity, some measure of choice is left open to the end-user in how she behaves within the geography set up by the code. For example, she is free to choose from a palette a highlight colour for her social media profile, and to attach up to five photos (or indeed no photo at all) to her social media post. Such 'regulative latitude', however, always operates within constitutive outer boundaries beyond which choice

---

[96] Hildebrandt, 'Legal and technological normativity' (n 2) 175.

[97] M Hildebrandt, 'A vision of ambient law' in R Brownsword and K Yeung (eds), *Regulating Technologies: Legal Futures, Regulatory Frames and Technological Fixes* (Hart 2008) 177–8.

[98] Flores et al. (n 21).

[99] J Weizenbaum, *Computer Power and Human Reason: From Judgment to Calculation* (Freeman 1976) 37–8, 113.

[100] J Grimmelmann, 'Regulation by software' (2005) 114 *The Yale Law Journal* 1719, 1723.

is unavailable – for example, there is no freedom to choose colours that are not included in the selection provided, or to attach a ZIP file or executable programme to the social media post.

All of these behavioural (dis)affordances are contingent on the choices made by the designer. She can enable a particular functionality or close it off entirely, or perhaps hide it from view. In each case she has exercised her private power to constitute the range of behaviour that the end-user can engage in.[101] She might also opt for affordances that are merely regulative of behaviour, using one of the less ruleish mechanisms above to allow the end-user to change the configuration (defaults) of the code or reinvent the space it opens up in ways unforeseen by the designer (multistability). I will return to these possibilities in Chapter 6 in the discussion of the digisprudential affordances.

(f) Technological Constitutionalism

So far, this chapter has explored how the normativity embodied in an arte-fact's design enables and constrains the behaviour of the end-user, focusing on relationship (d) of Figure 1.1 in Chapter 1. But there is, however, another aspect through which the designer is herself made to comply. Further back in the chain of production, the designers of products are themselves subject to normativities created by the designers of the more fundamental, 'infra-structural' elements of the process.[102] Not only are end-users subject to the effects of (dis)affordance, inscription, and mediation, but so too are product designers within the environments that they in turn use to create artefacts intended for end-users. The product designer is thus herself rendered a type of user by those described by Vismann and Krajewski as the 'programmer of the programmer' ('PoP'):

> The programmer of the programmer, designing the tools and methods of a coding language (such as the compiler, code syntax, abstract data types, and so on) maintains the ultimate power because he or she, as the constructor of the programming language itself, defines what the 'normal' programmer, as a user, will be able to do. Both types of programmers establish the condi-tions for using the computer, and, as such, they behave like lawmakers or, rather, code-makers. Implemented within the CPU and the hierarchy of the file system is the law governing communication with and through the com-puter. In this respect, code and law maintain a relationship of more than structural homology. The code is a law – as Lawrence Lessig pointed out

---

[101] Van den Berg and Leenes (n 57).
[102] This is relationship (e) of Figure 1.1 in Chapter 1.

when he described 'code' metaphorically as a synonym for the conditions under which the computer runs.[103]

In the hierarchy thus developed, the product designer-as-user is beholden to the (dis)affordances and inscriptions in the design environment that are themselves chosen and designed by the PoP.

Product designers do not operate in a vacuum, developing their products and services each time as if from a *tabula rasa*. To do so would in many cases mean reinventing the wheel – a costly, inefficient, and even dangerous prospect in the case of fundamental technologies that have developed over decades of research, such as networking and encryption. Designers utilise existing hardware, programming languages, libraries, and habitual development practices that are in place well before they embark upon the development of new code. Situated within a context of decades of this prior art, a designer's approach to her work will to a greater or lesser extent be guided by all those practices that have gone before, and the technological mediations that bear upon her ability to solve the problem at hand. The result is often a bricolage of the old and the new, brought together with the 'glue' of that particular designer's skills, knowledge, and interpretation of the brief she is required to implement.[104] Before she considers her immediate task, then, she is starting out within a context that is itself replete with inscription and (dis)affordance, which mediates how she goes about her work.

In this sense we can start to see that the PoP is not a single individual but rather the complex of tools and practices that frame the work of the designer before it begins. These include programming languages and their internal 'habits', development paradigms such as agile and waterfall, the integrated development environments (IDEs) where code is actually written, third-party libraries and application programming interfaces (APIs), and the design patterns used by programmers and designers to solve common programming problems or to build common inscriptions. Each of these is to some extent designed, and to a greater or lesser degree plays a role in the product designer's practice, structuring it both from the outset and while she works. Some elements of the PoP are of course more susceptible than others to themselves being structured towards some normative end, but at this point what is interesting is the idea of 'constitutionality' within the design process itself. Recall

---

[103] Vismann and Krajewski (n 1) 100 (emphasis supplied).

[104] P Swartz, 'White boys' code' in *Division III: Essays in Programs as Literature* (Hampshire College 2007) 34–6.

the model of normative relationships in Figure 1.1 in Chapter 1.[105] We can start to see a parallel between on the one hand the top-down arrangement of constitutive rules that bind the state 'to the mast' in its exercise of legislative and executive power,[106] and on the other a bottom-up framework of constitutive normativity that enables and constrains the scope of generativity available in the first place to the product designer. The (dis)affordances and inscriptions created by the PoP create a kind of *de facto* constitution, delimiting the framework within which the day-to-day 'parliamentary' work of the product designer takes place. The normative power of design is thus deeper than just that of the product designer; it extends into the technical 'constitution' that makes up the foundation of the design process itself. Like a legal constitution, this technical foundation has implications for the artefacts built upon it in the higher levels of the technical 'stack'.

This is only a very brief introduction to the notion of the PoP and the concept of technological constitutionality that it represents. In Chapter 7 I discuss in more detail elements of the PoP that can facilitate a desirable technological constitutionalism, whereby the privileged position of the PoP enables the imposition of limits on the product designer that can be leveraged for normatively desirable purposes, binding the work of the latter so that the code she produces exhibits the qualities of legitimacy that I set out in later chapters. In this way, just as a constitution binds the work of a legislature ex ante, so too can the design environment contribute to the creation of legitimate code.

2.3 Conclusion

The discussion in this chapter has set out how code constitutes and regulates the behaviour of end-users, as framed by the theories of affordance, disaffordance, inscription, and technological mediation. The more a design is constitutive of behaviour, the more the balance of power favours the designer – in this sense, code is thus 'more' than law in its capacity to regulate. It is possible, however, for design to embody regulative rather than constitutive normativity, thus shifting (some) power back to the end-user. Redressing this balance is essential to the notion of legitimacy I am advocating. Given that design environments themselves have a regulating effect on the work of product designers, this paves the way for a consideration of how the production of user-facing affordances might be guided by the 'constitutionality'

---

[105] See 'Normative Relationships in Code and Law' in Section 1.4.
[106] The Odyssean idea of constitutional binding is discussed in Section 3.1.

of designer-facing affordances. The latter act as guard rails, delimiting and constraining the possible shapes that code can legitimately take. In the next chapter, I deepen the theoretical connection between law and design, proposing the concept of 'computational legalism' as a foundation for the synthesis of the later chapters of the book.

3

A Legal Philosophy Perspective:
Code is *Less* than Law

The alternative to legality is not anarchism, it is legalism . . . '[N]ot thinking about it', if left to its own devices, tends to take over the entire social
world, or at least cyberspace.[1]

In the previous chapter, I used design theory and the philosophy of technology to describe how code constitutes and regulates end-user behaviour.
Demonstrating the material directness of code-based regulation was the first
task in setting out the theoretical grounding of digisprudence. This chapter
complements that analysis, turning towards legal philosophy to develop an
account of 'computational legalism'. This idea is borne of the parallel between
code's ruleishness – its reliance on strict, binary logic instead of interpretable
standards – and its conceptual equivalent in the juridical realm, known as
legalism. The latter is a perspective that disavows the holistic interpretation
of legal norms, instead requiring that citizens merely follow rules as they are
presented to them, without enquiring as to their efficacy or their legitimacy
beyond the question of where they came from. Code's characteristics exemplify a particularly strong form of 'legalism', and therein lies the problem of
unlegitimated code-based regulation and the claim that it is 'less' than law.
As Wintgens puts it, '[r]ule creation is a matter of choice, and this choice is
legitimated because it is based upon the democratic character of the regulating process.'[2] In very few cases are such aspirations reflected in the production
of code. End-users are 'induced, habituated and, if necessary, compelled, to
accept the norms of commercialized cyberspace',[3] all of which taking place

[1] Z Bańkowski and B Schafer, 'Double-click justice: Legalism in the computer age' (2007) 1
Legisprudence 31, 47–8.
[2] L Wintgens, *Legisprudence: A New Theoretical Approach to Legislation* (Hart 2002) 2.
[3] G Longford, 'Pedagogies of digital citizenship and the politics of code' (2005) 9 *Techné:
Research in Philosophy and Technology* 68, 71.

outwith democratic debate and legal processes of interpretation, contest, and remediation. As Longford suggests,

> whereas the terms and conditions of political citizenship in liberal demo-cratic states are, relatively speaking, subject to free, open and transparent deliberation and negotiation, the codes governing the citizen in the digital era are invisible and opaque, thanks to certain features of the technologies themselves and to the proprietary nature of many of the codes increasingly mediating our lives.[4]

To be clear, my aim is not to suggest that designers harbour a legalistic ideology; instead, I want to demonstrate how aspects of a legalistic mentality are closely reproduced in the material architectures of code, with the result that the ideological 'ought' of legalism becomes the technological 'is' of code. If we proceed from the starting point that legalism is an undesirable thing in a democracy, then the mechanisms for mitigating it in the traditional legal sphere might also have an ameliorating effect in the analogous context of code-based 'legislation'.

Drawing a parallel between legalism in the contexts of legal and techno-logical normativity sets the stage for an analysis of the ways in which its mit-igation in the former can be imported into the sphere of the latter. The aim is to investigate the 'new forms of interaction' that Bańkowski and Schafer suggest are necessary to 'promote the benefits of legality, and to prevent the disadvantages of legalism' in the code context.[5]

This chapter first sets out the notion of legalism, before demonstrating how it is that code, when it operates as an enforcer, mediator, and constitutor of behavioural reality, can be a particularly extreme incarnation of this ideological perspective. Wintgens suggests that 'long decades of legalism in legal reasoning [have meant that] the dominant views in legal theory . . . have barred the way for questioning the position of the legislator'.[6] In the parallel between code and law that I aim to construct, questioning the position of the designer *qua* legis-lator becomes a pressing concern and precisely what digisprudence seeks to do.

3.1 What is Legalism?

There are conflicting conceptions of legalism in the literature, it being occa-sionally confused with related concepts such as legality and the rule of law.[7]

---

[4] Ibid.
[5] Bańkowski and Schafer (n 1) 46.
[6] Wintgens, *Legisprudence: A New Theoretical Approach to Legislation* (n 2) 2.
[7] Bańkowski and Schafer note for example that legalism is 'often confused with legality, an altogether more reflexive and rational concept'. See Bańkowski and Schafer (n 1) 31–2.

MacCormick contended early on that legalism is 'a prerequisite of free government',[8] but this seemed for him to amount essentially to the ex post doctrine of *nulla poena sine lege* ('acts of government however desirable teleologically must be subordinated to respect for rules and rights'[9]), and is therefore different from the 'stronger' version of legalism with which I am concerned. Indeed, MacCormick explicitly distinguishes between that conception of legalism and the stronger conception identified in the literature.[10] MacCormick's conception of legalism is akin to Wintgens's idea of 'weak' legalism, which forms a part, rather than the whole, of the legisprudential conception of legitimacy that I draw on in Chapter 4. At any rate, this intermediate position, later adopted by MacCormick himself in work with Bańkowski, views some measure of legalistic rule-following as a necessary element, but not the whole, of a functioning legal order. This accords with the normative position developed here, where rules are an appropriate basis for regulating behaviour, but the process of their development is constrained so as not to be arbitrary. This idea is embodied in the Greek myth of Odysseus, in which the eponymous captain orders his crew both to tie him to the mast of his ship, so he cannot succumb to the enticement of the Sirens, and to block their ears with beeswax, so his orders to untie him in the face of that temptation will fall on deaf ears. The metaphor is of a sovereign limiting itself in order to avoid the temptation of iniquity (being bound to the mast) whilst also submitting to checks and balances that prevent that power being exercised should the sovereign's scruples change (the wax in the ears of the crew). Various scholars have considered the myth in their discussions of constitutionalism in the computational context.[11] Hildebrandt contrasts legality and legalism thus:

> Legality, in this sense, refers to justice (proportionality), to legal certainty (the legal ground in positive law, with the necessary safeguards) and purposiveness or expediency (the legitimate aim of the intervention, the requirement of effective remedies). Legalism, instead, reduces all this to the correctly enacted legal ground, which may or may not offer any protection, leaving the subject of government interventions dependent on a rule *by* law instead of the Rule of Law. Even if the sovereign that rules *by* law is the

---

[8] N MacCormick, 'The ethics of legalism' (1989) 2 *Ratio Juris* 184.
[9] Ibid. 184.
[10] Ibid.
[11] See for example M Hildebrandt, *Smart Technologies and the End(s) of Law: Novel Entanglements of Law and Technology* (Edward Elgar Publishing 2015) 156; L Lessig, *Code: Version 2.0* (Basic Books 2006) 313–14.

nation or the *Parliament*, legalism leaves individual subjects without effective remedies against arbitrary rule.[12]

One can see here the implication in the concept of legality that the rules promulgated must be designed to reflect certain ideals (proportionality, safeguards, the substantive legitimacy of the norm itself). Legalism, by contrast, is concerned only that the rule has been promulgated by a legitimate institution, and cares not what its content or substantive effects are.

Hildebrandt's characterisation of legalism, where there is an absence of protection against arbitrary rule, matches the stronger variant of the concept, described by Shklar as 'an ethical attitude that holds moral conduct to be a matter of rule following, and moral relationships to consist of duties and rights determined by rules'.[13] This deontological outlook – termed the 'morality of duty' by Fuller[14] – of course has a long pedigree in moral philosophy, exemplified in Kant's categorical imperative, he being the 'high priest for a rule based morality'.[15] Such an approach has moral force because it results in a normalisation and systematisation of behaviour across society, which in turn begets the kind of behavioural predictability that has been argued is a desirable goal in the development of a stable (capitalist[16]) society.[17]

Heteronomy, the condition of being dominated by an external sovereign, is antithetical to aspirations of reasoned interpretation and action, and thus to autonomy.[18] It is exemplified in what Wintgens calls the 'strong' variant of legalism, which he describes as a normative 'strategy', used historically to avoid contingency and promote legal certainty.[19] On the other hand, it is also

---

[12] M Hildebrandt, 'Radbruch's Rechtsstaat and Schmitt's legal order: Legalism, legality, and the institution of law' (2015) 2 *Critical Analysis of Law* 42, 56 (emphasis supplied). For the antinomian conception of law that Hildebrandt draws on, see G Radbruch, 'Legal philosophy' in K Wilk (ed.), *The Legal Philosophies of Lask, Radbruch, and Dabin* (Harvard University Press 1950).

[13] JN Shklar, *Legalism* (Harvard University Press 1964) 1.

[14] LL Fuller, *The Morality of Law* (Yale University Press 1977) chapter 1.

[15] Z Bańkowski and N MacCormick, 'Legality without legalism' in W Krawietz et al. (eds), *The Reasonable as Rational? On Legal Argumentation and Justification; Festschrift for Aulis Aarnio* (Duncker & Humblot 2000) 183. See also Z Bańkowski, 'Don't think about it: Legalism and legality' in MM Karlsson, Ó Páll Jónsson and EM Brynjarsdóttir (eds), *Rechtstheorie: Zeitschrift für Logik, Methodenlehre, Kybernetik und Soziologie des Rechts* (Duncker & Humblot 1993) 45; Bańkowski and Schafer (n 1) 33.

[16] Bańkowski (n 15) 48. See also L Wintgens, 'The rational legislator revisited. Bounded rationality and legisprudence' in *The Rationality and Justification of Legislation* (Springer 2013) 4.

[17] Shklar (n 13) 64.

[18] See, for example, Bańkowski and Schafer (n 1); Bańkowski and MacCormick (n 15) 194; Bańkowski (n 15) 56; MacCormick, 'The ethics of legalism' (n 8) 192.

[19] L Wintgens, *Legisprudence: Practical Reason in Legislation* (Routledge 2012) 159.

often thought that some measure of legalism (that is, respect for rules *qua* rules, or 'law as law') is necessary for a society to operate well, and indeed that legalism should be understood normatively not as being in opposition to legality but rather as a necessary element of it.[20] This is 'weak legalism', a viewpoint central to legisprudence, according to which rules remain the proper mechanism for regulating action, but the potential for their arbitrary definition is simultaneously constrained. Strong legalism undermines legality, whereas weak legalism is a necessary (although insufficient) component of it. Legality, properly understood, requires a complementary combination of adherence to rules with thoughtful interpretation of what is being commanded by the rule, with the appropriate response varying depending on the particular circumstances.[21] For Bańkowski and Schafer, it is sometimes appropriate for citizens mindlessly to follow a rule – to 'act like automata' – while at other times it is necessary to act autonomously, considering what the rule asks of us before deciding how to act. Strong legalism implies only the former approach, whereas weak legalism is the rule-based element of the broader concept of legality.

This strong conception of legalism is extremely relevant to a descriptive analysis of code, because as we shall see the latter not only exemplifies its characteristics but indeed amplifies them far beyond what is envisaged in most of the legal literature: '[code's] unrestricted anarchism in the absence of the state has indeed resulted in the most absolute form of legalism possible'.[22]

Subsequent references in this chapter to legalism are to this strong variant, unless otherwise specified. In the rest of this section I set out the theory of legalism and its approach to law-making in more detail, setting the stage for a comparison between it and code in the latter part of the chapter.

(a) Solipsism and Positivism

Legalism is rooted in a solipsistic view of law as a system of rules and practices that operates separately from the societal contexts within which it is embedded and which it serves. Law is a 'clean' system, 'self contained and autogenerative', subsuming the outputs of the 'dirty business' of politics (that is, legislation) and applying them according to its own *sui generis* processes, institutions, and vocabulary.[23] Already we have a glimpse of the parallel with code.

---

[20] Bańkowski (n 15); MacCormick, 'The ethics of legalism' (n 8).

[21] Bańkowski and Schafer (n 1) 48. I will return to legality in Chapter 4.

[22] Ibid.

[23] Bańkowski (n 15) 46. For a nineteenth-century expression of this perspective in Scots constitutional law, see *Edinburgh & Dalkeith Railway Company v Wauchope* (1842) 1 Bell 278,

'Legislation is a matter of politics, and politics is a matter of choice', and so the 'truthiness' of law requires that it remain separate from anything so contingent.[24] Law is viewed as a scientific practice that identifies and works with 'truths', which are the product of sovereign legislators. The content of those truths is not to be questioned: from the perspective of the law and legal practice the truth 'just is', it is handed down from the political realm where it is the sole province of the legislator to debate the substance of the norm. The jurist has no valid interest in what goes on there; politics is about choice, and therefore it does not deal in 'truth' because competing choices can never be objects of true knowledge.[25] Once the legislature chooses between the various possible options and crystallises one of them into a law, it becomes an item of 'true' knowledge within the science of law, whose objective (extra-legal) quality is irrelevant to the legal 'scientists' who, from that point onward, take it as a datum for application within their field.

In this way, legal thinking becomes 'fenced off' from 'all contact with the rest of historical thought and experience'.[26] The result is a positivistic view that the law is 'just there', and it is not the task of citizens or practitioners to enquire as to how it got 'there'.[27] What matters is whether it is a valid law, and not whether we agree with its substance and relevance to the present circumstances. The 'truth' ('is-ness') of a given legal norm derives from the validity of its creation vis-à-vis authorised actors and processes, and the question of whether its substance is desirable or not (its 'ought-ness') is properly to be viewed as separate from this.[28] The preoccupation with the ex post examination of what should and should not be considered 'law' is of course a core characteristic of Anglo-American analytical legal positivism. Strong legalism is connected with this outlook in its drive to classify rules according to those that are internal to the legal system and those that are external.[29]

---

per Lord Campbell: 'All that a court of justice can look to is the parliamentary roll; they see that an act has passed both Houses of Parliament, and that it has received the royal assent, and no court of justice can enquire into the manner in which it was introduced into parliament, what was done previously to its being introduced, or what passed in parliament during the various stages of its progress through both Houses of Parliament.'

[24] L Wintgens, 'Legisprudence as a new theory of legislation' (2006) 19 Ratio Juris 1, 5.

[25] Ibid.

[26] Shklar (n 13) 3. See also Bańkowski and MacCormick (n 15) 182, and Fuller, in his response to Hart in their classic debate: LL Fuller, 'Positivism and fidelity to law: A reply to Professor Hart' (1958) 71 Harvard Law Review 630, 635.

[27] Bańkowski (n 15).

[28] Bańkowski and MacCormick (n 15) 186.

[29] L Wintgens, 'Legislation as an object of study of legal theory: Legisprudence' in Legisprudence: A New Theoretical Approach to Legislation (Hart 2002) 20.

Thus, from a legalistic perspective, 'what ought to be done is confined to the knowledge of the rules that contain rights and duties. Following rules is a matter of knowledge, while their enforcement is a matter of application.'[30] Legal practitioners take that knowledge, provided from somewhere 'out there', and use it as a tool to achieve a given legal aim. Their practice is 'neutral' as to the substance of these materials (rules), and they become technicians whose task it is to manipulate those rules according to the mechanisms of legal reasoning.[31]

(b) Legalism According to Legisprudence

Strong legalism is thus concerned with the application rather than the design of rules.[32] In his comprehensive historical discussion of the origins of legalism, Wintgens discusses the theoretical mechanisms of legitimation in both natural law and analytical legal positivism, before identifying a set of specific characteristics of which the phenomenon of strong legalism is a 'conjugation', namely representationalism, a-temporality, concealed instrumentalism, *etatism* (the belief that the only true source of law is the state), and the scientific study of law.[33]

The orthodox source of a rule's legitimacy differs depending on the source of sovereignty – broadly, natural law or the social contract: respectively, that source is either a transcendent set of natural law norms, or a social contract which founds a sovereign law-making institution. In the case of a natural law perspective, this is because the source of its substantive content is the 'background' knowledge of natural law principles which are inherently true: such representational laws are 'a concretisation of natural law, or reflect a natural law conception that in its turn legitimises positive law'.[34] In the case of the sovereign, this is so because the social contract legitimises such pronouncements as a descendent of some original founding contractual act of the people that set up the institution to represent them[35] (perhaps a document with constitutional status, although the social contract can also be a hypothetical moment rather than a real instrument). That the state defines what is legal is in itself enough to legitimise the substance of the legal norms it chooses to

[30] Wintgens, 'Legisprudence as a new theory of legislation' (n 24) 5.
[31] Bańkowski and Schafer (n 1) 34.
[32] Wintgens, *Legisprudence: Practical Reason in Legislation* (n 19) 139.
[33] Wintgens, 'Legisprudence as a new theory of legislation' (n 24) 5. For an in-depth philosophical and historical discussion of these characteristics, see Wintgens, *Legisprudence: Practical Reason in Legislation* (n 19) chapter 5.
[34] Wintgens, 'Legislation as an object of study of legal theory' (n 29) 10–11. See also Wintgens, *Legisprudence: Practical Reason in Legislation* (n 19) 147 *et seq*.
[35] Wintgens, *Legisprudence: Practical Reason in Legislation* (n 19) 195.

declare; in constituting the field of play (the legal system), the state legitimises *de facto* that which it consequently promulgates as the rules of the game. One can detect in this hierarchical idea of legitimacy Kelsen's 'Grundnorm' and Hart's 'rule of recognition'.[36] The outcome in either case is the same, namely a legitimated foundational source from which laws can be promulgated that are themselves *de facto* legitimate as a result of the *a priori* legitimacy of the source, and that therefore ought to be followed.[37]

Wintgens describes this as 'one-shot' legitimation, operating continually thereafter to validate prospectively any norms promulgated within the ex ante framework that it sets up. Drawing on Hobbes and Rousseau, this is what he describes as the 'proxy model' of legitimation,[38] according to which the initial legitimation of the external decision-maker permits it to act on behalf of the people (that is, as a proxy) from that moment onward, despite the inability of either the sovereign itself or the people it represents to foresee all the rules, or 'limitations on freedom', that will in the future be imposed. The citizen is given the imperative 'not to think about it'; she need only act in accordance with the rule as it is given to her,[39] since by virtue of those constitutive facts the pronouncement of the sovereign is 'imputed to [the citizenry], as if they were its author'.[40] This legalistic idea of minimal interpretation is connected with Hart's discussion of the 'core' and 'penumbra' in the meaning of individual words, the former being deemed to be settled and uncontested, and the latter being where controversies of interpretation arise.[41] I discuss this further in the section on rules in computational legalism below.

In the commercial realm, society essentially gives the designer of code a one-shot 'legitimation' of this kind when (1) we endow her with the plasticity of code to create a near-infinite number of conditions which enable and constrain behaviour through technological normativity, (2) we protect her privatised practices through (legally sanctioned) commercial secrecy and a general absence of scrutiny, and (3) we submit to the *sui generis* opacity of code. I discuss each of these characteristics in more detail below.

From a computational perspective, perhaps the most relevant element of strong legalism is representationalism. This is the view of law as a

---

[36] Wintgens explicitly identifies the connection between the Rousseauian 'act of will' that creates the social contract, and the Hartian system of a founding rule of recognition that is followed by emergence of a combination of primary and secondary rules (ibid. 170).

[37] Ibid. 196 *et seq.*

[38] Ibid. chapter 6 generally.

[39] Bańkowski (n 15).

[40] Wintgens, *Legisprudence: Practical Reason in Legislation* (n 19) 208.

[41] HLA Hart, 'Positivism and the separation of law and morals' (1958) 71 *Harvard Law Review* 593.

representation of reality, either through the latter's reproduction (in the case of natural laws that need to be given force by positive law) or its construction (in the case of laws based on a founding social contract).[42] Wintgens embarks on a rich analysis of the philosophies of Hobbes and Descartes, discussing the relationship between realism and nominalism and how these, despite their seemingly fundamental differences, can both result in the 'naturalisation of positive law', according to which law is deemed to be a representation of objective reality.[43] What the law states is therefore held to be true, either because natural laws are hypostatically true or because the social contract is true and therefore so too are the rules that are based upon it.

The salient connection with the computational context is that there representationalism is even more concrete than in the ideology of strong legalism: whereas proponents of the latter hold the belief that the rule presents reality, in the computational context this is much more than mere belief because, as we saw in Chapter 2, code does not just represent reality but actively constitutes it (or, at least, a part of it). I have already talked about constitutive versus regulative technological normativity, a theme I will return to below.

The next salient component of strong legalism is 'a-temporality', which flows from the belief in law as a representation of reality. Because either the social contract or natural law represents reality ex ante, anything that flows from them is believed also to be true, since they are the genuine and true foundation of political space. That foundation is a-temporal because it is believed to be the universal principled basis for public law, something that is valid independently of human recognition.[44] Contingent laws built upon this foundation are deemed to 'uncover' the general will, rather than proactively to reflect it (those who disagree with a particular legislative proposition are in error as to what the general will is, rather than in disagreement *per se*). The general will exists at all times, ready to be uncovered and recognised by contingent legislative acts. Thus, 'acts of will then take on the appearance of time-lessness'.[45] The notion of the norms' timelessness connects with the immutable character of code discussed below, and the approach that Wintgens develops

[42] Wintgens, 'Legisprudence as a new theory of legislation' (n 24) 4. See also CM Campbell, 'Legal thought and juristic values' (1974) 1 *British Journal of Law and Society* 13.

[43] Wintgens, *Legisprudence: Practical Reason in Legislation* (n 19) 147–53. This metaphysical discussion centres around the distinction between the view of law as directly reproducing reality (realism), or the view that the creation of law constructs reality through the description of what is otherwise 'semantically empty' (nominalism). In either case, the result is a belief that law is representative of reality, of the world as it is.

[44] Ibid. 155.

[45] Ibid. 156–7.

to cope with timelessness in law-making – the legisprudential principle of temporality – also becomes relevant as a practical consideration.[46]

The final relevant aspect of strong legalism is 'concealed instrumentalism'. This is the idea of a 'veil of sovereignty', behind which the values or ends of the legislator are hidden. It is evidenced in textualism, where the policy goal of the legislator is less important than formalistic reasoning from the text. The fiction of timelessness previously discussed combines with this instrumentalism to form a strategy for converting the messy and contingent political into the clean and scientific legal.[47] This concealment finds its analogue in the legal and economic veils that protect code: enterprise is protected by trade secrets and anti-circumvention laws, while faith is placed in the market to curb any excesses.

As previously mentioned, whereas strong legalism is concerned primarily with the validity of a norm's source, legisprudence suggests that this is a necessary but insufficient condition for legitimacy. Not only must the sovereign be 'bound to the mast', but so too must it proactively legitimate the norms that it proposes. This is a type of validity that to an extent crosses the line between formal and substantive legitimacy – the substantive content of the norm is constrained according to certain formal qualities embodied in the principles of legisprudence. As Wintgens argues,

> [t]he basic idea of the rule of law or the *Rechtsstaat*, that both the ruler and the ruled are bound to rules, can be interpreted in two ways. The first interpretation is the path to strong legalism. According to this approach, the ruler's being bound to rules is tantamount to his 'not violating' them. This is both a necessary and a sufficient condition for rules to be valid and legitimate. Under the second interpretation – which is adopted by legisprudence – the idea of following rules by a sovereign counts only as a necessary and not as a sufficient condition for rules to be valid. Legal validity on this view is distinct from legitimacy. Legitimacy for its part can only be obtained through legitimation.[48]

The achievement of legitimacy thus requires an additional active step of legitimation, which means not just that the sovereign is subject to the same rules as everyone else (the rule of law; being 'bound to the mast'), but also that the rules which it seeks to promulgate reflect certain required formal

---

[46] This will be considered later in Chapters 4 and 5.

[47] Wintgens, 'Legislation as an object of study of legal theory' (n 29) 158; Bańkowski (n 15) 46.

[48] Wintgens, *Legisprudence: Practical Reason in Legislation* (n 19) 145.

characteristics, which in turn limit the breadth of possible content that those norms can legitimately have.

Strong legalism is clearly open to abuse: prioritising heteronomy undermines critical reflection and the application of principles of legality that are characteristic (and constitutive) of democracies. Without spaces for interpretation, rules become 'implements of tyranny' and legalism a 'vice of narrow governance'.[49]

By contrast, in addition to a formally valid source of the rule, legisprudence requires the legitimation of the proposed legislative act through its proactive justification. This justification is achieved according to the principles that legisprudence sets out, which guide the conduct of the ruler regardless of the political content of the norm she is making: 'through his ruling activity, while following rules, the ruler must supply reasons for his choices'.[50] One can thus see how legisprudence represents a form of constitutionalism. I will discuss the principles of legisprudence in greater detail in Chapter 4; the goal here has been to set out the problems of strong legalism that they seek to ameliorate. Those problems reach their apex in code, to which we can now turn.

3.2 Computational Legalism

Like strong legalism, code also requires citizens 'not to think about it' and simply to follow the rule as handed down. There is a difference of degree, however, since the legalistic mindset is at least something that can notionally be challenged by the citizen or rejected by the values of a given society. Even without such resistance, the interpretative or hermeneutic gap by definition creates space between the promulgation of the norm and any acquiescence to its requirements. Code, by contrast, admits of no opportunity for challenge: as we saw in Chapter 2, some measure of technological normativity is inherent in its very existence – the boundaries of the field of play, as well as the rules of the game, are determined from the outset, and there is little or nothing the end-user can do to change them, if she is even aware of what they are to begin with (which is far from a given, as we will see below). Not only is she made to 'not think about it', in many cases she is not given the opportunity to apprehend what it is that she is not thinking about.

Returning to the characteristics of legalism set out above, we can think about how they apply in the context of code to create what I call 'computational legalism', the particular species of legalistic obedience that flows from the *sui generis* nature of code as a regulator. First, we saw how legalism

---

[49] Bańkowski and MacCormick (n 15) 194.
[50] Wintgens, *Legisprudence: Practical Reason in Legislation* (n 19) 145.

concerns itself with rules that are to be followed as written. Code presents us with an extreme form of 'ruleishness', where conditions are hard-edged and admit of no latitude for interpretation. Second, legalism views those rules as a representation of reality. We saw in Chapter 2 how the code of digital architectures actively constitutes, rather than merely represents, the empirical and legal realities that the end-user is presented with (as well as those she cannot perceive). Third, under legalism rules are seen as a-temporal, or timeless – they reflect background truths, and they 'just are'. Similarly, code in a sense 'collapses' time, through a combination of the immediacy of its execution, its immutability at the point of execution, and the cumulative normativity of its pervasiveness. Fourth, the source of the sovereign's power is concealed so that the policy reasons behind the rules it promulgates are ignored, those norms being treated as simply 'there', to be followed without question by the end-user. The opacity of code and the privileging of commercial practices and trade secrets set up a similar concealment in the computational context – the 'sovereignty' of those who produce code is concealed by veils of both technical and legal-economic opacity.

The remainder of this chapter considers these characteristics in turn, demonstrating how the computational form of legalism is much stronger than even the strongest notion of its legal counterpart, in turn underlining the need for its ex ante mitigation through design.

(a) Ruleishness

Hildebrandt observes that textual norms have lives of their own beyond the author:

> Absent ostensive reference, the author is never sure how her text will be understood, while the reader cannot take for granted what the author meant to say. This provides for an inevitable latitude in the use of texts and turns law-making (enactment of legal codes as well as their application) into a creative process rather than a mechanical application.[51]

This is a historical consequence of the embodiment of law in text, implying the choice that text as a medium affords us as to whether or not to adopt a legalistic perspective.[52] This idea of law as a creative process reflects the aspirational view of legality, which I discuss in more detail in Chapter 4,

---

[51] M Hildebrandt, 'Legal and technological normativity: More (and less) than twin sisters' (2008) 12 *Techné: Research in Philosophy and Technology* 169, 172. This echoes R Barthes, 'The death of the author' in S Heath (ed.), *Image – Music – Text* (Fontana 1977).

[52] L Diver, 'Law as a user: Design, affordance, and the technological mediation of norms' (2018) 15 *SCRIPTed* 4, 30–2 ('4.3 *Operation* versus *formation* of law').

according to which the slow iteration of normative interpretation across heterogeneous circumstances builds towards a body of law that is simultaneously stable and flexible.[53] As we have seen, this is at odds with strong legalism's binary application of rules *qua* rules.[54] This 'ruleishness'[55] is one of the most salient connections between juridical and computational legalism. Taking the orthodox spectrum that at one end has absolute rules that admit of no interpretation, and at the other has more flexible standards that specify broader outcomes but not the detailed means by which they should be achieved, code is very much located towards the rule end.[56] Code execution represents the mechanical application of rules *par excellence*; as Zittrain puts it, 'execution is exquisite'.[57] Simultaneously, code's 'enactment' does not by default (or even generally) admit of the latitude of interpretation that Hildebrandt refers to. The rule as laid down by the designer is the rule that will be followed (not just by the end-user, but also, as we shall see, by the machine). Whereas text-based institutional laws are created in the knowledge that the passage of time and the ambiguity of language will permit consideration of exceptional circumstances or evolving social norms, code 'requires extreme precision and rigor not resident in analog law'.[58] Without that precision, the code will simply fail to execute.

As a result of this, three profound consequences flow from code's ruleishness, namely (1) its mindless execution wherever the conditions it requires are met, (2) the total absence of performance in circumstances where exactly those conditions are not met, leaving no possibility of sensitivity to edge cases, and (3) its inability to respond to changes in the world that lie outside of its predetermined and necessarily limited ontology. Each of these is explored below, followed by a discussion of the difference between the 'rules' the machine follows versus the rules *qua* technological normativity that they in turn create, and to which the end-user is subjected.

Mindless Execution

First, the rules specified ex ante in the code will be applied in all instances where the conditions they require are present, regardless of any ex post

---

[53] Hildebrandt, 'Legal and technological normativity' (n 51) 171–2.

[54] Bańkowski and Schafer (n 1) 34.

[55] I adopt this term from J Grimmelmann, 'Regulation by software' (2005) 114 *The Yale Law Journal* 1719.

[56] Ibid. 1723. See also K Yeung, 'Can we employ design-based regulation while avoiding *Brave New World*?' (2011) 3 *Law, Innovation & Technology* 1.

[57] J Zittrain, *The Future of the Internet and How to Stop It* (Yale University Press 2008) 107.

[58] LA Shay et al., 'Do robots dream of electric laws? An experiment in the law as algorithm' in R Calo, A Froomkin and I Kerr (eds), *Robot Law* (Edward Elgar Publishing 2016) 274.

considerations (although of course inputs at run-time, from the end-user or some other source such as a sensor or an oracle, will in many cases be required for the ex ante specifications of the rules to be met). In the technical context this is of course a major benefit: even the most complex body of rules can be expected to execute in predetermined ways under precisely defined conditions, giving a notional predictability that has facilitated the rapid innovation that society has observed over the past several decades of the silicon era.

This is connected with the automated and immediate nature of code, which means that once released into a production environment it can repeat the same set of operations millions or billions of times with little or no marginal cost, and with no human intervention required beyond the maintenance of computing and energy infrastructure and any input necessary for its operation.[59]

Again, provided the conditions specified in the code are met, the code will execute automatically, regardless of any other consideration, provided that it is formally valid. Indeed, this point about formal validity is one of the problems of code's instrumentalism: the machine will execute semantically correct commands faithfully and with no regard to their consequences, which, depending on the behaviour and the pervasiveness of the code in question, can be catastrophic.[60] Back in the legal realm, this is quite evidently undesirable. Even the most 'ruleish' of textual legal norms requires interpretation in order to move from the page to behavioural instantiation, and even where the rule is one of strict liability (for example a speed limit for drivers), enforcement still requires an active process of interpretation, in the course of which justificatory or excusatory reasons may come to light which modulate a strongly legalistic application of the original rule (for example the driver was rushing to get her injured passenger to hospital).[61]

---

[59] Grimmelmann (n 55) 1729. See also Yeung (n 56). The low marginal cost is part of the orthodox story, of course – focus is now beginning to turn to the vast amount of energy required to run the ballooning infrastructures necessary to meet demands for computation, and the contribution this is making to climate breakdown.

[60] H Surden, 'Values embedded in legal artificial intelligence' (University of Colorado Legal Studies Research Papers 2017) 5. For a recent example that continues to affect both hardware and software at the most fundamental level of execution, see 'Meltdown and Spectre' (2018) <https://meltdownattack.com/> last accessed 4 March 2021.

[61] Shay et al. use the example of speed cameras in their discussion of the practical difficulties inherent in transposing a textual norm into code. See Shay et al., 'Do robots dream of electric laws?' (n 58). For a fascinating discussion of techno-regulation of speeding that bridges Hartian and Latourian notions of law, see K de Vries and N van Dijk, 'A bump in the road. Ruling out law from technology' in M Hildebrandt and J Gaakeer (eds), *Human Law and Computer Law: Comparative Perspectives* (Springer 2013).

Hard Edges

Second, as long as the precise conditions specified in the rule do not exist, it will never be executed. No matter how closely the code-based rule matches the circumstances that arise in operation, if the two do not match then the code will remain inert. Taken together with the first characteristic, there is therefore in code an emphatic absence – and indeed impossibility – of Hart's concept of the 'penumbra of doubt':[62] there can only be the core of meaning, except that the core expressed in the code reflects the subjective understanding of the designer, and not necessarily the settled meaning understood by the legislature, courts, or society more generally.[63] As Grimmelmann notes, the 'hard edges' of software rules are not susceptible to blurring, no matter how complex the set of rules is that is being applied[64] (which, in the modern computing context, will invariably be staggeringly complex). Whereas a human's ability to apply simultaneous rules might result in less precision as the set increases, there is for practical purposes no such limitation for code (except that speed of execution might suffer).

Limited Ontology

Third, and as a corollary of the two characteristics above, code's ruleishness limits by definition the conditions that it will respond to. This limiting of possibilities is put in place by the designer, who of course is interested in solving a particular problem by a particular set of technical means, each of which is considered from the perspective of the underlying business model and the norms and assumptions about formalisation that are a part of whatever computing 'discourse' she inhabits.[65] In so doing, she may fail to consider the

---

[62] Hart (n 41).

[63] Work on fuzzy logic seeks to map the indeterminacy of language onto the determinacy of numbers, while defeasible and non-monotonic logic are aimed at countering the otherwise brittle logic of code rules. See, for example, R Binns, 'Analogies and disanalogies between machine-driven and human-driven legal judgement' (2021) 1 *Journal of Cross-disciplinary Research in Computational Law* <https://journalcrcl.org/crcl/article/view/5> last accessed 19 April 2021; G Governatori and S Sadiq, 'The journey to business process compliance' in J Cardoso and W van der Aalst (eds), *Handbook of Research on Business Process Modeling* (IGI Global 2009); L Philipps and G Sartor, 'Introduction: From legal theories to neural networks and fuzzy reasoning' (1999) 7 *Artificial Intelligence and Law* 115, 122 *et seq*. It remains to be seen how far such approaches extend into mainstream code development practice, however.

[64] Grimmelmann (n 55) 1733.

[65] PE Agre, *Computation and Human Experience* (Cambridge University Press 1997) 44–8; F Flores et al., 'Computer systems and the design of organizational interaction' (1988) 6 *ACM Transactions on Information Systems (TOIS)* 153. For a critique, in this vein, of machine learning, see D McQuillan, 'Data science as machinic neoplatonism' (2018) 31 *Philosophy & Technology* 253. All of this is mediated by the affordances of the tools the

other possibilities that were relevant to the situation, thus reducing the world to an inappropriately limited set of conditions and responses. From her perspective, she intends that in the operation of the system conditions A, B, or C will arise, and the system should respond with one or a combination of X, Y, or Z. These conditions comprise the entirety of the closed world that is assumed by the code's 'ontology', which once it is defined is rigid and cannot, without the code being altered, be made to be sensitive to conditions D and G, or responses W and Q. The designer's predetermined view of the code's operation (conditions A, B, and C, and potential responses X, Y, and Z) is thus reified, and although that reification will not reflect the empirical reality of the world,[66] or the requirements of substantive law, or some other relevant normative value such as legitimacy or the rule of law, this fact will pose no barrier whatsoever to the execution of the code on the basis of the ontology the designer builds her artefact around.[67] As Grimmelmann puts it, '[w]hen a programmer creates a program, she predetermines its responses to every possible input – to every possible "case" it may adjudicate. The algorithm is the rule.'[68] Once compiled into commands executable by the machine the code is 'closed', and no information that has not somehow been represented there can make its way in post hoc to alter the nature of that execution.[69]

There is a connection here with Hart's notion of the open texture of language, and his argument against attempts to regulate unambiguously in advance:

> If the world in which we live were characterized by only a finite number of features, and these together with all the modes in which they could combine were known to us, then provision could be made in advance for every possibility . . . Everything could be known, and for everything, since it could be known, something could be done and specified in advance by rule. This would be a world fit for 'mechanical' jurisprudence. Plainly this world is not our world.[70]

---

designer uses, from the programming language to the integrated design environment. I return to this important theme in Chapter 7.

[66] This is sometimes termed the 'map–territory relation'.

[67] Agre (n 65) 48.

[68] Grimmelmann (n 55) 1732.

[69] M Krajewski, 'Against the power of algorithms closing, literate programming, and source code critique' (2019) 23 *Law Text Culture* 119; P Swartz, 'How do programs mean?' in *Division III: Essays in Programs as Literature* (Hampshire College 2007) 78–80. Strictly speaking, compiled and interpreted languages differ on this point, but pragmatically they are the same, at least from the perspective of the end-user.

[70] HLA Hart, *The Concept of Law* (2nd edn, Clarendon Press 1994) 128.

Code makes this vision a reality, although not in the way Hart imagined. It goes further by *imposing* such 'mechanical jurisprudence' on a contingent and complex world. It reduces that complexity to the set of features that the designer thought to include, whether or not those features are sufficient in terms of their number or the appropriateness of the types of formalisation used, and whether or not they capture the necessary features of whatever context(s) the code will ultimately operate in.[71] This solipsistic ontology allows code to operate at great speed with immense predictability, but this is inherently limited in scope to only what has been anticipated (and will include the inevitable bugs that accompany its implementation).[72] By contrast, law must be capable of contingently accommodating, referencing, and interacting with systems external to itself (that is, the society it is intended to serve).[73]

Bańkowski made a connection early on between legalism and code-based regulation in his description of a hypothetical system for borrowing ebooks from a library.[74] His description shows how the transition from an 'offline' manual library system to an automated system affects the rules that governed the former. The rules state:

1. borrowers must complete a separate form for each volume borrowed,
2. books should be returned before the due date,
3. borrowers have a limited number of loans that must not be exceeded,
4. no further books will be loaned to borrowers who have overdue loans.[75]

These regulations are transposed into code, governing the 'borrowing' of an ebook that will 'self-destruct' after the appropriate borrowing period.[76] (This is of course an archetypal DRM system, where ex ante constraints on media use define its availability and are embedded in and enforced by the artefact itself.) The computational legalism of such a system becomes evident when we consider what happens to the textual rules listed above, which previously under the manual system were interpreted and applied by the human librarian. The rules are bright lines that admit of no interpretation – once the

---

[71] On this general theme, see GC Bowker and SL Star, *Sorting Things Out: Classification and Its Consequences* (MIT Press 2000). There is a significant overlap here with the problems of attempting to formalise 'ground truths' in machine learning research design.

[72] An example of the combined problem of bugs and code's limited ontology is the Post Office Horizon scandal, which I discuss in Chapter 6.

[73] M Hildebrandt, 'Code-driven law: Freezing the future and scaling the past' in SF Deakin and C Markou (eds), *Is Law Computable? Critical Perspectives on Law and Artificial Intelligence* (Hart 2020).

[74] Bańkowski (n 15) 54 ('Norms and Machines') *et seq*.

[75] Ibid. 55.

[76] Ibid.

borrowing limit is reached, if no appeal process is built into the code then no further books can be borrowed, regardless of any extenuating circumstances (recall the third consequence of code's ruleishness discussed above). Once the borrowing period is reached, the book 'self-destructs', again regardless of any extenuating circumstance that might have moved a human librarian to make an exception (for example a combination of illness and exams).

The Absence of Interpretation

In sum, these characteristics highlight the absence of interpretative possibilities in code. There is no tolerance of ambiguity, no possibility of discretion or subversion, and little space to reason separately from either interpreting or even, in the first instance, identifying the rule.[77] Digital systems are thus 'crude and inflexible, often brutal and not open to critical reason'.[78] Returning to the example above, the speed camera detects one of three conditions (the car is travelling below, at, or above the speed limit) and it has two responses (do not take photo; take and process photo). In spite of the legalism of such a system, there is nevertheless an ex post buffer to enable some interpretation – a human may interpret the photo and, upon realising the vehicle was an ambulance, override the automated decision. The decision to include such oversight (that is, a 'human in the loop'[79]) is a design choice and is by no means a given – there is no technological barrier preventing a speed camera and penalty system being fully automated with no ex post adjudication[80] but we choose not to do so because there are other important values that must be represented.[81] Such scenarios demonstrate how the three elements of ruleishness can come together to amplify legalism in the computational context, especially when they are combined with the automation and immediacy of code.

---

[77] P Swartz, 'A tower of languages' in *Division III: Essays in Programs as Literature* (Hampshire College 2007) 96–7; Grimmelmann (n 55) 1723. On reason as an element of decision-making that is distinct from the rule, see N MacCormick, *Rhetoric and the Rule of Law: A Theory of Legal Reasoning* (Oxford University Press 2005) chapter 2.

[78] Bańkowski and Schafer (n 1) 46.

[79] W Hartzog et al., 'Inefficiently automated law enforcement' (2015) *Michigan State Law Review* 1763, 1780 *et seq*. I return to this theme in Chapter 6, discussing the digisprudential affordance of delay.

[80] LA Shay et al., 'Confronting automated law enforcement' in R Calo, A Froomkin and I Kerr (eds), *Robot Law* (Edward Elgar Publishing 2016); C Gavaghan, 'Lex machina: Techno-regulatory mechanisms and rules by design' (2017) 15 *Otago Law Review* 123, 130–1.

[81] This is reflected in Art. 22 of the GDPR, regarding automated decision-making and the difference made by having a human involved.

(b) Representationalism

Representationalism is a key aspect of strong legalism: in both its *jusnaturalistic* and positivistic accounts of the origins of law, legal norms are held to represent reality. As discussed above, for the former legal validity is derived from the underlying truth of nature, while for the latter it comes from the founding social contract, rule of recognition, et cetera. If the underlying natural norms or the founding political act are true, then the rules which flow from them must also be true.[82]

The way in which code constructs a rule-based normativity is of course not the same as law's approach. The regulative force of law is (and indeed ought to be) limited by its instantiation in the technology of the script (that is, text), which creates an interpretative or hermeneutic gap between what the text requests and how the addressee(s) of that text interpret its terms and choose to reflect them in their behaviour.[83] The instantiation of code rules, on the other hand, is not so limited: technological normativity, as we saw in Chapter 2, can have a direct effect in a way that legal normativity – necessarily constrained by its textual embodiment – does not.[84]

Does Code Contain Rules per se?

One crucial way in which code can be said to be less than law is that it does not promulgate rules in the basic sense of providing citizens with a set of guidelines they can find, interpret, and adapt their behaviour to follow. Nor does an appreciation of code's representationalism require any metaphysical gymnastics to connect its rules with empirical reality or some contested notion of 'truth'. The rules of code work in a different way – they are not Austinian commands to be followed,[85] nor are they the ex post representations of the norms of a community, against which standards of conduct can be evaluated.[86] Instead, they are instrumental tools that crystallise behavioural possibilities and limits from the outset, with varying levels of normative 'force' (recall the

---

[82] Wintgens, 'Legisprudence as a new theory of legislation' (n 24) 4.

[83] Diver (n 52); Hildebrandt, 'Legal and technological normativity' (n 51) 175.

[84] Hildebrandt, 'Legal and technological normativity' (n 51) 176. For more on the consequences for law of text as a medium, see J Goody, *The Logic of Writing and the Organization of Society* (Cambridge University Press 1986) chapter 4 and, more generally, WJ Ong, *Orality and Literacy: The Technologizing of the Word* (3rd edn, Routledge 2012).

[85] J Austin, *The Province of Jurisprudence Determined*, ed. WE Rumble (Cambridge University Press 1995), *passim*.

[86] See P Winch, *The Idea of a Social Science and Its Relation to Philosophy* (Routledge & Kegan Paul; Humanities Press 1990) 24 *et seq.*, discussing L Wittgenstein, *Philosophical Investigations*, trans. GEM Anscombe (Blackwell 1968).

discussion of the spectrum of technological normativity in Chapter 2). The result is that the gap that otherwise exists between the text of a legal rule and its effect on behaviour in the physical world collapses. Whereas the law has used legal fictions to maintain its position as ultimate arbiter of the social world, it now has to compete with code that constitutes both empirical and normative landscapes.[87] More and more, it is losing this competition: 'the virtual is a mode of reality that evades the space-time categories of the law'.[88]

The extent to which the hermeneutic gap collapses is profound; its efface-ment in code is not only easy but is entirely normal, and not necessarily through malice or intentional obfuscation (although these are a significant concern), but simply by the very nature of the medium. The gap can so eas-ily be collapsed because the 'text' of the rule (the code) constitutes directly the geography of the artefact: they are not just isomorphic, they are one and the same, at least at the level of computation. Unlike law, whose 'carrier' has hitherto been the inherently passive medium of text, software code allows us to, in Latour's words, 'conceive of a text (a programming language) that is at once words and actions'.[89]

In code we find the collision of rules and reality, where what was 'ought' becomes simply 'is' (or, at least, a categorical 'will be'). In this way, represen-tationalism finds its apex: no appeal to metaphysical belief is required to see how computer code not just represents reality, but actively constitutes it (or at least a part of it). Behavioural possibilities are constituted, and not merely regulated, by code rules. If legal rules can ultimately be decomposed into an 'if this, then that' structure,[90] code rules exemplify and amplify this reality, given that is in practice exactly how they are expressed from the outset.

Returning to Bańkowski's library borrowing system, we can appreciate how in their translation into code the rules become simply descriptive rather than regulative. The tracking of library users and their loans is obviated by means of swipe-card authentication (rule 1 collapses); the end of loans and the 'return' of ebooks is automated by code, thus rendering rule 2 descriptive; and rule 3 merely describes the state of the system that rule 4 enforces (again,

[87] What Vismann and Krajewski call 'digital virtuality'. See C Vismann and M Krajewski, 'Computer juridisms' (2007) *Grey Room* 90, 92.

[88] Ibid.

[89] B Latour, 'Where are the missing masses? The sociology of a few mundane artifacts' in WE Bijker and J Law (eds), *Shaping Technology/Building Society: Studies in Sociotechnical Change* (MIT Press 1992) n 1.

[90] N MacCormick, *Institutions of Law: An Essay in Legal Theory* (Oxford University Press 2007) 24 *et seq*. Importantly, this point is only about the structure of the rule and not the reasoning which interprets and applies it – which of course is precisely the point of compar-ison with code.

automatically). The 'if this, then that' instantiation of rule 4's logic simply does not allow the function in the code that issues loans to be executed. As Bańkowski puts it, '[w]hat we see then, is how the normative has become the descriptive. This gives us an example of rule following which has the machine-like quality of heteronomy: we "don't think about it".'[91] The library's rules, which were once normative, have become descriptive – they are simply how the system, and the end-user within it, will inevitably operate. There is no gap or space between the rule and its imposition; the code rule constitutes reality. If the stored number of books is at a certain threshold, then no further loans will be permitted, regardless of any extenuating circumstances. The code rule means that the computer will simply say no.

There is more to the story, however. A full analysis of code rules requires us to think at more than one level of abstraction. In that vein, Asscher draws a distinction between rules on the 'conceptual level' and the 'technical commands within a certain computer language',[92] concluding that it is the former that is ultimately what matters. This is correct insofar as it is necessary to think abstractly when comparing instantiations of rules in code with the textual legal rules from which they may be derived (this would be the techno-regulation level, which I discuss in Chapter 5). However, we must not ignore the concrete materiality of the technical commands that are the building blocks of the normativity that ultimately implements those rules. Although it might quickly become cumbersome to focus on the minutiae of the individual commands in source code, the materiality of the system in operation is precisely where the action happens, and so it is necessary to focus our attention at that level, at least to some degree. The challenge is to find an appropriate abstraction threshold between individual commands and the technological normativities that collectively they bring into being. In the end, it is code that performs this translation of normativities, and for better or worse that code is necessarily designed, even if not all of its effects can be anticipated in advance.

At this more abstract level, Leenes and Koops suggest that the negligent production of privacy-eroding code can be viewed as akin to a rule stating that privacy is not important, or is less important than other values:

> Although this is perhaps stretching the term 'rule' rather far, we are inclined
> to think that the development and application of code that negligently fails
> to take privacy effects into account can indeed be seen as the embedding

---

[91] Bańkowski (n 15) 56.

[92] L Asscher, '"Code" as law: Using Fuller to assess code rules' in E Dommering and L Asscher (eds), *Coding Regulation: Essays on the Normative Role of Information Technology* (TMC Asser Press 2006) 83.

of a 'rule' in the technology, namely that privacy is unimportant and secondary to other values that the code primarily serves. Such technology does indeed serve to guide or control (what is perceived as) proper and acceptable behaviour, since privacy-infringement is considered an acceptable outcome of its use.[93]

One can appreciate how abstracted this perspective is from the idea of viewing individual code instructions as rules. In this case, the broader functionality of the code and how it guides behaviour according to a particular stance on a given value (in this case privacy) is interpreted as a kind of rule. Here we can see a connection with the design theories discussed in Chapter 2: we could frame the above in terms of the (dis)affordance of privacy-protecting functionality as being a *de facto* rule embodied in that particular code.

Adapting Leenes and Koops's formulation, one might say that code rules that fail to embody standards of legitimacy in effect represent 'rules' stating that those standards are not important and need not be valued. The (dis)affordances and inscriptions that the code embodies can be seen as 'rules' of this sort, the corollary being that code can and ought to be made compatible with those standards by providing certain affordances. If it does so, the likelihood of the code artefact's normativity being illegitimate is accordingly reduced.

From this level of abstraction, we can appreciate the normativity the code imposes without having to look directly at the underlying commands, which is one useful strategy for connecting orthodox notions of what makes a rule and the normativities that code rules in fact bring into being. Maintaining a holistic sensitivity to code's effects in this way can help us avoid too narrow a focus on just its purposive effects (that is, what its designers purport its functionality to be), a perspective that much of the literature adopts implicitly.[94] We saw in Chapter 1 how digisprudence is concerned with not just the intended regulatory effects of code, but also those wider 'techno-effects' that may not have a legal underpinning, whether public or private.[95] It is important to consider not just the intended normative effects of a system but also its potential unintended effects, and if those undermine the legitimacy of the code's normativity, this becomes a real cause for concern. The

---

[93] R Leenes and B-J Koops, '"Code" and privacy or how technology is slowly eroding privacy' in E Dommering and L Asscher (eds), *Coding Regulation: Essays on the Normative Role of Information Technology* (TMC Asser Press 2006) 191.

[94] Cf. B van den Berg and RE Leenes, 'Abort, retry, fail: Scoping techno-regulation and other techno-effects' in M Hildebrandt and J Gaakeer (eds), *Human Law and Computer Law: Comparative Perspectives* (Springer 2013).

[95] Ibid. 81.

relational focus of both affordance theory and postphenomenology requires us to think about what the code is actually doing, as opposed to merely what it is intended by its designer to do. By viewing code rules at these different levels of abstraction, we can conceptualise the role they play in constituting and regulating behaviour.

Constitutive and Regulative Rules

We saw in Chapter 2 the distinction between constitutive and regulative technological normativity.[96] Hildebrandt discusses the difference between legal rules that are constitutive of other (institutional) facts or rules, and those that aim to regulate behaviours which can take place independently of the rule's existence.[97] For example, the institutional fact of marriage cannot exist independently of a constitutive rule which creates or institutes it,[98] while it is possible to drive at 100 miles per hour even though there is a regulative rule which prohibits it.[99] Regulative rules are therefore aimed at regulating existing activities, while constitutive rules 'create the very possibility of certain activities'.[100] In a sense, then, constitutive rules are creative, or generative, while regulative rules are limiting. Searle discusses the example of chess: the rules of the game do not regulate what was already happening (that is, we do not tend idly to push around on a chequered board miniature figurines representing kings, queens, knights, etc.); rather, the rules in fact constitute the game. The game of chess does not exist outside of its constitutive rules – if people ignore those rules, they may be playing something, but it is not chess. The constitutive rules are thus creative in their bringing about (1) the general institution of 'chess', and (2) the contingent institutional fact of any given game of chess.[101]

This idea of an 'institutional fact' stems from the distinction between facts that are socially constructed, and 'brute facts' which exist 'out there' in

---

[96] See 'A Spectrum of Technological Normativity' in Section 2.2.

[97] Hildebrandt, 'Legal and technological normativity' (n 51) 172 *et seq.*

[98] MacCormick's suggested sub-division of constitutive rules into institutive, consequential, and terminative rules adds helpful pragmatic granularity to the broader scope of the former, but we can continue for present purposes to use the term as-is. See MacCormick, *Institutions of Law* (n 90) 36–7.

[99] Hildebrandt, 'Legal and technological normativity' (n 51) 172.

[100] JR Searle, *The Construction of Social Reality* (Free Press 1995) 27.

[101] Ibid. 27–8. One can also appreciate here the contrast drawn between 'broad' and 'narrow' normativity in M Piekarski and W Wachowski, 'Artefacts as social things: Design-based approach to normativity' (2018) 22 *Techné: Research in Philosophy and Technology* 400.

empirical reality.[102] Obvious examples of institutional facts include a 'university' and a 'doctoral degree'. Examples of brute facts include the distance between the earth and the sun at this very moment, or the amount of force I am currently exerting on my keyboard.[103] An 'institution' in this sense refers to an arrangement recognised within the relevant community or form of life, as in the game of chess, as opposed to an agency. (Having said that, the two concepts can overlap, potentially symbiotically, within the same entity. For example, a university is both an 'institution-arrangement' – like a game of chess, it is something whose character is borne of certain features being observed and maintained through time by those with the relevant capacities committing to doing so – and it is also an 'institution-agency', that is an organisation empowered *inter alia* to confer doctoral degrees.[104])

Because institutional facts are 'thought-objects'[105] that we create as part of our shared institutional world, they do not exist or make sense independently of that world and can therefore be brought into being only by following the criteria agreed to by the members of the relevant community. This is the creative work done by constitutive rules. One can appreciate the tension here between legalism on the one hand, which holds that the constitutive rules of law (quintessentially a system of institutional facts) are 'out there', and the viewpoint I am advancing, which seeks to question the design of those constitutive rules.

From a legalistic perspective, constitutive rules can be arranged in a hierarchy which creates the underlying framework (itself an institutional fact or set of facts, sometimes termed a 'constitution') within which other rules can be made. This is Wintgens's proxy model, discussed earlier, where the legitimacy of a given legal rule flows from some founding act which operates in the

---

[102] Searle (n 100).

[103] It should be noted, however, that the units we use to conceptualise these two facts are in a sense themselves institutional (that is, part of a shared social understanding), because the scientific practices that have resulted in them are not objective, even if the physical reality they seek to represent is. See for example Ihde's discussion of the 'hermeneutic relation' that mediates our experience of the world (or the universe) via the reading of scientific instruments in *Technology and the Lifeworld: From Garden to Earth* (Indiana University Press 1990) 80 *et seq.*

[104] MacCormick, *Institutions of Law* (n 90) 35–7.

[105] O Weinberger, 'The norm as thought and as reality' in N MacCormick and O Weinberger, *An Institutional Theory of Law: New Approaches to Legal Positivism* (Springer 1986). From an external perspective, a legal-institutional fact might be treated as brute: 'depending on one's perspective, any brute fact can be rearticulated as an institutional fact, while institutional facts can be "used" as brute facts to be regulated' (Hildebrandt, 'Legal and technological normativity' (n 51) 172).

background to validate those subsequently promulgated norms. As previously noted, the idea is connected with various accounts of law that culminate in a notional foundational legal rule.

As with the institution of chess, in law constitutive rules are necessary to inaugurate valid instances of what MacCormick calls institution-arrangements (for example a contract or marriage), institution-agencies (for example a university or local authority), and intangible institution-things (for example a patent or a stock portfolio).[106] The legal institution of marriage, for example, is defined by the requirements laid down in certain constitutive rules, and a particular institution-arrangement of marriage is an institutional fact brought into being by the following of those rules. To speak of a couple being 'married' outside the institutional framework (in both the universal and particular senses of 'institution') does not make sense, or at least does not point to a legally recognised institutional fact.[107]

How does all of this relate to code? Whereas the institutional facts created by legal constitutive rules are always only 'real' within the law's own 'regime of veridiction'[108] or institutional order, code-based rules are 'brute' in the sense that they are 'just there' and part of the 'physical' fabric of the system. Recalling the discussion of rules above, this is true in every case where the notion of 'rule' refers to the individual instructions given to the machine – the instructions are brute facts in the sense of manipulating physical reality at the level of the machine's hardware. Moving up towards more abstract notions of rules, code-based rules become potentially less brute, in the sense that spaces can be opened up in which more than one course of action is open to the end-user. The extent to which she is accorded this 'freedom' is down to the particular mix of intentional and unintentional (dis)affordance embodied in the design, but, as previously stated, whatever the level of flexibility the design provides, this too is necessarily bounded from the outset.

Code-based rules, then, are 'constitutive of our behaviour'.[109] Just as our notions of legal rules have moved beyond the earlier Austinian command model to encompass the broader 'creative' or empowering aspect of secondary or institutive rules,[110] so too does code represent an example of this 'creative', constitutive form of normativity-generation. A crucial difference in the code context, however, is that it is not the citizen who is so empowered by those constitutive rules to create the relevant normative constructs, such as

[106] MacCormick, *Institutions of Law* (n 90) 35–6.
[107] Hildebrandt, *Smart Technologies* (n 11) 145.
[108] Ibid.
[109] Hildebrandt, 'Legal and technological normativity' (n 51) 174.
[110] See, respectively, Hart (n 70) 91 *et seq.*; MacCormick, *Institutions of Law* (n 90) 36–7.

a contract, will, or whatever. Instead, the creative 'instituting' of the relevant form of normativity (technical, not legal) is performed by the designer of the code, who constitutes the terms of behaviour of the citizen as if the latter were a subject of the former's sovereign power. In including, excluding, and defining the limits of behaviour within the ambit of the system, code 'rules' limit end-user freedom in material ways. The qualitative difference is that, with code, these limits are not merely regulative, where the end-user, already engaging in whatever activity, is 'requested' to amend her behaviour this way or that (this is the equivalent of the speed limit which *ceteris paribus* can only ever 'request' that the driver travel at less than 70 miles per hour). Rather, the limits are constitutive, in that the salient features of the behaviour are themselves defined by code. Whereas the chess player can use the architecture of the artefact (the board and its pieces) in ways that are outside the rules of the game, for example to play something less complex like draughts, the architecture of code sets the rules in place ex ante, and does not by default allow them to be so adapted at the discretion of the end-user. To quote Lessig, 'one obeys these laws as code not because one should; one obeys these laws as code because one can do nothing else'.[111] The constraints and enablements of code are 'like laws of nature, like the world as we find it';[112] they are simply 'there', with the crucial difference between code and law being that rather than suggesting an 'ought', as law in its regulative capacity always does, code can simply impose an 'is'.[113] The three traditional phases of regulation (direction, detection, and correction)[114] are thus collapsed into a single step.[115]

We will see later that it is possible for code rules to be regulative so that the end-user is in fact invited to behave in certain ways, and of course many digital systems do allow a range of behaviours in end-users' interactions with them. Social networks, for example, give end-users fairly wide latitude on the volume and content of the text, images, and videos they can upload. But even within this seemingly unlimited freedom to upload there are nevertheless

[111] L Lessig, 'The zones of cyberspace' (1995) 48 *Stanford Law Review* 1403, 1408.
[112] Grimmelmann (n 55) 1740. Similarly, Bamberger notes that 'the fact that architectural technology embodies normative choices at all can escape notice, as the perfect constraints code places on behavioral possibility can seem as natural, immutable, and invisible as the laws of physics'. See KA Bamberger, 'Technologies of compliance: Risk and regulation in a digital age' (2010) 88 *Texas Law Review* 669, 724–5.
[113] R Brownsword, 'Lost in translation: Legality, regulatory margins, and technological management' (2011) 26 *Berkeley Technology Law Journal* 1321.
[114] C Scott, 'Regulation in the age of governance: The rise of the post-regulatory state' in J Jordana and D Levi-Faur (eds), *The Politics of Regulation: Institutions and Regulatory Reforms for the Age of Governance* (Edward Elgar Publishing 2004) 147.
[115] Brownsword, 'Lost in translation' (n 113) 1344.

constitutive limits – the code will accept only text, images, or video files (not PDFs, executables, or images/videos in formats the platform does not recognise), and only a certain quantity of data can be uploaded. For most ordinary usage these boundaries will never be approached, and so the end-user may be unaware of their existence, but they are nevertheless always and necessarily there.

In many cases, then, the normativity embodied in code is more constitutive than regulative of the practice in question. The more constitutive a digital system is of a given behaviour, the more control the designer has exercised in defining the nature of that behaviour. In many cases it will be more profitable to limit the 'regulative latitude' given to the end-user, channelling her behaviour in ways that are commercially beneficial (some of these were discussed in the previous chapter). Even on a practical level, building in or enlarging the contingent regulative space at the expense of constitutive certainty requires anticipation of more possible conditions, which in turn requires more code and therefore more expense in its creation, maintenance, and support. This will lend further commercial impetus towards taking a constitutive rather than a regulative approach to design.

Rules for Humans; Rules for Machines

One might detect an ambiguity in the discussion above as to who the addressee is of a rule found in code. In the abstract sense discussed above and in the previous chapter, the end-user's interactions with the system are constituted and delimited by the design of that system's code, facilitating some acts while preventing others. Continuing the analogy with legislation, the end-user is the 'addressee' of these 'rules',[116] what she can do being structured in all the ways previously discussed. This is the level that Asscher suggests we ought to focus on. But that level of rule is itself necessarily constituted by a further, deeper level of 'rule-following', where the machine is the 'addressee' of the instructions contained in the code, those instructions being intended in turn to produce that end-user-facing technological normativity at the higher level. We might conceptualise these relationships as shown in Figure 3.1, where source code directs the machine, creating the technological normativity that directs the end-user.

Without the 'internal', absolute ruleishness of the source code that directs the machine, the 'external', abstract ruleishness of the artefact that directs the end-user will never come to be. As we saw in Chapter 2, even where there are

---

[116] Assuming that is possible, bearing in mind the discussion in Chapter 2 of signifiers and the distinction between real and perceived affordances.

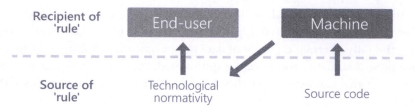

Figure 3.1 Sources of 'rules' in code

spaces in the latter that allow for contingent behaviours, these are themselves ruleishly delimited, simply because they must be – whatever nature those interactional possibilities might have, they could not exist without code that reflects the three characteristics of ruleishness described above. So, whereas technological normativity might be resist-able by the end-user, the machine has no choice or latitude as to whether or not it follows the instructions it is given – and so the configuration of technological normativity experienced by the end-user is itself necessarily structured by the absolutism of machinic rule-following.

These multiple roles that code plays – a text describing what its execution will do, a set of rules for the machine to follow, and, ultimately, the framework for the experience that the end-user will have – suggest some important sites at which practical approaches to ensuring legitimacy can be introduced. I will return to this theme of code deconstruction in Part III of the book, where I discuss how the text of code provides us with potential avenues for both interrogating and facilitating its legitimacy.

(c) Immediacy

Code's immediacy refers to the temporal aspect of execution. As discussed above, the hermeneutic gap between text and behaviour is collapsed, but not only does the text of code constitute both rule and reality, but the imposition of it is arranged prior to, and imposed immediately at the point of, execution. The conditions specified in that prior arrangement are imposed without delay and without consideration of alternative actions that might have been appropriate. There is no scope to 'hesitate well', as in Latour's description of judicial practice;[117] linear time is in a sense compressed, further distancing the character of code's operation from the role that law's more measured pace plays

---

[117] B Latour, *The Making of Law: An Ethnography of the Conseil d'Etat* (rev. edn, Polity 2009) 193–4.

in the stabilisation of societal expectations.[118] After the point of 'closure',[119] the compilation of whatever configuration of normativity is contained in the code, the machine will execute it faithfully and as quickly as it is physically capable of.

Grimmelmann refers to this characteristic as code's immediacy, where the ex ante nature of code means that '[s]oftware cannot – as law can – adapt its response in light of later-available information or a later determination that such information is relevant.'[120] As we have seen, whereas law as a prospective regulator is inert in the absence of the will to reflect its terms in real-world behaviour, the enablements and constraints of code, put in place by the designer, have latent efficacy even before the system is operational. Recalling the discussion of the library above, the end-user is simply subjected to the ex ante 'ruling' of the code: she may not borrow any more ebooks, the overdue ebook ceases to be accessible, et cetera. The code's swiftness is brutal and entirely impervious to external reason or extenuating circumstances.[121]

Default Configurations
Immediacy is embodied in code even where the design includes the possibility of altering its configuration. End-users tend to accept as a 'natural and immutable fact'[122] the configuration an artefact has when it is supplied to them. This may be due to automation bias, whereby the configuration and responses of a machine are assumed to be more appropriate or 'correct' than a human equivalent.[123] Clearly, the designer has significant power in choosing one starting configuration over another. As Tien notes, 'default settings may seem "normal" because the equipment is common, or have become "legitimate" as people have grown accustomed to the situation presented

---

[118] M Hildebrandt, 'A vision of ambient law' in R Brownsword and K Yeung (eds), *Regulating Technologies: Legal Futures, Regulatory Frames and Technological Fixes* (Hart 2008) 186–7. See also N Luhmann, *Law as a Social System*, ed. F Kastner et al., trans. KA Ziegert (Oxford University Press 2004) 205 *et seq*.

[119] Krajewski (n 69).

[120] Grimmelmann (n 55) 1730.

[121] Bańkowski and Schafer (n 1) 46.

[122] M Goldoni, 'The politics of code as law: Toward input reasons' in J Reichel and AS Lind (eds), *Freedom of Expression, the Internet and Democracy* (Brill 2015) 128. See also JP Kesan and RC Shah, 'Setting software defaults: Perspectives from law, computer science and behavioral economics' (2006) 82 *Notre Dame Law Review* 583, 591 *et seq*.

[123] DK Citron, 'Technological due process' (2008) 85 *Washington University Law Review* 1249, 1271–2.

by the equipment'.[124] Simultaneously, the 'is-ness' of default settings militates against enquiring as to whether other configurations might be more suitable for the end-user – instead, the defaults are accepted as immutable facts, and alternatives (should they even imagine them) as impossible or even unreasonable.[125] For many end-users, the assumption will in many cases be that the designer knows best.[126] Furthermore, they might lack the technical sophistication to investigate all the possible customisation options,[127] or they might not have the time to do so,[128] much less to think critically about what incentives might have motivated the designer to select a certain configuration of defaults or why these occasionally change in ways users do not necessarily support.[129] The behaviour-guiding quality of default configurations is often stripped away by the perception that they are 'mere design features';[130] as with legalism, they are taken to be part of what is 'just there'. Even where end-users do care about the underlying values that are impacted by the default configuration of the design, unless they are aware of the possibility of choice they will accept the default, even if it is injurious to the value.[131]

To further complicate matters, the designer must make a choice as to how to balance the number of defaults (that is, options which the end-user can change) against the amount of 'pre-wired' functionality: too many options or a complex interface can confuse, undermining the benefit of providing a choice.[132] Indeed, providing configurable options within interfaces that are antagonistic to exercising that choice is one means by which some unscrupulous (or perhaps just negligent) enterprises can argue that they are respecting end-users' autonomy whilst simultaneously undermining their interests in

---

[124] L Tien, 'Architectural regulation and the evolution of social norms' (2004) 7 *Yale Journal of Law & Technology* 1, 16.

[125] Kesan and Shah (n 122) 596, 601; Diver (n 52) 11. See also I Kerr, 'The devil is in the defaults' (2017) 4 *Critical Analysis of Law* 91, 98 *et seq.*

[126] This is known as the 'legitimating effect'. See Kesan and Shah (n 122) 603. For a study showing empirical evidence of the effect, see RC Shah and C Sandvig, 'Software defaults as de facto regulation: The case of the wireless internet' (2008) 11 *Information, Communication & Society* 25.

[127] Kesan and Shah (n 122) 611–12.

[128] Ibid. 598 *et seq.*

[129] Tien (n 124) 16. An example of this was Facebook's controversial move to the 'news feed' layout as the default for all end-users. See J Leyden, 'Users protest over "creepy" Facebook update' *The Register* (7 September 2006) <https://www.theregister.co.uk/2006/09/07/facebook_update_controversy/> last accessed 4 March 2021.

[130] Tien (n 124) 12.

[131] Kesan and Shah (n 122) 601–2.

[132] Ibid. 627. See also Brownsword's discussion of 'prudential choice' in 'Lost in translation' (n 113) 1345.

favour of commercial expediency. A recent example is the design change in Google's Chrome browser that obfuscates the circumstances in which end-users are logged into Google's services, even when they have enabled the 'block third-party cookies' preference that would normally prevent this kind of behaviour (and indeed still does in other browsers).[133] It is worth noting, too, that the 'block third-party cookies' preference itself is not the default set-ting on any mainstream browser, and thus its privacy-enhancing mechanism is something end-users must manually enable, which requires first that they are aware of the option and what it means.[134]

Pervasiveness

The pervasiveness of code is not difficult to appreciate. Code is all around us, its presence at both infrastructural and artefactual levels increasing at what seems like an inexorable rate. The market analysis firm IDC, for example, expects there to be 41.6 billion Internet of Things (IoT) devices connected by 2025, a compound annual growth rate of almost 29 per cent.[135] Earlier this decade, Cisco estimated that by 2020 there would be 250 'things' connecting to the Internet every second, up from 80 per second in 2013.[136] IoT devices are being integrated further into daily life through the development of more sophisticated low-power infrastructure[137] and the diversification of connected

---

[133] L Olejnik, 'Am I logged in or not? GDPR case study on the example of Chrome browser change' <http://blog.lukaszolejnik.com/am-i-logged-in-or-not-gdpr-case-study-on-the-example-of-chrome-browser-change/> last accessed 4 March 2021.

[134] This is in line with the evolution of the relevant IETF standards, which have changed from requiring a higher standard of privacy (RFCs 2109 (1997) and 2965 (2000) suggest that the default should be to reject persistent (cross-session) cookies) to permitting browsers to implement whatever default standard they wish, albeit while noting the 'worrisome' nature of third-party cookies (RFC 6265 (2011), section 7.1). At time of writing, it appears that third-party cookies may be in the process of being phased out, at least in relation to behavioural advertising, the efficacy of which is beginning to be questioned.

[135] IDC Media Center, 'The growth in connected IoT devices is expected to generate 79.4ZB of data in 2025, according to a new IDC forecast' *IDC Media Center* (18 June 2019) <https://www.businesswire.com/news/home/20190618005012/en/Growth-Connected-IoT-Devices-Expected-Generate-79.4ZB> last accessed 4 March 2021.

[136] K Tillman, 'How many Internet connections are in the world? Right. Now' *Cisco Blogs* (29 July 2013) <https://blogs.cisco.com/news/cisco-connections-counter> last accessed 4 March 2021.

[137] J Twentyman, 'IoT drives progress towards low-power technology' *Financial Times* (8 January 2018) <https://www.ft.com/content/f2b4de5a-d8ee-11e7-9504-59efdb70e12f> last accessed 4 March 2021. A salient example at time of writing is the use of Bluetooth Low-Energy (BLE) in the tracing applications that have become a central element in tackling the COVID-19 pandemic.

applications.[138] Similar trends can also be seen in blockchain adoption and machine learning, themselves also so often amalgamated with the data that flows from IoT devices.

Regardless of the truth of such numbers, what seems intuitively clear is that the hype around the 'fourth revolution' is resulting in an ever-greater reliance on code and data infrastructure that seems unlikely to abate any time soon.[139] In the end, as Ihde puts it, our 'technologies invent us as we invent them',[140] and given the accelerated blurring of the line between the off- and the on-line it becomes ever more pressing to protect the ability of citizens to question the 'inventive' normativities that code imposes. If the pervasiveness of code means we are entering a new phase of the 'onlife', we must not in the process surrender our capacity to have a say in the ways that code is reinventing us. As we find our behaviour being channelled this way and that by the many code artefacts that play a role in our lives, we might in our more sober moments find the aggregate of all this technological normativity somewhat troubling. The point, however, is not to push from one extreme to the other, but rather to mandate checks and balances that can facilitate our autonomy in amongst both the good and the bad that this brings.

Immutability
Surden notes how the subjective value judgements of designers, and the resulting effects of the rules embodied in their code, can be magnified when the systems are distributed and adopted widely.[141] The choice of rules becomes fixed in the code, enabling its exponential magnification as its effects compound with concurrent and successive execution.[142] Bamberger notes similar risks in his discussion of 'systemic effects': whereas at production time the designer has great freedom to choose how the code should behave, this

---

[138] Forbes Technology Council, '14 predictions for the future of smart home technology' *Forbes* (12 January 2018) <https://www.forbes.com/sites/forbestechcouncil/2018/01/12/14-predictions-for-the-future-of-smart-home-technology/> last accessed 4 March 2021.

[139] Even a global pandemic has done nothing to halt this trend – in fact, at time of writing the worldwide lockdowns due to COVID-19 have significantly increased the role played by code infrastructures in our lives. See for example BBC News, 'UK's internet use surges to new highs in lockdown' *BBC News* (24 June 2020) <https://www.bbc.com/news/technology-53149268> last accessed 4 March 2021.

[140] D Ihde, *Ironic Technics* (Automatic Press/VIP 2008) vi.

[141] Surden (n 60) 5.

[142] Ibid.

plasticity is to a great extent 'locked down' once production has ceased.[143] This is what Winner terms the 'initial commitments'; for him,

> technological innovations are similar to legislative acts or political foundings that establish a framework for public order that will endure over many generations. For that reason, the same careful attention one would give to the rules, roles, and relationships of politics must also be given to such things as the . . . tailoring of seemingly insignificant features on new machines.[144]

Without some ready means of altering the code after it is produced, the normative importance of those 'initial commitments' is all the greater. These observations strengthen the impetus to focus on ex ante production of code rather than ex post assessments of it. Goldoni summarises why this is so:

> Given the nature and the logic of architectural regulation, the emphasis on output legitimacy is misplaced for several reasons. First, since technology is often irreversible – once it is developed and applied in society, it is difficult to change it or remove it from society in those applications – the process which develops code as law becomes a key concern when normativity is at stake. In fact, it may well be too late when a particular version of a technology appears or is adopted . . . The difficulty of reversing embedded code is often evident and makes it fundamental to focus on the procedure and the actors involved in [its] development.[145]

Even where the code can be updated, its immediacy means its normative effect is in place before this happens, and so it is important that the design is produced in a legitimate fashion from the outset. Code is of course updated all the time, but this does not alter the reality that at the point of compilation it is immutable, pending some change at some point in the future. The technological normativity imposed upon the end-user is precisely that which was defined in the latest update, and it will not change until the next one comes along. In that sense, code is immutable insofar as its normative configuration is fixed for whatever length of time. The ability to update it is contingent on

---

[143] Bamberger (n 112) 710–11. Krajewski refers to this as a moment of 'closure' (n 69).

[144] L Winner, 'Do artifacts have politics?' (1980) *Daedalus* 121, 128.

[145] Goldoni (n 122) 128. Koops makes a similar argument, although he focuses nevertheless on ex post assessment. See B-J Koops, 'Criteria for normative technology: The acceptability of "code as law" in light of democratic and constitutional values' in R Brownsword and K Yeung (eds), *Regulating Technologies: Legal Futures, Regulatory Frames and Technological Fixes* (Hart 2008) 166. I consider both his contribution and the important difference between input and output legitimacy in Chapter 5.

the design – it is not a given – but it also requires oversight by its creator, who may not have any commercial incentive to provide updates (so-called 'planned obsolescence' means the trade-off between creating profitable new features and maintaining older code is one that usually favours the former at the expense of the end-user's interests).

(d) Opacity

We saw in Chapter 2 how design operates in ways which are not always within the conscious apprehension of the end-user. This opacity forms another fundamental way in which code *de facto* requires end-users to 'not think about it': if the end-user cannot comprehend the rules to which her behaviour is subject, she cannot possibly consider whether and how to respond to them. This foundational issue is problematic in traditional processes of democratic law-making. Waldron, for example, notes that 'those interested in democracy will have a direct interest also in this opacity itself – that is, in the sheep-like ignorance of the nature of the law one is ruled by'.[146] So too in the computational context, except that there the extent to which end-users *qua* citizens are rendered 'sheep-like' is qualitatively and quantitatively greater.[147] As Goldoni notes, 'given the opacity of architectural regulation, to be aware of how technology is directly or indirectly impacting upon agents' behaviours may prove to be too difficult in many cases'.[148] Longford's observations in relation to web technologies are apposite:

> A central feature of new media design, in fact, is that the source code for any particular application or program which structures an end-user's experience is hidden from them . . . HTML, IP addresses, and web browser software are exemplary of code's self-concealing character. HTML conceals the textual information which is ultimately responsible for the graphical web pages presented to surfers.[149]

Whereas most browsers have a 'view source' option that makes HTML relatively accessible (if not necessarily comprehensible, despite its human-readability[150]) to the end-user, the compiled code that implements specific rules in other digital artefacts is generally both inaccessible and inscrutable

---

[146] J Waldron, 'Can there be a democratic jurisprudence?' (2009) 58 *Emory Law Journal* 675, 696 *et seq.*, discussing the problematic nature of analytical positivism from a democratic perspective.

[147] Citron (n 123) 1254–5.

[148] Goldoni (n 122) 128.

[149] Longford (n 3) 82.

[150] This is the heart of the transparency fallacy, discussed in Chapter 6.

because of its translation (compilation) into machine-readable 'object code'. Regardless of the programming language used, however, end-users face difficulty in comprehending the totality of the system before them, and are in essence forced to accept a great deal on faith.[151] The user interfaces of digital artefacts are inherently limited in their communication of the myriad operations taking place behind-the-scenes. Even the apparently simplest of operations, for example clicking a hyperlink on a webpage, involves a host of unseen technical processes. Most of the time obscuring all of this is beneficial, in terms of avoiding the overwhelming cognitive load that trying to comprehend all that is really going on would entail. As mentioned above, it would be undesirable to enquire into the detail of every rule being followed in every computational operation, since the burden of comprehension is too great. The task, then, is to give information and control 'over the right things at the right time'.[152] This obfuscation of actual behaviour can, however, be used both for good and bad; the ability to hide the complexity of standard technical behaviours for the sake of the end-user can also be used to obfuscate technical behaviours that are antagonistic to her interests.[153]

We have seen on the one hand how end-users tend to accept defaults as-is, while on the other the immutable aspects of a system's architecture situate the end-user within an assemblage of behaviour-constraining rules that might admit of only minimal, if any, interpretation – a fait accompli, 'achieving compliance by default rather than through active enforcement'.[154] As Hildebrandt notes, whereas '[l]egal norms do not rule out disobedience, contestation of the technological defaults that regulate our lives may be impossible because they are often invisible and because most of the time there is no jurisdiction and no court.'[155]

The normativity of code is thus in no way contingent on it being intelligible to those whose behaviour is regulated by it (or indeed even those who created it). There is no requirement that its rules be made public, much less

---

[151] L Winner, *Autonomous Technology: Technics-Out-of-Control as a Theme in Political Thought* (2nd edn, MIT Press 1977) 284.

[152] B Friedman, 'Value-sensitive design' (1996) 3 *interactions* 16, 18. See also A Pols and A Spahn, 'Designing for the values of democracy and justice' in J van den Hoven, PE Vermaas and I van de Poel (eds), *Handbook of Ethics, Values, and Technological Design: Sources, Theory, Values and Application Domains* (Springer 2015). For a recent discussion of design sensitive to 'kairological time', see T Bucher, 'The right-time web: Theorizing the kairologic of algorithmic media' (2020) 22 *New Media & Society* 1699.

[153] See generally F Pasquale, *The Black Box Society: The Secret Algorithms that Control Money and Information* (Harvard University Press 2015).

[154] Tien (n 124) 12.

[155] Hildebrandt, *Smart Technologies* (n 11) 12.

in a form that can be understood by humans. Indeed, the complexity of code rules is such that they rapidly become unintelligible, even to the experts who created them. As discussed in Chapter 2, it thus becomes extremely difficult (and in most cases impossible) for the end-user to scrutinise the rules to which her behaviour is subject. We therefore have the blindest of legalistic 'blind rule following'.[156]

Code as a-legal 'Positivism'

What can hopefully be appreciated from the preceding discussion is the sheer 'is-ness' of code; its 'positivity' is of a form that is deeply challenging to a vision of law as a reasoned enterprise that reflects the democratically expressed outlook of a society, from and according to which its norms are articulated and subsequently interpreted and applied. As Vismann and Krajewski note, code's 'virtuality challenges the law's core concepts: corporeality, finitude, and authentication, concepts that are fundamental to any claim of territorial sovereignty as well as to imputations and rules of evidence'.[157]

This 'positivism'[158] removes the possibility of deliberation on the part of the end-user, resulting in a kind of instrumentalism that strips individuals of their ability to take part in the moral community, even where they disagree with what the code rule is making them do. End-users have no choice but to obey the rules, but simultaneously they have no standing in their formulation.[159] As Brownsword notes, design simply 'by-passes practical reason to eliminate all options other than the desired pattern of behaviour'.[160] One of the effects of this is to de-moralise citizens, blunting their sensitivity to social norms and thus their capacity for self-control and for doing good.[161] This latter point evokes Fuller's discussion of the morality of aspiration, and how it conflicts with a legalistic morality of duty according to which, as we have seen, the rule constitutes the entirety of what is required of regulatees,

---

[156] Bańkowski and Schafer (n 1) 31.

[157] Vismann and Krajewski (n 87) 92.

[158] Hoffmann-Riem for example refers to 'digital neo-positivism' in the context of techno-regulation. See W Hoffmann-Riem, 'Legal technology/computational law: Preconditions, opportunities and risks' (2021) 1 *Journal of Cross-disciplinary Research in Computational Law* <https://journalcrcl.org/crcl/article/view/7> last accessed 19 April 2021.

[159] Bańkowski and Schafer (n 1) 48. See also Longford (n 3).

[160] R Brownsword, 'Code, control, and choice: Why east is east and west is west' (2005) 25 *Legal Studies* 1, 4.

[161] Ibid. 19, quoting DJ Smith, 'Changing situations and changing people' in A von Hirsch, D Garland and A Wakefield (eds), *Ethical and Social Perspectives on Situational Crime Prevention* (Bloomsbury Publishing 2004). See also Brownsword, 'Lost in translation' (n 113) *passim*.

with no further expectation.[162] For Bańkowski, this minimal expectation is not enough; legalism and positivism collapse the aspirational aspect of legality and reduce the guiding normative value of social practices, because the presence of a 'critical morality' that invites self-scrutiny becomes displaced by a rote approach to the direction of citizens' conduct.[163] By removing the need to consider the proper course of action, our ability or habit of raising such questions becomes atrophied. Brownsword suggests that a community fully reliant on such forms of (state) regulation which obviate the possibility of moral deliberation is 'no longer an operative moral community'.[164] We require the opportunity to choose to do good, in the face of at least the possibility of doing otherwise, if we are to continue to exercise practical reason as moral actors.

I return to the topic of legality in Chapter 4, but for now, we can observe how computational legalism demonstrates the most certain of certainties, simultaneously hiding this from the end-user's comprehension under the veil of opacity. As we will see in Part III, the provision of spaces for the exercise of such reason and choice is not just about providing more choice, but is about providing the right quality of choice at the right time.

(e) The Veiling of Code's Production

Wintgens discusses the 'veil of sovereignty' that shrouds the work of the legislator, shielding it and her from the gaze of the legal philosopher and the citizen.[165] Legislative sovereignty is thus perceived as a black box.[166] The ultimate source of sovereignty is not in question and the mechanisms by which its outputs are arrived at are not to be questioned by jurists. Boyle noted this obscuring function early on when he suggested that '[t]he technology appears to be "just the way things are"; its origins are concealed, whether those origins lie in state-sponsored scheme or market-structured order, and its effects are obscured because it is hard to imagine the alternative.'[167]

---

[162] Fuller, *The Morality of Law* (n 14) chapter 1.

[163] Bańkowski (n 15) 49–50. Gardner resists this characterisation of legal positivism, although such arguments seem predicated on conflicting framings of the question – what counts as law versus what one ought to do with it. See J Gardner, 'Legal positivism: 5½ myths' in *Law as a Leap of Faith: Essays on Law in General* (Oxford University Press 2012).

[164] Brownsword, 'Code, control, and choice' (n 160) 19. See also Brownsword, 'Lost in translation' (n 113) 1355–6.

[165] Wintgens, *Legisprudence: Practical Reason in Legislation* (n 19) 2; Wintgens, 'Legislation as an object of study of legal theory' (n 29) 2.

[166] Wintgens, *Legisprudence: Practical Reason in Legislation* (n 19) 212 *et seq.*

[167] J Boyle, 'Foucault in cyberspace: Surveillance, sovereignty, and hardwired censors' (1997) 66 *University of Cincinnati Law Review* 177, 205.

In the computational context, the 'sovereignty' of the designer is protected by two 'veils' – one technical and the other legal. The first is the code-based opacity discussed in the previous section: this veil is one of technical inscrutability, which the ordinary end-user is usually ill-equipped to lift, if it is even possible to do so. The second veil protects enterprise by means of, for example, trade secrecy and anti-circumvention laws, which limit the scrutiny their code production practices can be put under, thus strengthening their quasi-sovereignty.[168] The prevailing neoliberal economic outlook sustains this second veil by shifting sovereignty away from the state and onto the market,[169] while simultaneously prioritising unfettered technological 'innovation' as a good in itself.[170]

The private 'sovereignty' of the profit-seeking enterprise is thus black-boxed unless and until a real-world harm is detected, which because of the technical veil might never happen. It is the task of the market and not the state to respond to the enterprise's designs in order to ascertain their value; meanwhile, the commercial entity is free to exercise its imperative for profit, while the market is trusted to curb any excesses. As Schulz and Dankert put it, 'code is essentially a resource through which the ones designing the code can pursue their interests'.[171] Similarly, Bańkowski and Schafer note that '[f]or the individual, more often than not, the absence of government is not experienced as liberating, but as subjugation to commercial interests which effortless [sic] project, and indeed magnify, their offline powers into cyberspace.'[172] Herein lies a paradox of commercial computational legalism: as discussed above, legalism is ideologically attractive in part because it helps establish a baseline of legal certainty which is advantageous to capitalist enterprise.[173] As those enterprises have developed into promulgators of code-based rules, however, their need for certainty has circumscribed the liberty of the ordinary citizen by the development of an imbalance of regulative power

---

[168] Pasquale (n 153) 15.

[169] BH Bratton, *The Stack: On Software and Sovereignty* (MIT Press 2016) 21.

[170] JE Cohen, 'The regulatory state in the information age' (2016) 17 *Theoretical Inquiries in Law* 369, 387–8. See also D Harvey, *A Brief History of Neoliberalism* (Oxford University Press 2005) 157 *et seq.*

[171] W Schulz and K Dankert, '"Governance by things" as a challenge to regulation by law' (2016) 5 *Internet Policy Review* 5 <https://doi.org/10.14763/2016.2.409> last accessed 19 April 2021. Hildebrandt and Koops term this a 'provider-centric scenario'. See M Hildebrandt and B-J Koops, 'The challenges of ambient law and legal protection in the profiling era' (2010) 73 *The Modern Law Review* 428, 457.

[172] Bańkowski and Schafer (n 1) 47.

[173] Wintgens, 'The rational legislator revisited' (n 16) 4; Bańkowski (n 15) 48.

between government and code,[174] and by the lack of incentives to ensure that their design processes and their products embody the values of legitimacy and legal protection intrinsic to that liberty. Hildebrandt and Koops suggest that cost, convenience, the difficulty of controlling risk, and the power imbalance between government and commerce all combine in the context of privacy to 'favour privacy-threatening technology far more than privacy-friendly "code"'.[175] In the absence of incentives to create the latter, code which is supportive of commercial interests but detrimental to end-users' interests is likely to win out; the features of computational legalism make it easy to take that route (and indeed 'rational', from an orthodox economic perspective). The same is true for the more fundamental form of user-antagonistic code I am concerned with. As with the aim of legality in law-making, we cannot appeal to market fundamentalism to prevent the creators of code from exploiting computational legalism to further their own ends – checks and balances need to be put in place at the design level.

3.3 Conclusion

We have seen how the characteristics of code come together to demonstrate a form of legalism that is significantly stronger than anything envisaged in the legal literature. With code we have the apex of legalism: from the end-user's perspective, code's architecture is 'just there', while simultaneously its constitutive nature defines what practices are possible, by definition ruling out all the possible alternatives that the plasticity of the code might otherwise have allowed. This, indeed, is one of the great ironies of code – a near-infinite range of design possibilities mean there is nothing in principle stopping it from being designed in a non-legalistic way, there are just few incentives to do so. Ultimately, whatever the (de)merits of the design, code confronts us with not just representationalism, but realism: it does not just represent reality, it actively constitutes it. The behaviour of the end-user is to a great extent structured and bound ex ante, and since she will in most cases not be aware of that binding she is, through no oversight or mistake on her part, forced to acquiesce blindly to the rules that are inscribed in the code: she is deprived of even the notional possibility of choosing whether or not to 'think about it'.

Taken together with the analysis in Chapter 2, the discussion here has set up the concept of computational legalism, strengthening the theoretical parallel between code and law as normative orders whose rules can be created in ways that are to varying degrees legalistic. By developing this parallel, I set up

---

[174] Hildebrandt and Koops (n 171) 444.
[175] Ibid.

the foundation for an analysis that imports into the design sphere measures that are intended to reduce or avoid legalism in the domain of law-making. Before I embark on that synthesis, we first move on to Part II, which does two things: first, Chapter 4 sets out the two legal theories from which I develop the digisprudential framework, and second, Chapter 5 reviews the existing legal literature on criteria for the use of code as a regulator.

Part II

What Makes a Good Rule?

4

Criteria for Laws

> [I]t is perfectly fair to ask regulators to justify both their purposes and the instruments (the rules or the designs) that they have adopted.[1]

The previous chapter looked at the characteristics of strong legalism, before considering how they are exhibited and amplified by code. This and the next chapter take a similar approach in structure, looking first at literature in the legal sphere before shifting the analysis to the computational domain. First I discuss various notions of legitimacy in the literature, before looking more closely at two sets of normative criteria for the creation of legal norms, namely Fuller's *internal morality of law*, and Wintgens's *legisprudence*. The next chapter then shifts focus to a critical review of the existing literature on normative criteria for code-making, including the application of Fuller's principles to code. From this discussion we gain a sense of the kinds of concern around computational legitimacy that exist in the literature, and what considerations are missing or less fully analysed: the most obvious limitation in the current literature concerns the production of private code, and the unintended creation of technological normativity. These gaps are then considered in the development of the digisprudence framework in the next and final part of the book.

4.1 Normative Criteria for Law-Making: The Aspirations of Legality

The strong legalism we saw in Chapter 3 might be described as the extreme end of a spectrum, at the opposite of which lies the open-ended particularism of certain strands of Critical Legal Studies scholarship.[2] Legality, on the

---

[1] R Brownsword, 'In the year 2061: From law to technological management' (2015) 7 *Law, Innovation and Technology* 1, 29.

[2] Z Bańkowski and N MacCormick, 'Legality without legalism' in W Krawietz et al. (eds), *The Reasonable as Rational? On Legal Argumentation and Justification; Festschrift for Aulis Aarnio* (Duncker & Humblot 2000) 191; Z Bańkowski, 'Don't think about it: Legalism and legality' in MM Karlsson, Ó Páll Jónsson and EM Brynjarsdóttir (eds), *Rechtstheorie: Zeitschrift*

other hand, is viewed by some as a more aspirational concept, somewhere in-between, which is of fundamental importance to constitutional democracy: according to Bańkowski, it is a crucial element in what makes a free and democratic society – it is 'something worth living for; something worth dying for'.[3]

Although legality is a contested notion, some common themes run through the literature. Bańkowski speaks of the operation of individual will ameliorating the blanket heteronomy of legalism, with legality representing the appropriate interplay, or placing of the threshold, between the moralities of duty and aspiration. Some rules can be followed 'mindlessly', like automata, while others ought to be considered more deeply before acting, sometimes with the help of the appropriate agency-institutions.[4] Brownsword views legality as a 'legal approach' embedding 'participation, transparency, due process, and the like'.[5] He also speaks of 'processual public law values of transparency, accountability, inclusive participation, reason-giving and the like together with the controls exerted by background fundamental values (such as compatibility with respect for human rights and human dignity)'.[6] Waldron makes a similar point: we aspire to a law which 'conceives of the people who live under it as bearers of reason and intelligence', even if the price of this is a 'diminution in law's certainty'.[7]

For Hildebrandt, legality is the combination of purpose binding with the imposition of checks and balances, 'tying the state to its own legal rules, but also [instantiating] a system of checks and balances that safeguards against the Sirens of tyranny or those of market fundamentalism'.[8] Fundamental rights play a role too, preventing the rule of law lapsing into a legalistic rule 'by' law.[9] She invokes the Greek legend of Odysseus as an illustration of the purpose

---

für Logik, Methodenlehre, Kybernetik und Soziologie des Rechts (Duncker & Humblot 1993) 51. See also N MacCormick, 'Reconstruction after deconstruction: A response to CLS' (1990) 10 *Oxford Journal of Legal Studies* 539.

[3] Bańkowski (n 2) 45.

[4] Ibid. 56–7. See also Z Bańkowski and B Schafer, 'Double-click justice: Legalism in the computer age' (2007) 1 *Legisprudence* 31, 36–7.

[5] R Brownsword, 'Lost in translation: Legality, regulatory margins, and technological management' (2011) 26 *Berkeley Technology Law Journal* 1321, 1363.

[6] Brownsword, 'In the year 2061' (n 1) 48.

[7] J Waldron, 'The rule of law and the importance of procedure' (2011) 50 *Nomos* 3, 18 *et seq.*, and also his 'How law protects dignity' (2012) 71 *The Cambridge Law Journal* 200.

[8] M Hildebrandt, *Smart Technologies and the End(s) of Law: Novel Entanglements of Law and Technology* (Edward Elgar Publishing 2015) 157–8.

[9] Ibid. 157.

binding principle – like its protagonist, in a constitutional democracy the government is bound by its own predefined rules, despite its notional power to redraw those rules and the evident temptation to do so.[10] Ultimately, this results in a 'modern law' that consists in 'self-rule, disobedience and contestability': (1) laws are constituted by a democratic legislator and are made visible and intelligible to those they seek to govern, (2) the governed have the ability to violate those laws, and so the decision to comply is an exercise of autonomy, and (3) the substance and interpretation of the legal norms, and the consequences of their violation, can be contested in a court of law.[11]

These various conceptions of legality have a certain liminal quality; they point towards a kind of open space for rational contemplation and the exercise of autonomy, lying somewhere between the two poles of heteronomy and anarchism.[12] Acting appropriately involves more than simply falling in line with legalism's rote morality of duty, but also something more structured than a chaotically subjective choice based on the particulars of each and every circumstance. Somewhere between these extremes lies a balance of autonomy and duty, provided by legal and social frameworks whose guiding force and institutions create spaces that allow for that consideration to take place. The 'intimate justice' of particularity cannot be real justice because of its lack of even-handedness, while simultaneously an 'aloof' and 'objective' justice will at times be harsh and unforgiving.[13] The ideal of legality aims to tread a difficult line between these poles, providing a measure of institutional guidance and rule-bound certainty whilst also maintaining freedom of choice and reflection. In that respect, then, it encompasses aspects of legalism; the latter is a necessary element of legality, providing a level of predictability that is necessary to avoid the need to enquire into the particularities of every circumstance.

For Bańkowski and MacCormick, the strong legalism described in the previous chapter is a 'negative ideology'. Their conception of legality, which as we saw maps onto Wintgens's idea of 'weak legalism' (discussed below), does make use of the legalistic outlook insofar as positive law and legal certainty

---

[10] Lessig also invokes the Odyssey to highlight the difference between what he calls a 'codifying constitution' (the codification of existing norms to maintain stability – Odysseus being tied to the mast) and a 'transformative constitution', in which new significant societal changes are sought to be implemented (as in the French Revolution). See L Lessig, *Code: Version 2.0* (Basic Books 2006) 313–14.

[11] Hildebrandt, *Smart Technologies* (n 8) 10.

[12] Recall the discussion at various points in Part I of the spectrum of technological normativity.

[13] LL Fuller, *The Morality of Law* (Yale University Press 1977) 72.

are necessary for the ordering of 'durable social organizations',[14] but it rejects heteronomy untempered by rational and critical reflection:

> It remains true, however, that rules without underlying principles of a kind that could be assented to by a rational autonomous being are rules that can be implements of tyranny. It is also true that every application of a rule is also an interpretation of it. Approaches to interpretation that ignore or undervalue the need for attention to principles, and to the consequences of decision [sic] judged against implicit values and principles of law, are undesirable on the same ground if to a lesser degree. Legalism as vice is indeed the vice of this narrow governance of rules, unleavened by the principled approach of interpretation.[15]

This view of legality thus encompasses legalism as far as is necessary to create a predictable and reliable institutional order, but leaves a space in which the individual can deliberate about what her course of action ought to be. Unlike the strong legalism set out in the previous chapter, legality on this view does not confuse the rules and heuristics with the entirety of the law – it allows a dignified space for reflexive exercise of reason, intelligence, and freedom,[16] in contrast to the 'one shot' at autonomy allowed in the proxy model of strong legalism.[17] Radbruch captures this qualified role of legal certainty in his antinomian theory of law. For him, the legal certainty provided by posited rules is indeed fundamentally important, but as a goal it sits in continual and productive tension with the aims of justice and purposiveness – a balance that is constantly reinvigorated as particular cases entail new interpretations and reasoning taking the three elements into account. The ever-present tension between legal certainty, justice, and purposiveness is what holds the law aloft.[18]

Bańkowski draws on Fuller to argue that whereas the legalistic attitude cares only to meet the threshold of the morality of duty and no more, legality expands this to include the idea of a morality of aspiration. Here the question is not simply of what is 'owed'; instead, less strictly limned values

---

[14] Bańkowski and MacCormick (n 2) 194.

[15] Ibid.

[16] Waldron, 'The rule of law and the importance of procedure' (n 7) 19–20.

[17] L Wintgens, *Legisprudence: Practical Reason in Legislation* (Routledge 2012) 206.

[18] G Radbruch, 'Legal philosophy' in K Wilk (ed.), *The Legal Philosophies of Lask, Radbruch, and Dabin* (Harvard University Press 1950) 111–12. For a valuable discussion of Radbruch's contribution to legal philosophy, which seems to have had less of an impact in Anglo-American jurisprudence than it deserves, see H Leawoods, 'Gustav Radbruch: An extraordinary legal philosopher' 2 *Journal of Law and Policy* 28. This qualified perspective is also central to MacCormick's notion of 'post-positivism' – see his *Institutions of Law: An Essay in Legal Theory* (Oxford University Press 2007) 278.

come into play, such as authenticity.[19] It is, he argues, not sufficient simply to meet the minimum standard represented by a bald interpretation of the rule; instead, these exist on an 'aspirational scale'[20] and there are times when it is appropriate to expect more of an actor (or indeed perhaps 'less', in the consequentialist sense where disobeying a rule can be morally desirable if it means a better outcome, *pace* the legalistic categorical imperative). The morality of duty is one point on the aspirational scale and represents (*ceteris paribus*) the minimum action that is required. But the scale goes further; it is possible to do more. Aspiration goes beyond the morality of duty's 'rules of grammar', aiming instead for what Smith called 'what is sublime and elegant in composition'.[21] As we shall see, the question of where the threshold between duty and aspiration should lie also arises in the context of code: to what extent should the concrete behaviour of the technical design be legalistic (fixed configuration; the heteronomous end-user), and to what extent should it build in the aspirations of legality (flexible configuration; the autonomous end-user)?

(a) Input and Output Legitimacy in Law

We can see from the above views of legality that it is to some extent an amorphous ideal. Conceptions focus sometimes on the ex ante criteria that dictate the process of norm creation and the formal qualities of the resulting rules, sometimes on ex post criteria that provide for due process and non-arbitrariness in administration (this latter perspective is what I understand by the rule of law[22]), and sometimes both.[23] Waldron makes a similar distinction between what law is (the 'concept of law', or what constitutes the legal), and how it is administered and applied (the 'rule of law').[24] Legality on this account speaks to the formal qualities of the rules, while the rule of law speaks

---

[19] Bańkowski and Schafer (n 4) 33; Bańkowski and MacCormick (n 2) 183; Bańkowski (n 2) 45.

[20] Bańkowski (n 2) 51.

[21] Fuller, *The Morality of Law* (n 13) 6, quoting A Smith, *The Theory of Moral Sentiments* (2nd edn, Millar 1761) 257. One can find hints of this notion in contemporary discussions around the boundary between compliance with 'bare law' and the ethical requirement to do more; see for example L Floridi, 'Soft ethics, the governance of the digital and the General Data Protection Regulation' (2018) 376 *Philosophical Transactions of the Royal Society A* 20180081. For a recent discussion of this crucial distinction in relation to code, see M Hildebrandt, *Law for Computer Scientists and Other Folk* (Oxford University Press 2020) chapter 11.

[22] Cf. J Raz, 'The rule of law and its virtue' in *The Authority of Law: Essays on Law and Morality* (Oxford University Press 1979).

[23] This is true both of Raz's principles (ibid. 218) and Fuller's, the latter of which I discuss in detail below.

[24] J Waldron, 'The concept and the rule of law' (2008) 43 *Georgia Law Review* 1.

to how those rules are applied in practice. Neither of these ideas concerns the substantive content of the rules directly – the question is one of process, both before promulgation (that is, in the design of the norm), and after (in its application).[25]

Scharpf and Waldron each contrast the concepts of input (process) and output (result) legitimacy within the contexts of legislation and judicial review. Input legitimacy concerns the process being followed, which in the traditional sphere requires participation or representation of some form.[26] Scharpf calls this 'government by the people';[27] Waldron gives the obvious examples of political equality and enfranchisement.[28] Output legitimacy, on the other hand, is about the 'proof being in the pudding' – legitimacy is established through an assessment of the results of a rule's operation. Scharpf calls this 'government for the people', where a result is deemed legitimate because it solves the problem it was aimed at.[29]

Disagreement about the desirability of a norm's substantive content (its output) can exist alongside an agreement that the norm was arrived at and formulated in a proper way (its input legitimacy). This is how the norm, despite its divisiveness, attains (political) legitimacy.[30] As we will see, the distinction between input and output reasons chimes with the Fullerian ideas of the inner and external morality of law, the former being constituted by his principles of legality, discussed below. Whereas input criteria speak to the procedural aspects of the creation of a given rule or judicial decision, output criteria speak to its efficacy or desirability in the world. Goldoni describes the distinction in the following terms:

> Input reasons are those reasons that apply to the procedural aspects of decisions, that is, to how a decision is reached. As a measure for legitimacy, input reasons take into account the fairness of the adopted procedure. Output reasons concern the content of decisions and they represent a moral yardstick for judging the legitimacy of technologies. What counts

---

[25] Waldron appears to consider 'procedure' to relate only to ex post due process, arguing that Fuller's use of the word is misplaced and that the latter is in fact referring to formal validity. See Waldron, 'The rule of law and the importance of procedure' (n 7) 8.

[26] F Scharpf, *Governing in Europe: Effective and Democratic?* (Oxford University Press 1999) 7; J Waldron, 'The core of the case against judicial review' (2006) 115 *Yale Law Journal* 1346, 1372.

[27] Scharpf (n 26) 6.

[28] Waldron, 'The core of the case against judicial review' (n 26) 1373.

[29] Scharpf (n 26) 11. Recall the goal of purposiveness – what the rule-giver aims to achieve by promulgating a particular norm – in Radbruch's tripartite antinomy. See Radbruch (n 18).

[30] Waldron, 'The core of the case against judicial review' (n 26) 1387.

as legitimate, according to the output-based perspective, is the end result of a decision and its normative content, not how the decision was reached.[31]

Very crudely, then, a focus on input criteria is deontological, while a focus on output criteria is consequentialist. As with Fuller, the two perspectives interact – the quality of the rule in action (that is, its consequences or output) is shaped by the conditions that channel how it was made; those conditions can tend towards normatively undesirable as well as desirable substantive rules[32] (although, in his debate with Hart, Fuller argued that the principles of legality do tend towards less substantive iniquity[33]). Thus the inner, input, morality constrains the substantive content of its outer, or output, morality; form circumscribes substance.[34] Wintgens's theory of legisprudence makes a similar claim: whether a given proposed legislative rule is legitimate or not is contingent on it being justified according to the principles of legisprudence, whose formal qualities dictate, apart from any substantive political content, the base level required in order for legitimacy to obtain.

We can identify from this analysis a roughly four-part classification of the various types of criteria, according to their target and temporal position. In terms of input (ex ante) criteria, these can be split into (1) procedural criteria that govern the process of deliberation that leads to a given norm being created,[35] and (2) criteria that constrain what formal qualities the norm should have, assessed separately from its substantive content.[36] In terms of output (ex post) criteria, we have (3) mechanisms of due process, transparency, and accountability to enable the detection and remedy of wrongs in operation,[37] and (4) assessments of the moral or political content of the norm itself.[38]

As we shall see, most theorists' frameworks include criteria from more than one of these categories. Of course, computational legalism requires greater focus on the first two of these classifications, although in the private sector, at least, ex ante procedural criteria are less likely to be readily applicable than ex ante formal criteria, given the lack of incentives and resources to

---

[31] M Goldoni, 'The politics of code as law: Toward input reasons' in J Reichel and AS Lind (eds), *Freedom of Expression, the Internet and Democracy* (Brill 2015) 127.

[32] Cf. Waldron, 'The core of the case against judicial review' (n 26) 1374.

[33] LL Fuller, 'Positivism and fidelity to law: A reply to Professor Hart' (1958) 71 *Harvard Law Review* 630, 636.

[34] Ibid.

[35] Broadly, this view requires democratic participation, and encompasses the analyses of Brownsword, Hildebrandt, and Goldoni.

[36] This would encompass Fuller's and Wintgens's analyses, as well as my own.

[37] This is the ex post conception of procedure that Waldron refers to and includes Hildebrandt's requirement of contestability. I too include the latter in the digisprudential framework.

[38] This would encompass Brownsword's and Koops's analyses.

facilitate participation. The digisprudential theory I am developing is primarily concerned with the second classification (formal ex ante, or input, criteria), part of which is intended to facilitate the ex post criterion of contestability (the third classification). In this way, the former operate simultaneously to constrain iniquity and to facilitate the latter. I return to the question of criteria for code in the next chapter, but for now I set out more fully Fuller's and Wintgens's normative frameworks for the design of legal norms.

(b) Fuller's Internal Morality of Law

Perhaps the most prominent and influential discussion of formal normative standards for law-making can be found in Fuller's *The Morality of Law*.[39] Explicitly aspirational, Fuller's eight 'principles of legality' are intended to appeal to 'a sense of trusteeship and to the pride of the craftsman'.[40] They are about trying to achieve excellence (not to say perfection) in the business of law-making and application – a primary consideration arising from his principles is how best to design a law, as distinct from what its political content is or ought to be. Indeed, Fuller uses the language of design on various occasions, referring to law-making as a 'craft',[41] and to the eight principles as 'those laws respected by a carpenter who wants the house he builds to remain standing and serve the purpose of those living in it'.[42] As can be appreciated from the principles, listed below, they are not just about making good law from the perspective of the conscientious law-maker, but can also be viewed as constraining the unconscientious law-maker to prevent the possibility of (excessive) iniquity.[43]

Fuller's eight principles are as follows:
1. **The generality of law.** In order for conduct to be regulated, rules must be laid down that display 'reasoned generality' rather than the 'patternless exercise of political power'.[44] Arbitrariness is to be avoided. (Recall the discussion of legality above, and the threshold between duty and aspiration.)
2. **Promulgation.** The rules must be made available to those who will be governed by them, who are thus empowered to interpret and criticise them, and observe how they are applied and enforced.[45]

---

[39] Fuller, *The Morality of Law* (n 13).
[40] Ibid. 43.
[41] Ibid. 43, 156.
[42] Ibid. 96.
[43] Fuller, 'Positivism and fidelity to law' (n 33) 636.
[44] Fuller, *The Morality of Law* (n 13) 46–9.
[45] Ibid. 49–51.

3. **Retroactive laws.** This principle overlaps with the others: if laws are promulgated which render conduct unlawful that was not prohibited at the time it took place, the possibility of citizens knowing and obeying the law becomes fatally undermined. This principle is not absolute, however: Fuller notes that while retrospective law-making is *prima facie* 'a monstrosity', in some cases a holistic view of the principles will require it in order to cure some other 'shipwreck' in the enterprise of legality.[46] This hints at the non-absolute, deliberative nature of legality.

4. **Clarity of laws.** Fuller views this as one of the most essential of the principles. Whereas legalism deems that what looks like law is law (that is, formal validity begets law, regardless of its substantive merits), this principle requires the legislator to do more. As Fuller puts it, 'it is obvious that obscure and incoherent legislation can make legality unattainable by anyone, or at least unattainable without an unauthorized revision which itself impairs legality'.[47] If a rule is so unclear that its interpretation distorts either its original expression or the intention behind it, then recursively we hit the buffers of legality again, whereby the law as practised is not the law as promulgated.[48]

5. **Contradictions in the laws.** Fuller suggests that dealing with contradictions in legal norms is not simply a case of logic, that is to say it is not enough to observe that norm *A* cannot be the same as not-*A*; clearly, such a statement does not on its own assist in resolving the contradiction. Determining whether two laws are contradictory requires something more: an appeal to extra-legal factors is necessary to determine the state of the world, what he calls the 'whole institutional setting of the problem – legal, moral, political, economic, and sociological'.[49]

6. **Laws requiring the impossible.** Fuller's treatment of this principle is complex and includes a discussion of criminal and delictual liability, unjust enrichment, and tax law that is not of relevance here. The essential concept is simple, however: a law should not compel the impossible, for example that 'one should become ten feet tall'.[50] The promulgation of laws which are impossible to follow risks 'doing serious injustice or . . .

---

[46] Ibid. 51–62.

[47] Ibid. 63.

[48] Ibid. 63–5.

[49] Ibid. 65–70, quote at 70. This idea of 'peering in' to the legal system from some outside vantage point, to garner from that external perspective information necessary to the interpretation of the rule, is echoed strongly in Wintgens's principle of coherence, discussed below.

[50] Ibid. 70 n 29.

diluting respect for law'.[51] Although in other contexts, such as the classroom, the exhortation to impossible ends can be an incentive to aspire to better results, in the legal context the stakes are different, and higher.[52]

7. **Constancy of the law through time.** This requirement is interesting from the perspective of the dignified pace of law. Fuller observes that both retrospective laws and constantly changing laws are apt to create injustice. If one of the aims of law is to normalise expectations, this can only be achieved if norms have a chance to settle in to the society in which they are promulgated.[53]

8. **Congruence between declared rule and official action.** Fuller describes this as the most complex principle, such congruence being potentially undermined in various ways, including 'mistaken interpretation, inaccessibility of the law, lack of insight into what is required to maintain the integrity of a legal system, bribery, prejudice, indifference, stupidity, and the drive toward personal power'.[54] This is in a sense a catch-all requirement, under which practices and institutions such as procedural due process, contest, and judicial review operate to identify and address such problems. It relates also to the constancy and retroactivity principles; the settling of arrangements over time may be necessary for latent incongruence to emerge as circumstances evolve.

The 'inner morality' that the principles engender is distinct from the 'external' morality of law, which represents the substantive content of legal norms. On this account a legal norm can be simultaneously 'internally moral' and 'externally immoral' – the assessment of external morality will differ according to each individual's moral and political outlook whereas, Fuller argues, the internal morality of law requires certain standards which are universal in a democratic polity. Internal morality should not be optional, whatever one's political persuasion.

Fuller's principles are a mix of input (ex ante formal) and output (ex post procedural) criteria. Principles three to six govern the form of a proposed rule, constraining ex ante what its substance can possibly be: the rule cannot be retroactive (with exceptions); it must be reasonably clear in order to enable interpretation by regulatees; it cannot contradict extant rules without amending or repealing them; and it cannot require the impossible. Principles two and eight are examples of ex post procedural criteria: the former requires

---

[51] Ibid. 71.
[52] Ibid. 70–9.
[53] Ibid. 79–81.
[54] Ibid. 81.

that the rules once made are publicised, while the latter binds the implementing authority to operate according to a reasonable interpretation of the substantive content of the rule (subject to the overarching contestability requirement).

As will become apparent, there are significant parallels between Fuller's inner morality and Wintgens's legisprudence, although the latter's formal prescriptions constrain even more tightly the substantive content a norm can have. The same concern, adverted to above, applies however, whereby any and all norms ought to demonstrate those formal characteristics in order to be deemed legitimate, regardless of the political content (external morality) each seeks to instrumentalise.

(c) *Wintgens's* Legisprudence

Legisprudence combines criteria for ex ante formal validity with additional criteria that constrain the possible substance of a rule, rejecting a strong-legalistic perspective in order actively to peer behind the 'veil of sovereignty'[55] to find additional legitimation of the proposed norm. Given the sovereignty of the legislator, Wintgens says that there is no notional limit to the theoretical foundation of a rule: the rationale could for example be economic, sociological, technical, or, presumably, ideological. The important point, however, is that there must always be justification from some theoretical basis other than just bare sovereign whim. Unlike strong legalism, which as we have seen is content not to lift the veil of sovereignty to reveal the reasoning that motivated a particular exercise of power, the legisprudence framework requires both formal qualities in the norms that are promulgated, and enquiries as to the other, extra-legal, theoretical bases that provide the necessary additional justification.

This provides some useful, and I think necessary, theoretical grounding for a critique of computational legalism and for the guidance of the production of technological normativity. The remainder of this section sets out the main parts of the theory of legisprudence, before moving on to discuss each of its principles.

What is Legisprudence?

Legisprudence aims to shift jurisprudence away from a focus on the ex post reasoning of the judiciary and legal professionals towards a greater consideration of the ex ante reasoning of legislators. The intention is to provide an

---

[55] Wintgens, *Legisprudence: Practical Reason in Legislation* (n 17) 2. Recall the discussion in 'The Veiling of Code's Production' in Section 3.2.

explicitly legal-theoretical (as opposed to ethical or political) framework for the creation of legal rules, instead of ignoring the latter as an aspect of the 'dirty business' of politics. Shklar's fences of legalism – those boundaries that surround law, separating it from other human endeavours – are thus broken down. Wintgens summarises legisprudence like this:

> A different position is to study legislative problems from the angle of legal theory. This approach I propose to call *legisprudence*. Legisprudence has as its object legislation and regulation, making use of the theoretical tools and insights of legal theory. The latter predominantly deals with the question of the *application* of law by the *judge*. Legisprudence enlarges the field of study to include the *creation* of law by the *legislator*.[56]

Legisprudence is a practical approach through which those who legislate can avoid succumbing to a strongly legalistic ideology. It aims to foster 'weak' legalism, under which fidelity to rules is accepted as necessary but only on the condition that the form of those rules meets certain criteria and the rules are subject to ongoing justification. As Wintgens puts it,

> [l]egisprudence can therefore be taken to be a meta-theory of morality, in that it allows for the formulation of principles that justify external limitations [of freedom, that is legal norms]. It is the latter that make morality possible, without enforcing any substantive moral principle whatsoever.[57]

The framework thus constrains the substance of the rules to which it is applied regardless of the subject area they are concerned with. If we consider that the principles of legality in a constitutional democracy are broadly about fairness and accountability, legisprudence can be viewed both as a tool to achieve legality at the outset of the legislative process, and as an ongoing means of upholding it as time passes and circumstances change.[58] It views the law-making process in a holistic fashion that seeks to achieve not just formal validity but also a broader rationality in the enterprise of making new norms.[59]

The Requirement of Justification
Wintgens contrasts strong legalism, described in Chapter 3, with its weaker alternative, under which the legalistic perspective is tempered by a central

---

[56] L Wintgens, *Legisprudence: A New Theoretical Approach to Legislation* (Hart 2002) 2 (emphasis supplied; references omitted).
[57] Wintgens, *Legisprudence: Practical Reason in Legislation* (n 17) 297.
[58] L Wintgens, 'The rational legislator revisited. Bounded rationality and legisprudence' in *The Rationality and Justification of Legislation* (Springer 2013).
[59] Wintgens, *Legisprudence: Practical Reason in Legislation* (n 17) 234–5.

test requiring the limitation by law of individual freedom to be justified.[60] Whereas strong legalism is satisfied by the presence of an authorised sovereign and does not enquire (indeed, prohibits enquiry) as to how or why a particular rule was made, weak legalism permits the lifting of the 'veil of sovereignty', to enquire as to the reasons behind its exercise.[61] The justification for a new rule cannot simply be the 'bare sovereign power' of the legislator, and neither can any natural law or social contract she might purport to instrumentalise.

Whereas under strong legalism the hierarchy of powers means the subordinate may not (in most cases) question the superior, under weak legalism the requirement of justification enables precisely this – the hierarchy of power can, for this purpose, be reversed. This is the work of legisprudence, which provides a framework for this temporary reversal, to legitimate the work of the legislator which the strongly legalistic perspective requires to be ignored. In this way the appropriate level of justification for a particular limitation on freedom (legislative norm) can be ascertained, both in advance of its promulgation (ex ante), and as an ongoing test of its efficacy in the world (ex post).

Freedom and the Trade-Off Model

For Wintgens, there is a *principium*, or foundational principle, of individual freedom. This has two elements. The first is descriptive, akin to the 'state of nature' in political philosophy: '[i]n the absence of any norm, anyone is free. In the beginning that is, there is freedom. From this perspective, freedom is at the origin of our philosophical inquiry.'[62] The second is normative, in that individual freedom should be a *leitmotif*, or guide, for both politics and law.[63] By definition, legislative rules constrain that foundational freedom for some individual or group in some place at some time. According to legisprudence, the fact that a proposed norm constrains foundational freedom means it should be rejected *a priori*, unless and until its imposition is sufficiently justified. Requiring citizens to acquiescence to rules simply because they are 'there', as strong legalism does, is not a legitimate exercise of power

---

[60] Ibid. 220; L Wintgens, 'Legisprudence as a new theory of legislation' (2006) 19 *Ratio Juris* 1.

[61] Wintgens, *Legisprudence: Practical Reason in Legislation* (n 17) 2.

[62] Ibid. 124, 207 and see generally ibid. chapter 4.

[63] Wintgens, *Legisprudence: Practical Reason in Legislation* (n 17) 207. This notion of a 'rational' law is not the preserve of a liberal conception of law. Shoikhedbrod argues that Marx's critique of liberal legality, for example, was founded not on a distaste for liberal rights *per se*, as is often assumed, but on the basis that positive law and the exercise of those rights is often at odds with maximising human freedom – with rational law. See I Shoikhedbrod, *Revisiting Marx's Critique of Liberalism: Rethinking Justice, Legality and Rights* (Springer 2019).

according to this conception of freedom as *principium* – it is merely the arbitrary exercise of sovereignty, regardless of any teleological value it might have.[64] Individuals' subjective conceptions of what freedom is (and is not) should not be interfered with lightly by the political project of the legislator.[65] Under legisprudential theory, with the primacy it places on individual freedom, the individual's idea of substantive freedom therefore takes precedence over the state's external view of it.[66]

As Chapter 3 discussed,[67] under strong legalism the sovereign is given a 'general proxy' to promulgate rules, and the resulting legislative acts are thus *de facto* legitimated – the veil is not lifted to consider whether or not they are justified; they are *a priori* deemed to be so. Under this model, the individual circumscribes her absolute freedom from the beginning through the 'outsourcing' of its limitation to the sovereign, thereafter accepting whatever limits the latter promulgates under that arrangement. The proxy model provides the sovereign with generalised justification for imposing limitations on the freedom of the individual.

By contrast, Wintgens's alternative 'trade-off' model requires that such limitations be justified in each case, in order that the *principium* of maximising individual freedom (or, expressed another way, the minimising of external limitations on individuals' conceptions of freedom) be honoured each time a new rule is considered.[68] Under weak legalism, then, there is no proxy that 'takes control' of the individual's conception 'of' freedom and is able unilaterally to limit it. There is instead a trade-off, in which the sovereign's desire to impose regulation based on its conceptions 'about' freedom must be balanced with the individual's subjective conceptions of freedom:

> Legislative ruling on the trade-off theory is not a priori legitimate as it was in the proxy theory. Legitimation, according to the trade-off model, consists of a justification as to why acting on a conception about freedom is preferable to acting on a conception of freedom. The legitimation of law under the trade-off theory, in short, consists in a justification of each external limitation of freedom that is a priori presumed to be legitimate or justified under the proxy model.[69]

---

[64] Wintgens, 'Legisprudence as a new theory of legislation' (n 60) 10.
[65] Wintgens, *Legisprudence: Practical Reason in Legislation* (n 17) 126, 254.
[66] Ibid. 254–7.
[67] See 'Legalism According to Legisprudence' in Section 3.1.
[68] Wintgens, *Legisprudence: Practical Reason in Legislation* (n 17) 229.
[69] Ibid. 220.

The primacy of moral (individual) conceptions of freedom mean political (sovereign) conceptions about freedom must be justified, and if the standards of the latter are not met, the balance cannot be tipped legitimately in favour of the limitation on freedom (that is, the creation of the rule). Wintgens summarises the test as follows:

> It is on the basis of freedom as *principium* that a norm giver is to justify why freedom is limited, that is, because (1) social interaction is failing, and (2) weaker alternatives are insufficient. In addition, freedom as principle requires that (3) the norm giver justify why he is issuing an external limitation at a certain time, in addition to an upholding of the limitation of freedom over time, and (4) a justification of its relation to the legal system as a whole.[70]

Those requirements map onto the four principles of legisprudence, which in turn become duties the legislator must consider in the course of making a new norm.

The Principle of Coherence (PC)[71]

Wintgens views the legal system as a complex system of dynamic and intertwined rules, which has grown exponentially (rules beget rules, in order to facilitate the 'operative closure' of legalism[72]). Within this he identifies four levels of coherence, LoC_0–LoC_3, which apply to ex ante legislative as well as ex post judicial reasoning. The PC is cumulatively normative: its levels are stepped through, and in order to be properly justified on the basis of the PC, a legislative act should attain coherence at each level. Wintgens argues that '[c]oherent legislation as the upshot of freedom as *principium* takes citizens morally seriously in legislative and not only in judicial decision making.'[73]

LoC_0 ('internal or synchronic coherence'). The basic vocabulary and grammar of a discourse, this level of coherence is about the building blocks of intelligibility, without which the substance of the concepts that make up the system cannot be communicated.[74] This level is concerned with the basic elements of language (grammar, semantics, the logic of individual norms), and their compatibility with one another. In an earlier paper Wintgens labels

---

[70] Ibid. 283–4 (emphasis supplied).
[71] Wintgens, 'Legisprudence as a new theory of legislation' (n 60) 15–22; Wintgens, *Legisprudence: Practical Reason in Legislation* (n 17) 235–57.
[72] N Luhmann, 'Self-organization and autopoiesis' in B Clarke et al. (eds), *Emergence and Embodiment: New Essays on Second-Order Systems Theory* (Duke University Press 2009).
[73] Wintgens, *Legisprudence: Practical Reason in Legislation* (n 17) 256 (emphasis supplied).
[74] Ibid. 242; Wintgens, 'Legisprudence as a new theory of legislation' (n 60) 16.

this first level of coherence 'simultaneous consistency', which has the slightly different meaning that no inconsistencies or contradictions be permitted within a particular decision or instrument.[75] These two elements – the alignment of individuals' understanding of the intension of a concept and the absence of logical contradiction between those understandings – can be read together to make up LoC_0. As Fuller notes, difficulties in avoiding contradictions can arise both within and between legislative instruments, and it is in part the 'legislative carelessness about the jibe of statutes with one another' that is ultimately 'very hurtful to legality'.[76] The aim of the coherence principle is to mitigate this kind of carelessness.

This level relates to Hildebrandt's discussion of the printing press as essential to the affordance of modern legality. Without an agreed vocabulary of relatively stable meanings, facilitated by the communicative affordances of writing and later the printing press, this level of coherence will always be contingent on the accuracy and consistency of verbal communications between practitioners and between generations.[77] The idea of epistemic continuity is closely related to the Level of Coherence 1, which begins to look at the relations between the elements of the discourse rather than their individual intelligibility.

LoC$_1$ ('diachronic or rule coherence'). This level considers consistency over time – similar cases should attract similar judgments. This is in large part the consistency required by the rule of law: everyone is equal before the law, and the external limitations on freedom should be uniform across every individual who is addressed by them (*ceteris paribus*). From the perspective of the legislator, who as the sovereign is not bound by *stare decisis*, this translates into the principle that the rules should not be changed too frequently, but when they are, good reasons should be given for doing so.[78] If an element of doing justice is the modulation of expectations over time, it follows that injustice arises from the excessive promulgation of new rules that arbitrarily override what has gone before.[79]

LoC$_2$ ('compossibility or system coherence'). Despite LoC$_1$, circumstances of course can and do change over time, and therefore so can and

---

[75] L Wintgens, 'Legislation as an object of study of legal theory: Legisprudence' in *Legisprudence: A New Theoretical Approach to Legislation* (Hart 2002) 36–7, citing Fuller, *The Morality of Law* (n 13) 65–70.

[76] Fuller, *The Morality of Law* (n 13) 69.

[77] Hildebrandt, *Smart Technologies* (n 8) 47 *et seq*. ('3.3.1 Affordances of Information and Communication Infrastructures (ICIs)'). See also J Goody, *The Logic of Writing and the Organization of Society* (Cambridge University Press 1986) chapter 4.

[78] Wintgens, 'Legislation as an object of study of legal theory' (n 75) 38.

[79] Fuller terms this 'legislative inconstancy'. See Fuller, *The Morality of Law* (n 13) 79–80.

should legal norms change, provided this is otherwise legitimated by the justification principle. The arguments that warrant this departure from precedent are provided by LoC$_2$; they take into account not just the individual facts of a particular case, but the legal system as a whole. Through 'systematic interpretation', which views the legal system holistically, it may be that another part of it invites, permits, or justifies a different interpretation and thus a different judgment from that which came before.

A paradigm example given by Wintgens is the question of whether to view a lease through the lens of contract or of property law.[80] Either choice is *prima facie* legitimate, but the legal implications differ significantly. Stopping at LoC$_1$ would require continuity with past similar decisions, so no change in approach would be mandated. In this situation, however, a departure could be justified under LoC$_2$: the judge views the legal system as a systematic whole and observes that there are parts of it other than those elements used in preceding cases that can legitimately influence her ruling. Wintgens illustrates this with a case from Belgium where it was ruled that a husband is eligible for a 'spousal premium', despite there being no precedent in Belgian law of a male being the recipient.[81] The justification for departure on LoC$_2$ (in direct contradiction of LoC$_1$) was demonstrated by other instruments expressing a general principle of spousal equality, including domestic legislation such as Belgium's Matrimonial Act 1976, and international human rights treaties. In this instance, the judge took a holistic view of the system, rather than just the precedents immediately relevant to the instant case, and found external, but justifying, reasons to rule differently. Indeed, when viewing the system as a whole, coherence is improved by such a ruling because it brings judicial precedent with respect to the spousal premium into line with the principles expressed in those various legislative instruments. A departure from LoC$_1$, justified by LoC$_2$, resulted in a more coherent legal system; judicial interpretation was realigned to fit legislative principle.

Whereas the judge assumes the possibility of viewing the legal system as a coherent whole, it is the legislature's duty to facilitate that systematic 'wholeness', *contra* the latitude of its sovereignty. Of course, this is a difficult task, replete with possibilities for carelessness and oversight.[82] The point is that the legislator 'has to justify his external limitations so that they allow the judge to make coherence$_2$ arguments'.[83] The unbridled sovereignty of the legislator means that he or she is not constrained in the way that the judge

---

[80] Wintgens, 'Legisprudence as a new theory of legislation' (n 60) 19.
[81] Ibid. n 6.
[82] Fuller, *The Morality of Law* (n 13) 65–70.
[83] Wintgens, 'Legisprudence as a new theory of legislation' (n 60) 20.

is by the assumption that the legal system is coherent. The onus on her is all the greater, then, to justify her legislative 'activism', in order that its effects cohere with the rest of the system, including ex post adjudication.[84] One can see how this contrasts with strong legalism, according to which the legislator's promulgated rules are law, to be grappled with by the adjudicator regardless of how incoherent they may turn out to be. Whereas LoC_0 was concerned with mere logical coherence, LoC_2 is about 'compossibility', the requirement that norms do not contradict one another's substantive effect.[85]

LoC_3 ('environmental coherence'). According to this level of coherence, attaining a holistic view of the system is not possible from a standpoint within that system – an external perspective is required to make sense of it.[86] Wintgens suggests that to get such a perspective is possible only by 'leaning over the edges of what is considered the whole'.[87] Whereas LoC_1 and LoC_2 are concerned with the internal rationality of the legal system, LoC_3 places that coherence within a wider, non-legal, context. This is where Shklar's fences of legalism are broken down; not only do we observe that law does not operate in a vacuum, but we require that sensitivity to this fact be embodied in it through its justification according to the broader societal context within which it operates.[88]

This required sensitivity is what Wintgens calls 'theory dependence'; at LoC_3 the legitimacy of the legislator's proposed rule is dependent on some extra-legal theory that can justify it – it is not enough to look for justification from within the legal system. Unlike strong legalism, where the perspective of the sovereign legislator is held to be a direct conduit to reality and so her pronouncements are isomorphic with that reality, under LoC_3 there is a requirement for an external mediating theory that justifies, according to the

---

[84] Ibid.

[85] Wintgens, *Legisprudence: Practical Reason in Legislation* (n 17) 252.

[86] Wintgens, 'Legisprudence as a new theory of legislation' (n 60) 21.

[87] Ibid. This brings to mind the notion of the 'hermeneutic circle', where the whole cannot be understood separately from its parts, nor they separately from the whole. See N MacCormick, *Rhetoric and the Rule of Law: A Theory of Legal Reasoning* (Oxford University Press 2005) 48; and generally LD Introna, 'Hermeneutics and meaning-making in information systems' in RD Galliers and WL Currie (eds), *The Oxford Handbook of Management Information Systems: Critical Perspectives and New Directions* (Oxford University Press 2011) 241 *et seq.*

[88] On the importance of viewing law as an integral part of a broader social good, see Z Bańkowski, 'Bringing the outside in: The ethical life of legal institutions' in T Gizbert-Studnicki and J Stelmach (eds), *Law and Legal Cultures in the 21st Century* (Wolters Kluwer 2007).

requirements of its own 'regime of veridiction',[89] the legislative rule that is to be made. From the perspective of that external theoretical framework, the law will take on a shape that is different from that of the sovereign who operates in a strong legalistic bubble, or indeed even that of the enlightened legal practitioner whose perspective is nonetheless circumscribed by her professional background. Fuller makes a related argument about identifying contradictions between rules as part of his fifth principle, noting that it is not 'merely or even chiefly technological' incompatibilities that must be taken into account but the 'whole institutional setting of the problem – legal, moral, political, economic, and sociological'.[90] Wintgens gives the law and economics school as one example of this – the study of law from the external viewpoint of some other field.[91]

On LoC_3, then, the legal system must be viewed holistically and in context. It is not simply a question of applying the rules according to the internal logics of LoC_1 or LoC_2 – something more is required (again we detect the distinction between the moralities of duty and aspiration in the search for legality, compared with legalism[92]). There is a connection here with MacCormick's 'post-positivist' theory of rules, whereby the legislator has both an internal view of the legal system and an external view of its coherence vis-à-vis the social context. Quoting him, Wintgens says:

> Since law or a legal system refers to a 'form of life', as MacCormick and Aarnio rightly puts [sic] it, coherence, then, is not a matter of logic alone, but a matter of 'making sense as a whole'. This 'making sense as a whole' refers to 'the whole corpus of the normative system', and thus brings MacCormick to state: 'To put it crudely, legal decisions must make sense *in the world* and they must also make sense in *the context of a legal system*.'[93]

From the perspective of rule-making, the proposed norm can be observed then from both the legal (internal) perspective and its broader social (external) perspective. Viewing it only from the 'inside' begets legalism, while the

---

[89] This is Hildebrandt's terminology, borrowed from Latour. She makes a related argument that '[t]he ends of law – though deeply entwined with their internal validation – are thus co-determined by the needs of the society it serves and co-constitutes.' The first part of this quote maps onto LOCs 1 and 2; the latter part onto LOC_3. See Hildebrandt, *Smart Technologies* (n 8) 144–5 citing B Latour, 'Biography of an inquiry: On a book about modes of existence' (2013) 43 *Social Studies of Science* 287.

[90] Fuller, *The Morality of Law* (n 13) 70.

[91] Wintgens, 'Legislation as an object of study of legal theory' (n 75) 22 and n 47.

[92] See ibid. 26 *et seq.* and Fuller, *The Morality of Law* (n 13) 5 *et seq.*

[93] Wintgens, 'Legislation as an object of study of legal theory' (n 75) 35, citing N MacCormick, *Legal Reasoning and Legal Theory* (Oxford University Press 1994) 103 (emphasis supplied).

addition of extra-legal justification consolidates its legitimacy – its ability to make sense 'in the world' that it is intended to serve. The norm must be justified, therefore, according to both the internal logic of the legal system (LoC_1 and LoC_2; the 'cognitive internal' aspect in MacCormick's language[94]), and the external reality of society (LoC_3), it being reflected in whatever external theoretical framework provides the extra justification that is required under legisprudence.[95] Rationality in the project of legislating arises from the legislator taking such a hermeneutic perspective: the rational quality of a rule consists not just in (legal) formal validity, that is the internal perspective, but also in the validity that flows from an investigation into the 'external social data' that have been produced and rendered as knowledge by other scholarly fields.[96] Legal reality is thus made to relate to social reality.[97]

The Principle of Alternativity (PA)[98]
The PA requires that the creation of a legislative rule must be preferable to the absence of that rule. Creating a rule that prohibits certain conduct removes or circumscribes the possibility of agonistic conflict,[99] which thereby contracts to that extent 'social space' while simultaneously expanding 'political space' to fill the gap that is created. Social space involves practices whose dimensions are discernible partly by the observation and resolution of conflict according to the practice's internal rules, and if that possibility is removed, which an external rule threatens to do, the practice itself might also cease to exist. By imposing an external legal rule, the ability of individuals to choose is removed, thus potentially reducing their scope to exercise moral autonomy. The imposition of a rule can only be justified, then, to correct a dysfunction that the practice cannot resolve according to its own internal processes.[100] This relates to contestability as an inherent part of legitimacy, and legislators should be loath to promulgate rules without first considering whether an alternative scheme might have the desired effect.

The PA is concerned not with the substantive content of the proposed rule, but with whether it is justified to have a rule at all – because freedom is notionally infinite prior to the imposition of a rule, the proposed

---

[94] MacCormick, *Legal Reasoning and Legal Theory* (n 93) 290 *et seq.*
[95] Wintgens, 'Legislation as an object of study of legal theory' (n 75) 17 *et seq.*
[96] Ibid. 31.
[97] Ibid. 38.
[98] Wintgens, 'Legisprudence as a new theory of legislation' (n 60) 10–11.
[99] Ibid. 11. See also M Hildebrandt, 'Algorithmic regulation and the rule of law' (2018) 376 *Philosophical Transactions of the Royal Society A* 20170355.
[100] Wintgens, *Legisprudence: Practical Reason in Legislation* (n 17) 257.

limitation must be *a priori* justified, regardless of its actual content.[101] The PA is therefore a threshold requirement, which once passed is connected particularly intimately with the principle of normative density with respect to the behavioural impact of the design mechanism that is chosen (this principle is discussed below). This idea of a threshold is related to the discussion in Chapter 2 of the spectrum of technological normativity.[102]

The Principle of Temporality (PT)[103]

The PT signals a significant departure from the 'single moment' focus of strong legalism. Whereas legalism wants to 'switch time off',[104] the PT requires a recognition that legislative rules exist in a historical context. Unlike physical laws, which are constant, the contexts within which legislation must operate are evolving, and so the process of enacting a legislative provision must take account of, and be responsive to, such contingency.

Over time the justification for a legislative norm may change. Whereas strong legalism takes no account of this (the law is the law until the legislator changes it; the morality of duty requires obedience to the rule as-is, regardless of any consideration that might merit a different response), the weak legalism of legisprudence requires that the passage of time be taken into account. In terms of equality, distinctions that obtained at the time of the rule's creation may no longer hold, leading to unjust discrimination.[105] More broadly, justificatory reasons that held true at time of promulgation may no longer apply. The legislator's focus is the future, but she cannot foresee all the possible circumstances that might undermine the justification of the norm she proposes in the present.[106] Justifying the promulgated rule is thus an ongoing process: circumstances must be continually assessed to ensure that the legislative norm continues to be an appropriate purposive response to what was originally targeted for change.[107] Failure to do so is to fall back into legalism, where the rule is viewed as 'just there', to be followed without further consideration of its legitimacy. Legitimacy under legisprudence is therefore an ongoing process that requires continual renewal in response to the requirements of each of the principles.[108] The PT requires consideration of the prospective effects

---

[101] Ibid. 297.
[102] See 'A Spectrum of Technological Normativity' in Section 2.2.
[103] Wintgens, 'Legisprudence as a new theory of legislation' (n 60) 13–15.
[104] Wintgens, *Legisprudence: Practical Reason in Legislation* (n 17) 268.
[105] Ibid. 269.
[106] Wintgens, 'The rational legislator revisited' (n 58); Wintgens, *Legisprudence: Practical Reason in Legislation* (n 17) 268–9, 281.
[107] Wintgens, *Legisprudence: Practical Reason in Legislation* (n 17) 269–70.
[108] Ibid. 270–1, 300–3.

of the rule, but because some effects are likely to be unintended, ongoing assessment and (if necessary) subsequent rectification and rejustification are also required.[109]

The Principle of Normative Density (PN)[110]

The PN is related to, but more nuanced than, the notion of proportionality. The extent of the limitation on freedom that a legislative norm imposes must be in proportion to its justification. In other words, the stronger the regulative force of the rule (the more 'dense' or 'intense', in Wintgens's terminology[111]), the greater the level of justification that is required to legitimate it. Normative density exists on a spectrum: criminal sanctions represent the highest density, while other options include 'regulatory techniques such as information, incentives such as tax relief, self-regulation based on codes of conduct or agreements, labelling and the like'.[112] The PN expects there to be a proportionate connection between a policy aim and the means by which it is achieved; the impact on freedom should be as close to the minimum required to achieve the policy aim as is possible, in order not to over-regulate.[113] The use of a technique with a particular normative impact must therefore be justified against any techniques that would have a lesser impact on freedom.[114] Again, one can appreciate the connection to the spectrum of normativity discussed in Chapter 2, from wired-in configuration to greater openness of behavioural possibilities.[115]

4.2 Conclusion

We can see that the legisprudential principles are about legitimising an incursion on freedom, and without sufficient justification that incursion is *a priori* illegitimate. Although the principles have equal weight, like Fuller's principles of legality they do not apply equally in every case. The justification under each principle can therefore operate more or less strongly depending on the circumstances.[116] They are aspirational and might never be fully embodied in a proposed norm, but the idea is to reach for the best possible laws, rather

---

[109] Ibid. 301–4.
[110] Wintgens, 'Legisprudence as a new theory of legislation' (n 60) 11–13.
[111] Wintgens, *Legisprudence: Practical Reason in Legislation* (n 17) 271.
[112] Ibid. 299–300; Wintgens, 'Legisprudence as a new theory of legislation' (n 60) 12–13.
[113] Wintgens, *Legisprudence: Practical Reason in Legislation* (n 17) 276, 279.
[114] Wintgens, 'Legisprudence as a new theory of legislation' (n 60) 13.
[115] See 'A Spectrum of Technological Normativity' in Section 2.2. This topic is returned to in Chapter 6.
[116] Wintgens, *Legisprudence: Practical Reason in Legislation* (n 17) 280. I consider this further in the code context in Chapter 6.

than to achieve a perfection that is unattainable due to the contingencies of time and the limits inherent in trying to anticipate the future.[117]

Returning to the discussion of input and output legitimacy above, we can appreciate how the principles of legisprudence expand upon the categories previously mentioned. The principle of coherence is an ex ante formal standard for assessing the intelligibility of the proposed norm vis-à-vis both existing legal norms and one or more potentially legitimating extra-legal theories. The principle of alternativity is both ex ante procedural (it speaks to the decision of whether or not to institute the proposed norm at all) and ex ante formal (it asks whether a rule is the correct format for achieving the desired outcome). The principle of temporality is both ex ante and ex post procedural, in that it requires justification at the time of promulgation that that was the correct thing to do, and ongoing (ex post) legitimation that it continues to be legitimate.

Fuller's principles are to an extent more hands-off than Wintgens's; the latter constrain more forcefully what the substantive content of a rule can possibly be. We can identify overlaps between them, however. Fuller's first principle requiring the use of rules connects with the legisprudential principle of alternativity – whether or not to use a rule in the first place. The second principle (promulgation) also connects with the principle of alternativity – can the mechanism chosen, if not a rule, be promulgated such that regulatees are able to understand how they are being regulated? It also connects with the principle of normativity, where the extent of normative force may be such, and in so many forms, that promulgation in the usual sense becomes impossible. The third, fifth, and seventh principles of legality (against retroactivity, against contradiction, and in favour of constancy, respectively) speak to the levels within the principle of coherence.

In this chapter I have considered two influential normative frameworks aimed at facilitating the creation of legitimate legal rules. For Fuller, achieving this is about respecting the 'internal morality' of law, which in turn minimises the potential for iniquity in the substance of the norms that can subsequently be promulgated from within that framework. For Wintgens, legitimate rules respect as far as possible individual autonomy, requiring justification of incursions on freedom only when they are in accordance with the legisprudential principles. As with Fuller's theory, these limit what the content of the resulting rules can possibly be. These theories identify the expectations we ought to have of legislators when they are trying to make good laws, regardless of the political content of those laws.

---

[117] Ibid. 282, 305–7.

In Part III of the book I will adapt these criteria to the design environment, on the basis that if they are the kinds of formal features we ought to expect from a normative order that constitutes and regulates our behaviour, then we might reasonably expect them (or their analogues) to be present in all such orders. Before I move on to that synthesis, the next chapter explores and assesses the existing literature on normative criteria for code, identifying gaps – especially regarding ex ante analysis and the practicalities of code's production – that digisprudence aims to begin filling.

5

Criteria for Code

[T]he genie may then be out of the bottle never to be put back in . . . criteria addressing the process of technology development – 'rules of the game' – should be a key part of our acceptability criteria.[1]

The previous chapter discussed criteria intended to govern the creation of legal rules, to ensure that they meet standards of legality and legitimacy regardless of their political content. This chapter mirrors that analysis, reviewing the existing literature on criteria for the use of code in regulating behaviour.

The literature on the regulation of and by technology is large, but analysis of what criteria can legitimate its design is very limited indeed.[2] Goldoni suggests that this is due to a scepticism developing in the decade following Reidenberg's and Lessig's work on *lex informatica* and 'code as law', respectively.[3] Ohm and Frankle have recently made a similar argument:

Too many scholars have interpreted Lessig as doing little more than issuing a license to imagine that anything is possible online, falling into a 'science fiction trap'. Too rarely do they consider the process of *how* code ends up the way it does (let alone how regulators can make use of this process), leaving a significant void in the utility of this body of work.[4]

Ironically, the scepticism Goldoni refers to embodies aspects of the legalistic ideology discussed earlier in the book, where an unwillingness to consider extra-legal sources of normativity leads lawyers to retreat to their intellectual

---

[1] B-J Koops, 'Criteria for normative technology: The acceptability of "code as law" in light of democratic and constitutional values' in R Brownsword and K Yeung (eds), *Regulating Technologies: Legal Futures, Regulatory Frames and Technological Fixes* (Hart 2008) 166.

[2] M Goldoni, 'The politics of code as law: Toward input reasons' in J Reichel and AS Lind (eds), *Freedom of Expression, the Internet and Democracy* (Brill 2015) 123.

[3] Ibid. 117.

[4] P Ohm and J Frankle, 'Desirable inefficiency' (2019) 70 *Florida Law Review* 1, 23 (emphasis supplied).

bunkers, from where they can continue to view law as a separate enterprise, 'fenced off' from other concerns. This strengthens the instinctive belief that code is not – and should not be seen as – law, and that legal thinking should therefore not concern itself with it other than as a subject of legal regulation like any other. Noting this tendency, Brownsword has suggested that the domain of jurisprudence should be 'redrawn' to sensitise it to a 'bigger regulatory picture', including forms of a-legal normativity that are 'at least as important as legal norms in the daily lives of people'.[5]

As Chapter 1 discussed,[6] the purpose of the analysis in this book is not to validate private enterprises as producers of law *per se*. Instead, its aim is to enquire as to how code which has normative effects can be legitimated, which is to say how it can embody effects, features, or affordances alongside its commercially purposive functionality that ameliorate the negative effects of computational legalism. The issue then is not one of the 'legal-ness' of code rules *per se*, that is of viewing them as a source of law, but rather the question of how the 'non-law' of code can, in spite of those negative effects, be produced in ways that are legitimate from the perspective of the law and of constitutional democracy.[7] A failure to do so leaves a significant and serious deficit in our understanding of how citizens, as end-users, have their behaviour enabled and constrained by the often unintelligible code created by unelected private enterprises.

The rest of this chapter considers the current literature on normative criteria for the production of code. Following the analysis in the previous chapter, it is possible to discern a broad separation between those arguments which focus on input criteria and those which focus on output criteria. First, I discuss briefly what these classifications mean in the context of code, and why input criteria deserve much greater focus, before summarising the most relevant contributions in the literature. We can then take stock before moving on to Part III of the book, where I build on the criteria discussed in this and the previous chapter, setting out a framework of affordances whose presence in code can serve to provide a baseline of legitimacy.

5.1 Input and Output Legitimacy in Code

We saw above how a norm's legitimacy can be considered by focusing on its production and/or the effects it has in operation. Chapter 2 set out why, in

---

[5] R Brownsword, 'In the year 2061: From law to technological management' (2015) 7 *Law, Innovation and Technology* 1, 10–14, 30.

[6] See Section 1.4.

[7] Cf. J Waldron, 'The concept and the rule of law' (2008) 43 *Georgia Law Review* 1, 12, discussing how by characterising something as 'law' we 'dignify it with a certain character'.

the computational context, the deontology of input legitimacy is necessary: the ex ante characteristics of computational legalism demonstrate that an ex post consequentialist perspective is not, on its own, sufficient to ameliorate those negative characteristics. When we move from the traditional legislative sphere into the computational context, though, things pivot somewhat. The focus on process is not just one of participation – indeed, the participatory aspect will in a great many cases be minimal, owing to the private spheres within which code artefacts are developed. Rather, the 'input' aspect shifts to have more of a temporal focus, where more granular design decisions about particular aspects of the code's functionality are the focus of legitimation according to binding criteria. Their private production means they might not be the product of a participatory democratic process *per se*, but they are 'input' in the sense that they are crucial constituents of the products (outputs) of the design process that ultimately are responsible for the code's effects in the world.

The distinction is a subtle but crucial one in the context of computational legalism: if we only assess a system according to its operation in the real world (we apply only criteria that assess output) then the production ship has already sailed, and the opportunity to amend the design to remedy any defects we discover may be limited or gone altogether. Furthermore, limiting our focus to operation assumes that assessments of output are capable of detecting all salient negative effects, which is of course far from guaranteed, especially owing to the opacity of code. The shift towards input criteria puts the focus on the design process, to ensure *ab initio* that certain design characteristics are in place that allow for better output assessments but simultaneously reduce the need for them, because the initial configuration of the system is more legitimate from the outset.

Within the sphere of privacy by design, Hartzog argues in favour of focusing on processual standards because 'even certain risky designs can be tolerated so long as companies take the right steps to mitigate potential harm and ensure that debatable design decisions were justified'.[8] Thus, mandating certain processes can potentially mitigate risk through the requirement to consider, during the process of design, the extent to which the proposed code embodies the standards we wish to see in a legitimate normative order. This approach also has practical appeal in terms of reducing the expense and delay of having to reconfigure a design once ex post assessment uncovers that it does not meet one or more of the requirements. Because of the integrated

---

[8] W Hartzog, *Privacy's Blueprint: The Battle to Control the Design of New Technologies* (Harvard University Press 2018) 179.

nature of software development processes, such ex post 'patches' are often less effective than approaches that take matters into consideration from the outset. As Luger and Golembewski note in the sphere of privacy by design,

> [a]ddressing these concerns at the end of a design cycle leaves the creators of the system with little time or agency to manoeuvre, and leads to a situation where potential privacy problems are addressed – if at all – as afterthoughts, with inelegant solutions and imperfect implementations bolted on to a mostly-complete design.[9]

Importing the distinction between input and output reasons into the computational sphere, Koops observes that

> [i]nput legitimacy implies legitimacy through rules-of-the-game and the procedure followed, output legitimacy means that the result establishes legitimacy . . . [I]n the context of normative technology input legitimacy is a primary concern. Because technology is often irreversible – once it is developed and applied in society, it is hard to fundamentally remove it from society in those applications – the process of developing technology is a key focus when normativity is at stake. After all, it may well be too late when technology simply appears in society to ask whether it is acceptable to use this technology; quite often, the genie may then be out of the bottle never to be put back in . . . [C]riteria addressing the process of technology development – 'rules of the game' – should be a key part of our acceptability criteria.[10]

Input criteria are important because the characteristics of computational legalism militate against the effectiveness of ex post assessments of effects in the world (outputs). Goldoni argues along similar lines:

> Given the nature and logic of architectural regulation, the emphasis on output legitimacy is misplaced for several reasons . . . The difficulty of reversing embedded code is often evident and makes it fundamental to focus on the procedure and the actors involved in the development of the technology. Second, given the opacity of architectural regulation, to be aware of how technology is directly or indirectly impacting upon agents' behaviours may prove to be too difficult in many cases. Last but not least . . . the importance

---

[9] E Luger and M Golembewski, 'Towards fostering compliance by design; drawing designers into the regulatory frame' in M Taddeo and L Floridi (eds), *The Responsibilities of Online Service Providers* (Springer 2017) 296. See also L Diver and B Schafer, 'Opening the black box: Petri nets and privacy by design' (2017) 31 *International Review of Law, Computers & Technology* 68, 74–5.

[10] Koops (n 1) 166.

of default technology cannot be underestimated. What appears to be default in code is often taken as a natural and immutable fact.[11]

He concludes therefore that 'input-based legitimacy should become the primary concern in choosing normative criteria'.[12] Moving from a focus on output (ex post) to input (ex ante) legitimacy is necessary if the public dimension involved in traditional rule-making is to be imported into the computational sphere, particularly when so much of the latter is privatised. Crucially, however, the latter does not replace the former – ex post measures remain necessary, to maintain a connection with institutional legal processes. Goldoni thus advocates for a shift from a 'descriptive to a normative approach' to code as law (recall that this is a reversal of the effects of computational legalism, where the normative becomes the descriptive[13]).

Goldoni categorises the literature between analyses of input and output criteria, noting a tendency towards the latter. This is perhaps to be expected, because observations of the real-world effects can be more easily subjected to an orthodox critique from a compliance perspective. The problem with this view is that it does not address directly those who produce the very code that is in question – it sustains the 'fencing off' of jurisprudential analysis from the object of that analysis. Lawyers continue to be viewed as ex post assessors of code, without acknowledging designers as the ex ante producers of it.

Ultimately, Goldoni suggests that two principles should govern code production: transparency and 'publicness'.[14] The first suggests that rules embodied in code must be knowable in order that they can be observed and their creators held accountable, while the second implies that there must be opportunity for those subject to the rules to have a say in their creation.

In the remainder of this section I consider the literature on the question of normative criteria for code, following Goldoni in separating the works broadly into those who focus on substantive output criteria and those who focus on input criteria. Again, my argument is that the latter is the more appropriate focus for criteria that can assist in guiding the design of digital artefacts. While ex post assessments are also important, we have seen how

---

[11] Goldoni (n 2) 128.
[12] Ibid.
[13] See Chapter 3. Bańkowski uses this exact formulation: 'What we see then, is how the normative has become the descriptive. This gives us an example of rule following which has the machine-like quality of heteronomy.' See Z Bańkowski, 'Don't think about it: Legalism and legality' in MM Karlsson, Ó Páll Jónsson and EM Brynjarsdóttir (eds), *Rechtstheorie: Zeitschrift für Logik, Methodenlehre, Kybernetik und Soziologie des Rechts* (Duncker & Humblot 1993) 56.
[14] Goldoni (n 2) 128–9.

computational legalism tends towards obfuscation, and thus the ability to carry out the assessments is itself contingent on ex ante design decisions that ensure they are possible. This complementarity of input and output criteria is therefore a part of the framework I develop in the next chapter.

5.2 Output Legitimacy

(a) Brownsword's 'Technological Management'

Brownsword's primary criterion for assessing techno-regulation is that of justification, which he characterises as a judgement on 'whether we are over-regulating or under-regulating'.[15] This has a bearing on the central theme of Brownsword's work more generally: the acceptability of techno-regulation assessed from the perspective of human rights and human dignity. He views the latter as a question of 'empowerment', which consists of three elements: 'that one's capacity for making one's own choices should be recognised; that the choices one freely makes should be respected; and that the need for a supportive context for autonomous decision-making (and action) should be appreciated and acted upon'.[16] This conception of dignity leads ultimately to the suggestion, in the computational context, that individuals always retain the choice not to follow the rule as inscribed in the artefact.

To encourage the development of 'moral community',[17] the individual should where appropriate be empowered to take moral rather than merely 'prudential' choices (that is, choices that are in her own interest).[18] Technological management is problematic not because it naturally favours a particular form of (a)moral reasoning, but because it has the capability of bypassing practical reason altogether,[19] effacing opportunities for either moral or prudential choice.[20] Without the opportunity to exercise such choice, the possibility of moral community falters through individuals being 'de-moralised', that is having their capacity for moral judgement corroded through the removal of

---

[15] R Brownsword, 'What the world needs now: Techno-regulation, human rights and human dignity' in R Brownsword (ed.), *Global Governance and the Quest for Justice*, vol. 4 (Hart 2004) 205.

[16] Ibid. 211.

[17] A concept characterised as a community that is built on publicly proclaimed principles that are open to review according to processes that are inclusive of its members. See R Brownsword, 'Lost in translation: Legality, regulatory margins, and technological management' (2011) 26 *Berkeley Technology Law Journal* 1321, 1335 *et seq.*

[18] Ibid. See also Brownsword, 'In the year 2061' (n 5) 32–3.

[19] R Brownsword, 'Code, control, and choice: Why east is east and west is west' (2005) 25 *Legal Studies* 1, 13.

[20] Brownsword, 'In the year 2061' (n 5) 34–5.

opportunities to exercise it.[21] The result is a blunting of sensitivity to social norms, and a breakdown in moral community.[22] Indeed, the very concept of morality might disappear altogether if the possibility of infringing rights (doing harm) is removed by techno-regulation.[23]

In his earlier work on techno-regulation, Brownsword maintains a focus on state regulators as its source, suggesting that any movements from what he terms normative regulation (that is, measures which invite compliance) towards non-normative regulation (measures that do not permit scope for choice) should be ventilated by means of a 'regulatory margin' that can 'facilitate deliberation about, and review of, changes to the complexion of the regulatory environment'.[24] In later work he suggests that this must take place ex ante in order to ratify the use of technological management before it is rolled out. Failure to do so will result in the potentially unlegitimated use of code which, because of the efficiency with which it enforces rules (its immediacy), closes the gaps in enforcement that previously permitted civil disobedience and the resulting friction and conflict that can be a driver for positive social change.[25]

This overarching goal is welcome at a policy level but does not engage with the practices of producing the code that implements the techno-regulation. The essential concern is that we ought to be wary of decisions that might lead to unfettered use of code for regulation. Brownsword's overarching goal of respect for human dignity, embodied in the preservation of the ability to reason practically and to exercise choice, is important. In later work he expands beyond the focus on dignity and moral community to consider more explicitly legal-theoretical ideas, for example Fuller's principles of legality (his analysis of which is considered below). For him, Fuller's characterisation of legality as involving a reciprocal relationship between the end-user and the

---

[21] Brownsword, 'Code, control, and choice' (n 19) 4. See also A Le Sueur, 'Robot government: Automated decision-making and its implications for Parliament' in A Horne and A Le Sueur (eds), *Parliament: Legislation and Accountability* (Hart 2016) 192–3, discussing the passage of the Social Security Act 1998 and the potential effects of the increased use of automation in public administrative decision-making.

[22] Brownsword, 'Code, control, and choice' (n 19) 19, quoting criminologist DJ Smith, 'Changing situations and changing people' in A von Hirsch, D Garland and A Wakefield (eds), *Ethical and Social Perspectives on Situational Crime Prevention* (Bloomsbury Publishing 2004). See also Brownsword, 'Lost in translation' (n 17), especially 1355–6.

[23] Brownsword, 'What the world needs now' (n 15) 231.

[24] Brownsword, 'Lost in translation' (n 17) 1351. At the level of design, this margin might be manifest in the digisprudential affordance of delay, discussed in the next chapter.

[25] Brownsword, 'In the year 2061' (n 5) 36–7. I discuss the role of this 'agonism' in democratic societies in the next chapter.

state is key to the latter's use of code, and therein lies his prescription for the 'regulatory margin' that can facilitate the participatory mechanisms that will legitimise such regulation.[26] Brownsword's earlier focus on the public regulation of citizens means that his analyses do not venture far beyond relationship (b) in Figure 1.1 in Chapter 1 (depicting the normative relationship between the state and the citizen/end-user[27]).

I return to Brownsword's more recent work on input legitimacy below, but for now three criteria can be identified for the proper application of 'techno-regulation'. These are (1) respect for individual dignity through the preservation of choice (and more choice is better), (2) reciprocity between the regulator and the regulatee in the designing of norms, and (3) the need for a delaying 'regulatory margin' that can facilitate this reciprocity.

(b) Leenes's 'Techno-regulation'

Leenes expands the concept of techno-regulation to include as producers of code the private sector as well as the state.[28] He maintains a focus on techno-regulation as regulation borne of identifiable legal sources, namely state legislation or private contracts. This focus sets his analysis apart from my own, although he does obliquely reference the kinds of extra-legal normativity I am concerned with:

> In the case of techno-norms implementing contractual terms or deriving legal status from the law . . . the legal status of the norms embedded in the artifact and the legal effects of breaching the norms are clear. In other cases the norms may be legally null and void and hence not legally bind individuals, yet as long as the norms remain embedded in the technology they in fact do regulate behaviour: legitimacy and effectiveness may be disjoint in practice.[29]

The latter class of norms that Leenes refers to is of course the focus of digisprudence, although he does not say much more about it (later work, discussed below, does consider this aspect). Ultimately, for Leenes the key factor is transparency of the 'techno-norms' and the process by which they are arrived at. For him, in an ideal situation regulatees consider the norms promulgated by privately produced code to be legitimate, the latter being achieved by 'engaging this community in deliberate discourse' which 'requires a free flow

---

[26] Brownsword, 'Lost in translation' (n 17) 1363–4.
[27] See 'Normative Relationships in Code and Law' in Section 1.4.
[28] R Leenes, 'Framing techno-regulation: An exploration of state and non-state regulation by technology' (2011) 5 *Legisprudence* 143.
[29] Ibid. 168.

of unhindered vital information'.[30] This overlaps with Brownsword's regulatory margin and Goldoni's transparency and 'publicness' requirements. I will consider below the limitations of this kind of participation in the privatised design process.

(c) Koops's 'Criteria for Normative Technology'

Koops provides an overview of criteria to be considered when assessing what he calls 'normative technology'.[31] He notes many of the concerns we have already seen in the discussion of computational legalism, around the ability of code to establish new norms, the effect of translating textual norms into code, and the applicability of democratic and constitutional values even in the context of private sector code production.[32]

Koops's survey of the literature provides a useful, complex, overview of the criteria that are discussed. His analysis conflates or bundles concepts that I believe should be kept apart, however. For example, he classifies due process, legality, and 'checks and balances' all under the umbrella of the 'rule of law', and refers to them as substantive (as opposed to procedural or formal) criteria.[33] Similarly, 'transparency of rule-making', 'transparency of rules', and accountability are listed as 'secondary criteria', while 'rule of law' and 'democracy' are listed as primary.[34] It is not clear that these concepts are quite so easily distinguished or prioritised.[35] They are all contested of course, but without clearer theoretical delineation Koops's criteria are somewhat limited (a point he acknowledges, and something he suggests be left to further research).

This is reflected in Koops's 'pragmatic, bottom-up' approach, where his aim is to identify the criteria suggested by other scholars, as opposed to taking an alternative 'top-down . . . theory-based interpretation of law'[36] (another point of departure). Although he acknowledges the fundamental importance of procedural (input) legitimacy, Koops's analysis is explicitly concerned primarily with what he calls 'outcome justice', and the ex post assessment of specific technologies. The set of criteria he ultimately develops is intended as a heuristic for structuring the process, rather than a means of performing it. His fourth level of abstraction begins to push towards concrete practices,

---

[30] Ibid. 167.
[31] Koops (n 1).
[32] Ibid. 159–61.
[33] Ibid. 168.
[34] Ibid. 169.
[35] For a useful overview separating out these various concepts, see J Tasioulas, 'The rule of law' in J Tasioulas (ed.), *The Cambridge Companion to the Philosophy of Law* (Cambridge University Press 2019).
[36] Koops (n 1) 162.

particularly in his class of 'secondary criteria', where he includes for example review, audit, the possibility of choice, optimal default settings, and context-adaptability.[37] He notes that the 'proof of the pudding is in the eating',[38] suggesting that what matters is testing of the criteria against concrete technologies. This will never, he says, 'be a straightforward or uncontested exercise. For one thing, several of the criteria are culture-dependent, in their interpretation (for example moral values and democracy) or in their importance (for example human rights and choice).'[39]

Like other authors, this is the ex post 'output' legitimacy that represents a kind of 'thick' version of legitimacy. As a result, the substantive aspects of, for example, human rights become part of the assessment, contributing to both the difficulties that Koops refers to and to the complexity of his criteria. I doubt whether such assessments of substantive legal requirements can ever be expected to be carried out by designers all across the private sector, particularly in light of the complexity and nuance of the law and the limited resources of companies (especially SMEs) who do not have dedicated legal departments with the expertise required to find the relevant law and interpret it on behalf of designers.

Koops's perspective seems, as mentioned above, to privilege the position of the lawyer as code assessor, thus maintaining an inbuilt bias towards legalistic ex post assessment.[40] The gaps between lawyers and designers, and between a product's design and runtime phases, are thus maintained rather than bridged. Koops also suggests that the list of criteria itself will require periodic reassessment,[41] but again this is made necessary because the focus is on substantive rather than formal or procedural legitimacy. The latter should be able to stand the test of time, as in Fuller's internal morality of law, because a procedure that follows legitimising formal principles ought to underpin the making of all code-based norms regardless of their substantive content.[42] Indeed, in a constitutional democracy we might say that it is a prerequisite

---

[37] Ibid. 168.

[38] Ibid. 171.

[39] Ibid. 170.

[40] Goldoni observes that '[i]n a rather typical legalistic and formalist fashion, Koops would also have lawyers testing the set of normative criteria.' See Goldoni (n 2) 127–8.

[41] Koops (n 1) 171.

[42] Although the legisprudential principle of temporality also requires periodic reassessment, this is of the substance of the rule and not the affordance of reassessment itself. The latter (that is, providing the ability to reassess) is timeless, while the justification for a rule may change over time or indeed disappear – it is the principle of temporality (and its concordant affordance) that allows for this to be determined.

of those rules being legitimate.[43] Furthermore, focusing on procedure also potentially simplifies the criteria that need to be applied, at least at this level, since (as we shall see) there are fewer of them, and they are more or less constant.

Koops finishes with an enjoinder to consider the question of 'ambient law', or the incorporation of legal norms and values of legality into technological infrastructure itself. This notion, developed alongside Hildebrandt,[44] is the precursor to the latter's concept of 'Legal Protection by Design', discussed next.

5.3 Input Legitimacy

In contrast to Koops's explicitly 'bottom-up' approach, Hildebrandt, Brownsword, and Asscher each take a legal-theoretical approach to assessing legitimacy, and in so doing they push the focus away from output legitimacy towards input, or production, legitimacy.

(a) Hildebrandt's 'Legal Protection by Design'

The concept of 'Legal Protection by Design', or 'LPbD', is very closely aligned with the spirit of digisprudence. In earlier work Hildebrandt used the term 'ambient law',[45] arguing that we must 'find ways to articulate the legal framework of democracy and the rule of law into the technological architecture it aims to regulate, creating what has been called "Ambient Law"'.[46]

Chapter 1 discussed the use of the term 'by design' to denote the separate concerns of substantive compliance with particular fields of law (most commonly data protection, as in privacy/data protection by design) and the more general and indeed fundamental[47] goal of achieving legal protection. It is therefore more of a philosophical project about the nature of law and its operation in and through computational architectures, rather than the application of substantive doctrine within the computational context.[48] Hildebrandt

---

[43] Cf. M Hildebrandt and B-J Koops, 'The challenges of ambient law and legal protection in the profiling era' (2010) 73 *The Modern Law Review* 428, 454.

[44] Ibid.

[45] M Hildebrandt, 'A vision of ambient law' in R Brownsword and K Yeung (eds), *Regulating Technologies: Legal Futures, Regulatory Frames and Technological Fixes* (Hart 2008).

[46] Ibid. 176.

[47] As Hildebrandt and Koops suggest, 'the challenge of Ambient Law is altogether far more fundamental than transposing "legal" norms into "technical" architectures'. See Hildebrandt and Koops (n 43) 460.

[48] M Hildebrandt, 'Legal protection by design: Objections and refutations' (2011) 5 *Legisprudence* 223, 238–9. Recall the discussion of this crucial distinction in 'Why Not "Compliance by Design"?' in Section 1.4.

suggests that LPbD as an umbrella concept is concerned with both aspects – on the one hand, technological normativity should comply with substantive law, and on the other it should be both resist-able and contestable in a traditional court of law.

As I have previously discussed, the first requirement (substantive compliance) is not the focus of the present analysis. The second and third requirements point to the design of an artefact, and what it enables the end-user to do: can she exercise choice, and can she contest the design in a court? For Hildebrandt, '[t]he "resistability" requirement rules out deterministic environments, and the contestability requirement rules out invisible regulation.'[49] The goal is that 'the exercise of . . . rights should not be obstructed by the intended or unintended effects of new technologies'.[50] In essence, then, there are for her two criteria for the non-doctrinal (input) aspects of LPbD, namely choice and transparency.[51] I have already set out in detail in Part I of the book how computational legalism creates the conditions she is arguing against. The challenge now is to move beyond them to suggest ways forward. Hildebrandt does not provide concrete suggestions on how these can be achieved, instead setting out the overarching goals of LPbD. She sounds a warning, too: '[d]eveloping a methodology for LPbD entails a vertiginous challenge to traditional doctrinal research methods within legal scholarship and to the scientific methods of computer science, requirements engineering and electronics.'[52] This challenge is precisely what Part III will begin to grapple with, building on the design theory set out in Chapter 2 to suggest ways that the second aspect of LPbD might be achieved. This answers Hildebrandt's second enjoinder that we

> should always include attention to the 'resistability' and contestability of the ensuing normativity, and should always involve testing how the configuration or design of the affordances can best serve the goals of justice, legal certainty and purposiveness.[53]

As we saw earlier, these latter three elements of justice, legal certainty, and purposiveness are drawn from Radbruch's antinomian theory of law.[54] The

---

[49] M Hildebrandt, *Smart Technologies and the End(s) of Law: Novel Entanglements of Law and Technology* (Edward Elgar Publishing 2015) 218.

[50] Hildebrandt, 'Legal protection by design' (n 48) 240.

[51] See also Hildebrandt and Koops (n 43) 456.

[52] Hildebrandt, *Smart Technologies* (n 49) 218.

[53] Ibid.

[54] G Radbruch, 'Legal philosophy' in K Wilk (ed.), *The Legal Philosophies of Lask, Radbruch, and Dabin* (Harvard University Press 1950) 111–12.

implication here is that the focus is on the design stage, where the affordances of the product are developed and where it can be considered whether or not they meet both the product's commercial requirements and those of legitimacy so conceived.

More generally, LPbD requires that the design of a product's 'commercial' affordances (what makes it attractive or useful to the end-user) must take account of its legal affordances; in (dis)affording particular behaviours for the end-user, the code must at all times permit the operation of the ideals of legality, which means the possibility of the end-user (1) observing the rules to which the system is subjecting her, (2) exercising choice as to which rules apply, and (3) contesting those rules in court.[55] Hildebrandt's analysis thus concerns input criteria, even though the focus is about the end-user having the ability to exercise her rights ex post. Her discussion of affordance and the 'designing in' of mechanisms to facilitate LPbD is inherently concerned with input criteria and the requirement that the design process reflect those ex ante requirements; if that is achieved then the ex post operation of the system will by definition embody the procedural, if not necessarily the substantive, aspects of output legitimacy (*ceteris paribus*).

(b) Applying Fuller to Code

Both Brownsword and Asscher have considered how to adapt or apply Fuller's principles of legality in the context of code.

Brownsword

In recent work Brownsword has focused more on conventional legal theories with respect to code, demonstrating a pluralist perspective that is sensitive to the private production of code and its capability to 'compete with or complement, or simply supersede Hartian legal norms'.[56] For him, the principles of legality are an example of 'cosmopolitan values' that normatively bind all regulators, regardless of the substantive content of the regulations they promulgate.[57]

Brownsword appears throughout to maintain an ontological separation between the 'rule' or decision which animates the use of a particular code measure, and the substantive effect of the measure itself (this is made explicit in his treatment of the second principle, as I will explain below).

---

[55] M Hildebrandt, 'Law as an affordance: The devil is in the vanishing point(s)' (2017) 4 *Critical Analysis of Law* 116, 122.
[56] Brownsword, 'In the year 2061' (n 5) 10–14, 19.
[57] R Brownsword, 'Technological management and the rule of law' (2016) 8 *Law, Innovation and Technology* 100, 113.

This creates a distance between his analysis and the materiality of code, and therefore the design questions (what an artefact (dis)affords, and how it mediates reality for the end-user) that, as I explore in the next chapter, some of the Fullerian principles can usefully point towards. Nevertheless, alongside Asscher, Brownsword's is one of only two analyses of code from the perspective of Fuller's principles that I am aware of. The discussion below follows Brownsword's ordering of the principles.[58]

Promulgation of rules (Fuller's second principle). Brownsword claims that code environments are not governed by rules *per se* (and therefore there can be no operation of the first Fullerian principle, which states that there must be rules). Thus, for him, the second principle is converted into a requirement of transparency vis-à-vis the proposed use of technological management (that is, code).[59] The result is that regulatees should be given 'a fair opportunity to participate in the processes that will determine whether such a use is authorised',[60] the idea being that 'the purpose of promulgation is to invite public debate about the use of [code] measures'.[61] As mentioned above, whether this is workable in the commercial contexts where digital artefacts are designed is questionable, not least given the lack of incentives designers have to consult end-users or the communities who will be affected by their code. Brownsword aims at transparency of intent rather than actual technical transparency, but as I will discuss later, the distinction – and gap – between the two is problematic. At any rate, while the role of participation in the design process may be a desirable one, it is at most complementary to digisprudence, because it speaks to either (1) organisational processes (Brownsword's focus on the decisions to use code, rather than the code itself), or (2) the substantive functionality that makes the code attractive to a given class of end-user, at which point the question has moved beyond the 'constitutional' standards of legitimacy that should be present in all digital artefacts regardless of their commercial purpose. (This is a theme I return to below.)

Rules should be prospective, not retrospective (third principle). Although it is possible for retrospective acts in technologically managed environments (Brownsword gives the examples of database records being deleted, or contractual provisions being altered), he suggests that in general changes to the environment are prospective and therefore technological management

---

[58] Set out in LL Fuller, *The Morality of Law* (Yale University Press 1977) chapter 2. I discussed Fuller's principles within the legal context in the previous chapter.

[59] Brownsword, 'Technological management and the rule of law' (n 57) 117.

[60] Ibid.

[61] Ibid. 118.

does not introduce any new risk of 'unfair retrospective penalisation of conduct'.[62]

Rules should not require the impossible (sixth principle). Brownsword's discussion here focuses on the notional mental state of the regulatee, and how various legal systems deal with criminal attempts that are frustrated because of their impossibility.[63] Here, though, his focus shifts to the subjective position of the regulatee, rather than the legitimacy of the technological management measure, and so his analysis of this principle is not strictly relevant here.

Rules should be clear (fourth principle). The channelling of regulatees' behaviour 'should be done with less friction and confusion where the regulatory signal is clearly and decisively transmitted'.[64] Regulatees ought to have it communicated clearly that their conduct will be limited in some way by a technological measure.

Rules should be relatively constant (seventh principle). Brownsword suggests that frequent changes in what an application of technological management permits and denies, either because of malfunction or because of a deliberate change to the 'regulatory coding', might invite the uncertainty in regulatees that the principle aims to guard against. He warns against causing confusion to regulatees, caused by frequent code changes, resulting in their contravention of the 'terms' of the system and thus the levying of what are therefore unfair penalties because of a lack of constancy.[65]

Rules should not be contradictory (fifth principle). In the technological management context this principle should be 'consistent in allowing or disallowing a certain "act"'.[66] This would appear more or less to match his proposal for the seventh principle, discussed above. He suggests further that where the system permits or renders possible a particular act, the regulatee should be given the benefit of an assumption against levying a penalty where it was the 'fault' of the system that what should have been a prohibited act (presumably owing to some other legal requirement) was in fact made possible.[67]

The practical administration of rules must match their content (eighth principle). Again, Brownsword maintains the ontological separation between code and the 'offline' rules that sit 'behind' the technological measure and animate its use. This is perhaps necessary for this particular principle.

---

[62] Ibid. 120.
[63] Ibid. 120–2.
[64] Ibid. 122.
[65] Ibid. 123.
[66] Ibid. 124.
[67] Ibid.

Here, his focus is on the translation of rules into code, and it is there where his concern over congruence arises: whether the rule as stated (or written) is properly reflected in the technological management measure.[68] This is the well-known problem of compliance by design discussed in Chapter 1, and also of the translation of '"law in the books" to "law in other technologies"'.[69]

Rules should be general (first principle). Here Brownsword shifts focus onto the question of algorithmic profiling, whereby the technological management system can feasibly have as many bespoke rules as there are regulatees subject to it.[70] Whether or not the code in question is 'data-driven', the concept of generality is relevant here. For example, end-users can believe themselves to be having the same experience as one another, when in fact this is not the case (an evocative example is the Facebook 'emotional contagion' experiment, an example of so-called 'A/B testing' discussed in Chapter 2[71]). Another example is when designers release 'alpha' and 'beta' versions of software, where end-users elect to access new features in a system before they are fully completed and ready for widespread distribution. In some cases, updates are released that fragment the uniformity of the code across the userbase.

Brownsword summarises his understanding of Fuller's principles in the context of technological management as requiring 'openness, or transparency, in authorising the use of measures of technological management for particular regulatory purposes, supported by ideals of fairness and due process'.[72] As I previously mentioned, this focus on authorisation maintains an ontological separation between the policy animating the use of technological management and the code that actually implements the normativity. The focus too on ex ante deliberation, the 'regulatory margin', is sensible from the perspective of large public regulatory bodies but is, I think, less plausible in the context of small commercial enterprises creating low-margin digital artefacts. The suggestion that such firms submit to 'special procedures possibly akin to applications for planning permission'[73] seems unlikely to receive much purchase given the fecundity of the Internet as a generative platform and the ease with which almost anyone can get started creating code that has normative effect. Where Brownsword does discuss the private sector, he sets up

---

[68] Ibid. 124–5.

[69] Hildebrandt and Koops (n 43) 452, *et seq.*

[70] Brownsword, 'Technological management and the rule of law' (n 57) 125–6.

[71] R Booth, 'Facebook reveals news feed experiment to control emotions' *The Guardian* (29 June 2014) <https://www.theguardian.com/technology/2014/jun/29/facebook-users-emotions-news-feeds> last accessed 4 March 2021.

[72] Brownsword, 'Technological management and the rule of law' (n 57) 127.

[73] Ibid.

a dichotomy between ex ante 'approval and authorisation' on the one hand, and ex post 'challenge and review' on the other. Where the ex ante measures are not present, the ex post measures are thus necessary.[74] This is a good starting point for thinking about the responsibilities of software designers and their employers, but on its own does not go far enough. As I have argued throughout, and as we saw from the discussion of computational legalism in Chapter 3, an either/or approach is insufficient; if we rely only on ex ante measures, we cannot account for emergent and/or unexpected regulatory effects, while if we rely only on ex post measures, there may be significant harm done that will not be detected in order for those processes to be invoked.

Brownsword's application of Fuller boils down to the need for openness, transparency, and due process in the authorisation of the use of technological management, together with the requirement – a longstanding theme in his work – that the conditions for moral community be maintained. As I discussed earlier in the chapter, for him the latter conditions are provided where there is preservation of individual choice and the ability to make a moral decision.[75] Brownsword does not engage with the concrete materiality of design, beyond a passing reference to transparency 'about how the particular technologies work'.[76] For present purposes, this observation is particularly apposite: 'while it is certainly a *necessary* condition for the acceptability of a particular use of technological management that the underlying rule or policy is compatible with the Rule of Law, it might not be *sufficient*'.[77] Indeed, digisprudence views it as not sufficient, because it does not engage with the materiality of the design that actually implements the normativity. This will be discussed in the next chapter, but for now I turn to Asscher's application of Fuller's principles to code.

Asscher

Asscher's analysis is more closely focused on the idea of code *per se*, as opposed to Brownsword's focus on the legitimacy of the rules operating behind the code. His approach in adapting Fuller's principles is to pose numerous questions for the assessment of code.[78] First, is it transparent: can citizens discern the rules they are subject to, or, in computational terms, can we be sure of

---

[74] Ibid. 117.
[75] Ibid. 129–31.
[76] Ibid. 139.
[77] Ibid. (emphasis supplied).
[78] L Asscher, '"Code" as law: Using Fuller to assess code rules' in E Dommering and L Asscher (eds), *Coding Regulation: Essays on the Normative Role of Information Technology* (TMC Asser Press 2006).

what the code is doing, and is this what we expect to happen?[79] Second, is the code consistent, both in the temporal sense (that is, it is not updated arbitrarily), and in the sense of congruence both with other code rules and with legal rules? This speaks to the trust that end-users can have in the system. Third, is its provenance clear, that is can end-users identify who is responsible for its production? ('[C]an a sovereign be distinguished that can also be held accountable for the influence of the software?'[80]) Fourth, is autonomy respected through the preservation of the choice of whether or not to obey?[81] He distils these adaptations of Fuller's principles into the following 'checklist':

1. Can *rules* be distinguished in the code?
2. Can they be *understood*, i.e., is it understandable how code works and what it does? If so, are those rules transparent, are they accessible to the general public?
3. Can the rules be *trusted*, is there any guarantee that rules are not changed during the game? Are code rules *reliable* in the sense that they are predictable?
4. Is there a sovereign? An *authority* who makes the code rules?
5. Is there a choice? Can consumers/citizens choose not to obey the rules? Can consumers/citizens freely *choose* another system of law/code?[82]

If the answer to the first question is negative, the rest can be ignored (I discuss below why things are not quite so simple). Questions two and three are connected, while the fourth is a practical concern. Interestingly, Asscher connects the fifth question – whether the end-user retains choice – explicitly with the issue of competition (contrast this with Brownsword's framing of choice as a foundation for moral reasoning and community).[83] For Asscher, the questions are about restoring balance between code and law. This is connected with the traditional process of legislation and law-application, one element of which is the practice of balancing competing interests. Asscher suggests that his Fullerian analysis of code is apt to assess whether the balance of power has tipped away from institutional law, in favour of the 'code world', and thereby whether some kind of state intervention is required to restore it.[84]

---

[79] Ibid. 84.
[80] Ibid.
[81] Ibid. 84–5.
[82] Ibid. 85 (emphasis supplied).
[83] Ibid.
[84] Ibid. 85–6.

Asscher's criteria can be summarised as follows. When there are rules enforced by code, (1) the code must be transparent (understandable to those regulated by it), (2) the code must be trustworthy and reliable (it operates as expected, and is not changed arbitrarily), (3) the producers of the code must be identifiable, and (4) end-users must have the choice of whether or not to obey its rules. We will see in the next chapter how these considerations are adopted in the framework of digisprudential affordances.

In Chapter 3 I considered Asscher's suggestion that 'rules should not be confused with the technical commands within a certain computer language but must be understood on the conceptual level'.[85] As discussed there, the rules at the conceptual level that Asscher refers to (that is, rules *qua* techno-logical normativity) are necessarily dependent, at the lower level, on 'technical commands within a certain computer language'. The issue of code-as-rules *per se* thus cannot be quite so easily dismissed. It is appropriate (and indeed necessary) to focus, at least to some extent, on what the code actually says and does. It may be that Asscher is implying that code does not present us with rules in any conventional legal-theoretical sense, and that insofar as there are 'subtle examples of the intertwined effects of legal policy and software effects'[86] our focus should nevertheless remain at the conceptual level. As I have argued throughout, however, the failure to engage with the normativities that code in fact generates is precisely what allows its illegitimacies to go undetected, given cover by the notion, at the 'conceptual level', that the code 'underneath' does what it purports to do, or implements the orthodox rule its designer says it does.

5.4 Conclusion

To conclude, we can summarise the various contributions from the literature surveyed above. Brownsword and Koops are interested mostly in substantive assessments of code's real-world effects. Brownsword's earlier contributions focused on public regulation, arguing that 'techno-regulation' must maintain scope for individual choice in order that the possibility of moral decision-making, as a foundational element of moral community, is retained. Koops, apart from providing a useful interpretation of other scholars' criteria, focuses on ex post assessments of specific technologies as they operate in the world. The criteria he identifies are mixed, although he prioritises the substantive

---

[85] Ibid. 83. See 'Does Code Contain Rules *per se?*' in Section 3.2.
[86] Ibid. 87.

(output) criteria of human rights and 'other moral values' before the rule of law and democracy.

Hildebrandt, Asscher, and Brownsword (in his later work) include a focus on input criteria, the latter two applying Fuller's principles to code. Hildebrandt's 'Legal Protection by Design' requires transparency in the rules which technological normativity embodies, the ability of the end-user to exercise choice (that is, to resist the default configuration), and the possibility of contesting the rules in a court of law. Brownsword surveys Fuller from a rule of law perspective, but his ontological separation between code itself and the policy rule which animates its use means that his target of assessment is not the design of the code *per se*, but rather the decision of whether or not to use it. He requires transparency and due process in the authorisation of the use of code regulation, as well as the original requirement of the retention of the possibility of (moral) choice on the part of the individual. In contrast to Brownsword, Asscher maintains a closer focus on code *per se*. His distillation of the Fullerian principles requires that code be transparent, that it works as expected and is not changed arbitrarily, that its producers can be identified, and that end-users retain choice as to whether or not to obey its rules. I adopt various of these requirements in the framework of digisprudential affordances developed in the next chapter.

This chapter has surveyed the literature on normative criteria for code, noting certain gaps in existing analysis, particularly with respect to the private production of code (as opposed to state-sanctioned use of code as a regulator), the production of unintended normativity, and the focus on ex post assessments of an artefact's operation instead of the ex ante design decisions which lead to those effects.

The analysis in this part of the book has sought to provide both a legal-theoretical view on legitimate normativity, and the state of the art in the literature on criteria for code as a normative order. As we saw in Part I, with code there is an inevitability about the initial configuration – once the decision to build something has been made, that something by definition embodies a set of initial commitments that necessarily privileges one configuration of normativity over all the other possibilities. Furthermore, as the discussion of input and output legitimacy showed, in the code realm we cannot simply await a determination by the courts of a particular (legal) issue; in code the 'decision' is by definition ex ante. Restating the central concern of the book, the composition of the system, chosen by the designer, has the potential to introduce significant path dependencies in how it regulates end-user behaviour. This is coupled with the plasticity of software, which empowers the designer to impose such regulation in a vast, near-infinite number of ways. We must therefore interrogate critically that initial configuration in order to ensure its legitimacy from the outset. The next part of the book uses the understanding gleaned here both to develop a framework of design strategies that can help to ameliorate computational legalism, and then to suggest some concrete practices that can serve as a starting point for implementing the framework.

Part III

Legitimating Code:
Theory and Practice

6

The Digisprudential Affordances

> To promote the benefits of legality, and to prevent the disadvantages of
> legalism, we will require new forms of interaction with these systems.[1]

This third part of the book represents its main practical contribution. In this
chapter, I synthesise the theoretical ideas from the past four chapters into a
framework of 'digisprudential affordances' that can provide a baseline of regulative legitimacy. By employing affordances not just to describe what code
does but also as a conceptual lens for what it *ought* to do, I provide a novel
way to identify those new forms of interaction referred to in the quote above
from Bańkowski and Schafer. One can appreciate from the review of the literature in the previous chapter that although the work in this area has considered criteria for the use of code as a regulator, this scholarship has not engaged
in depth with the relational theories of design that I set out in Chapter 2, and
has therefore not considered the desirability, efficacy, or indeed legitimacy of
code from that perspective. This chapter contributes such an analysis through
the synthesis of the legal-theoretical perspective of legitimacy with design
theory, the outcome of which is a set of affordances that code ought to exhibit
in order to be deemed legitimate.

I begin by mapping the characteristics of computational legalism onto
the Fullerian and legisprudential principles. From this mapping relationships
can be identified between those principles and the affordances that can help
to embody their aims within the design of code. The affordances provide
both a way of asking what features a given design provides, and a set of goals
for what should be afforded in order to achieve legitimacy. Designers should
not think only about what their code is intended to do from a commercial perspective; they ought also to make informed assessments of whether

---

[1] Z Bańkowski and B Schafer, 'Double-click justice: Legalism in the computer age' (2007)
1 *Legisprudence* 31, 46.

it is, and if not how it might become, legitimate. The digisprudential framework is a mechanism for guiding those anticipations from a legal-theoretical perspective.[2]

6.1 Assessing Decisions, or Assessing Design?

We saw in the previous part of the book a tendency to focus on background decisions as the target for tests of legitimacy, a perspective that implicitly views the code that embodies them as a separate product of those decisions. By contrast, digisprudence is concerned with the legitimacy of the resulting design itself, whatever those decisions were. This means that any ontological separation between the normativity of the code and the preceding decision animating its use must not result in a focus on only the latter half of the whole: the code is what does the work of instantiating whatever normativity ultimately comes into being, so to ignore it is to introduce a fundamental blind spot into our analysis. This involves grasping the technical nettle, but that is unavoidable. We saw in Chapter 2 how design has a direct influence on end-user behaviour. We also saw in Chapter 3 how representationalism means that the text of the 'rule' (that is, the source code) and its operation are two halves of a whole: isomorphism between source code and the materiality of the artefact is to a great extent a given in the computational context. Rather than querying the motivations behind the design of a particular artefact's code (important though this is), the task then is to query what the code in fact does, and whether the normativity that it imposes is itself legitimate, separately from those anterior motivations. The distinction is nuanced but fundamental, for if we focus on only the motivation behind a design but fail to look critically at how that motivation is in fact instrumentalised, we risk not only failing to observe what the artefact actually does, but also – and potentially worse – sanctioning it in the erroneous belief that because the decision to use code was sound the implementation must also have been.

The aim therefore is to guide production of the 'moreness' of code (its instrumentality; Chapter 2) in ways that reduce its 'lessness' (its computational legalism; Chapter 3). The question is ultimately one of what the design affords the end-user (contestability, choice, transparency, and delay), legal institutions (appropriate and sufficient quality of evidence), and its own designer or manufacturer (oversight). The ultimate goal of digisprudence is fidelity to the input criteria of legality (Chapters 4 and 5) that ensure that

---

[2] There is a parallel here with Verbeek's discussion of anticipating the morality of a given set of technological mediations, and imposing restrictions where necessary. See P-P Verbeek, 'Materializing morality: Design ethics and technological mediation' (2006) 31 *Science, Technology, & Human Values* 361, 370, 372.

its technological normativity, whatever its substantive output functionality, includes mechanisms that ameliorate the path dependencies of computational legalism.

6.2 Mapping the Criteria

Below I map the Fullerian and legisprudential principles discussed in Chapter 4 onto the relevant characteristics of computational legalism, showing how they apply across the separate normative orders of institutional law and code. I then consider how the digisprudential affordances reflect the purposive goals of the principles, providing a baseline of legitimacy. There are overlaps between the characteristics and the suggested affordances – any given affordance does not apply only to ameliorate the specific characteristic indicated; instead, the idea is to consider them in a holistic fashion, the goal being to achieve more legitimate technological normativity through a concurrent sensitivity to each of the issues raised. Wintgens makes a similar claim about legisprudence, plotting the notional justifications of various norms on a 'graph', the horizontal axis representing at one side the principle of normativity and at the other the principle of temporality, and the vertical axis similarly representing the principle of alternativity and the principle of coherence (Figure 6.1).[3]

A given norm will be more or less justified according to each of the four legisprudential principles; a notional norm that is equally justified according to each of the principles would be plotted in the centre of the graph. An important point is that the particular circumstances surrounding the proposed norm will affect the extent to which it must be justified by each of them. For example, emergency legislation following a natural disaster might be justified despite a relative lack of in-depth fact-finding or foresight, because the alternatives would not implement the powers and duties necessary to facilitate the (presumably widely supported) purpose of mitigating the disaster.[4] This might mean there is strong justification under the principle of alternativity, but less under the principle of coherence, but that on balance the former is sufficient to justify the norm in the circumstances. In that situation, respecting the principle of temporality can provide justification from another direction – because of the emergency the design of the norm may not perfectly cohere to the rest of the system of norms, but if mechanisms

---

[3] Figure 6.1 is reproduced from L Wintgens, *Legisprudence: Practical Reason in Legislation* (Routledge 2012) 282.
[4] Ibid. 307.

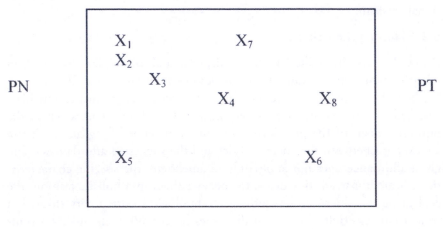

Figure 6.1 Differing justification of norms

for oversight are put in place, this may nevertheless justify its imposition, all things considered.[5]

In a similar fashion, the digisprudential affordances are not intended to be viewed in isolation, but rather to be seen as a set of elements that work in concert to achieve more legitimate configurations of technological normativity. Depending on the purpose and intended use of a particular artefact, the relevance of each principle will vary, and therefore so too will the justificatory contribution of each affordance. An artefact that includes none of the affordances is on balance unlikely to be legitimate.

The intention here is to contribute a set of 'normative anchor points'[6] that are explicitly oriented towards legal-theoretical concerns.[7] The exercise is

---

[5] At time of writing we are seeing this phenomenon play out in real time in relation to the COVID-19 pandemic, where lockdown regulations have built-in requirements for periodic reassessment. For an example, see section 12 of the Coronavirus (Scotland) (No. 2) Act 2020.

[6] E.g. R von Schomberg, 'A vision of responsible research and innovation' in R Owen, J Bessant and M Heintz (eds), *Responsible Innovation* (John Wiley & Sons 2013) 63 *et seq*.

[7] Cf. other frameworks for computer ethics. See for example Association for Computing Machinery, 'ACM Code of Ethics and Professional Conduct' (2018) <https://www.acm.org/about-acm/acm-code-of-ethics-and-professional-conduct> last accessed 4 March 2021; BC Stahl et al., 'From computer ethics to responsible research and innovation in ICT' (2014) 51 *Information & Management* 810.

necessarily qualitative to an extent, and therefore it requires human judgement and the willingness to do the right thing on the part of the designer. Table 6.1 maps the characteristics of computational legalism onto the Fullerian and legisprudential principles, and suggests the digisprudential affordances that can embody the purposive aims of those principles within code.

(a) Contestability as an Overarching Affordance

The central importance of facilitating contestability must be borne in mind as an overarching concern. This means keeping open the possibility of questioning the code (and by implication its creator) in a court of law. As we saw in the previous chapter, contestability is a central criterion for the maintenance of the rule of law in the computational context. From a strictly legal point of view, the ability to 'return' from the normative order of code to that of institutional law is an important part of retaining the role and the rule of law within the a-legal realm of code. Computational legalism militates against contestability: end-users must be able to understand the normativities they are being subjected to in order to mount any kind of legal challenge to them. As I will discuss below, resistance and transparency are aspects of this that are concerned with the ability of the end-user to 'see' and question the norms to which she is subjected. This is the user-centric side of the contestability coin, but on the other side are legal institutions, most importantly the courts.

Affording Evidential Scrutiny to Courts

In order for contestability to be properly embodied in code, courts must be afforded proper evidential scrutiny. If the end-user seeks to contest the code, she must be able to bring evidence of her complaint, and that evidence must be intelligible to the trier of fact. Whatever happens in the code-based normative order, the judicial process must retain its role as ultimate arbiter of any dispute. The affordance of contestability, then, is necessary not just to enable the end-user to understand the code's normativities sufficiently well that she can choose to contest them, but is necessary also to enable legal institutions to grapple with the code from an evidential perspective. This raises questions of due process vis-à-vis evidential quality and propriety, and how these interact with the design process. From an evidential perspective, certain standards must be met in order for an action to succeed; from a computational perspective, this means that affording those standards must be considered during the design process if valid contestability – and therefore legitimacy – is to be achieved. Without consideration of the need for contestability at the point of production, it will not be possible (or will be that much more difficult) at the stage of operation.

Table 6.1 Mapping legitimacy across domains: the digisprudential affordances

Characteristic of Computational Legalism	Fullerian Principle	Legisprudential Principle	Digisprudential Affordances
Ruleishness	Contradictory (5) or impossible (6) rules	Alternativity (PA); Normative density (PN)	**Transparency (provenance & purpose); Choice**
Opacity	Promulgation (2); Intelligibility (4)	Alternativity (PA); Normative density (PN); Coherence (PC) LoC_3	**Transparency (provenance & purpose); Transparency (operation)**
Immediacy	Contradictory (5) or impossible (6) rules; Frequency of change (7)	Normative density (PN); Temporality (PT)	**Delay; Choice**
Immutability	[In]frequency of change (7)	Temporality (PT); Coherence (PC) LoC_3	**Oversight; Choice**
Pervasiveness	–	Normative density (PN)	–
All of the Above	–	–	**Contestability**

The consequences of failing to afford contestability are demonstrated by the Post Office Horizon scandal, only recently resolved in favour of the sub-postmistress/sub-postmaster 'end-users' whose livelihoods were destroyed in part as a result of that failure.[8] There, a presumption of the infallibility of the Horizon computer system led in effect to a strict liability presumption that any discrepancies in the accounts of a Post Office branch could only be the result of fraud. At common law there is a presumption that deems a computer to be operating as expected unless there is explicit evidence to the contrary.[9] The evidential burden that this placed on the sub-postmistresses and sub-postmasters whose accounts showed discrepancies could not in practice be discharged, because the Horizon system removed their access to relevant system logs upon detection of an accounting shortfall.[10] Without access to evidence of the system's operation, those subsequently accused of fraud were unable to mount an effective defence to the effect that there must be bugs in the code causing the erroneous shortfalls. The code did in fact contain numerous bugs responsible for the mis-accounting, but these were not directly considered by the courts until *Bates* in 2019.[11] In the ensuing period – well over a decade – more than 1,000 sub-postmistresses and sub-postmasters lost their livelihoods, over 900 of them being wrongfully convicted of false accounting, fraud, and theft.[12]

Following *Bates*, it has been proposed that the common law presumption be reversed, so that code is assumed, instead, to be fallible.[13] This is on the

---

[8] K Peachey, 'Postmasters' huge step towards quashing convictions' *BBC News* (2 October 2020) <https://www.bbc.com/news/business-54384427> last accessed 4 March 2021.

[9] P Marshall, 'The harm that judges do – misunderstanding computer evidence: Mr Castleton's Story' (2020) 17 *Digital Evidence and Electronic Signature Law Review* 25, 26. The presumption has operated at common law since 1999, following (misguided) recommendations by the Law Commission of England & Wales that led to the repeal of s. 69 of the Police and Criminal Evidence Act 1984 that had required evidence of the computer's proper operation. See Law Commission, 'Evidence in criminal proceedings: Hearsay and related topics' (Law Commission 1997) LC245 para. 13.13–13.14.

[10] Marshall (n 9) 26–7. See *Bates & Ors v Post Office Ltd (No 6: Horizon Issues)* [2019] EWHC (QB) 3408, *per* Fraser J at [1000].

[11] For a summary of the issues likely to result in further litigation, see *Bates* (n 10), *per* Fraser J at [965]–[1030].

[12] Marshall (n 9) n 14. The article provides an upsetting account of the experiences of those affected by a combination of unethical behaviour on the part of the Post Office/Fujitsu (Horizon's developer) and the courts' uncritical trust in the Horizon code.

[13] PB Ladkin et al., 'The Law Commission presumption concerning the dependability of computer evidence' (2020) 17 *Digital Evidence and Electronic Signature Law Review* 1. For an argument that this does not adequately take into account the asymmetries of information inherent between the roles of designer and end-user, see A Hicks, 'The role of usability, power

basis that code is rarely if ever bug-free, even in safety-critical applications.[14] Viewed this way, the notion of reliability can be reframed as both a social and a technical standard,[15] thus wresting assessments of efficacy away from the lure of automation bias that were so evident in the Horizon scandal. Affording contestability necessitates access, and a system that is designed to prevent that access will, without appropriate additional safeguards, struggle to meet an appropriate standard of legitimacy. I discuss in the next chapter some approaches that can assist in implementing this institutional aspect of contestability during production.

Contestability is thus an overarching concern; a necessary backstop. Whatever the other merits or demerits of the design from a digisprudential perspective, it must in the end always be possible for the end-user to resort to court action to determine illegality (of whatever substantive form). This ensures the continuing role of the rule of law, notwithstanding code's existence as a separate a-legal normative order.

6.3 From Characteristics to Affordances

We come now to a central part of the book's synthesis, where the analysis of computational legalism and its negative effects meets the affordances that can ameliorate them. What follows is aspirational; the idea is to aim for legitimacy in privately designed code in the knowledge that on the one hand attaining absolute perfection is unlikely, but on the other that the characteristics of computational legalism make the attempt all the more important.

(a) Ruleishness

Code is extreme in its precision; it is not flexible by nature. While code rules can exhibit non-discrimination, in that they apply to every end-user completely regardless of their characteristics, this is a virtue only if the rule is

---

dynamics, and incentives in dispute resolutions around computer evidence' *Bentham's Gaze* (23 June 2020) <https://www.benthamsgaze.org/2020/06/23/the-role-of-usability-power-dynamics-and-incentives-in-dispute-resolutions-around-computer-evidence/> last accessed 4 March 2021; A Hicks and SJ Murdoch, 'Transparency enhancing technologies to make security protocols work for humans' in J Anderson et al. (eds), *Security Protocols XXVII*, vol. 12287 (Springer 2020).

14 In that context, reliability rates of one defect per 1,000 lines of code may be deemed 'robust' (Ladkin et al. (n 13) 2). By way of comparison, the Windows 10 operating system contains 50–60 million lines of code.

15 On which, see PB Ladkin, 'Robustness of software' (2020) 17 *Digital Evidence and Electronic Signature Law Review* 15, observing the central role of human concepts such as trust and the contextual acceptability of failure rates and severity in assessing code. This is relevant to the concept of 'tussle', discussed below.

legitimately designed.[16] As set out in Chapter 3, code rules execute in every situation where their predetermined requirements are met, they execute in no situations where those requirements are not met (no matter how close the circumstances are), and the exact consequences specified within the rule are all that will or can flow from its execution. They are thus by nature brittle in the extreme. This aspect of ruleishness lies at the heart of computational legalism.

This relates to the earlier discussion of constitutive norms and the threshold between a design's 'constitution', or the behavioural constraints which are 'wired in', and its merely 'regulative' aspects which provide the end-user with the latitude to decide whether or not to acquiesce to a suggested limitation on her freedom.

Digisprudential Affordance: Choice

Default configurations of code contribute to shaping an end-user's understanding of the behavioural possibilities it affords her. End-users tend to trust that the designer has made the 'right choice' for them, even where the code permits alternatives – the situation presented to the end-user is perceived to be normal, and even legitimate in pervasive systems. Once the artefact is operating, the outputs of its processes tend to be trusted by end-users, due in part to automation bias.[17]

The effects of immediacy and immutability can be countered through the appropriate affordance of configurability. For the latter characteristic, the ability to change the configuration of the system is by definition in opposition to the state of immutability. But the mere provision of choice is not sufficient on its own. To ameliorate ruleishness and empower the end-user, the choice must be between appropriate options and must be given at the appropriate time,[18] otherwise we have the code equivalent of long terms of use documents which notionally inform the end-user but which in practice leave her bewildered. Configurability *per se* can thus become a counterproductive burden, particularly for naïve end-users who may be confused and intimidated by too many options.[19] At any rate, customisation is viewed by many end-users as time-consuming, and so they avoid it even where objectively it could benefit them by enabling them to choose options that reflect their interests

---

[16] Bańkowski and Schafer (n 1) 46.

[17] DK Citron, 'Technological due process' (2008) 85 *Washington University Law Review* 1249, 1271–2.

[18] JP Kesan and RC Shah, 'Setting software defaults: Perspectives from law, computer science and behavioral economics' (2006) 82 *Notre Dame Law Review* 583, 601.

[19] Ibid. 627.

and/or preferences.[20] Thus, the ways in which code affords configurability must be considered in advance if the relevant audience is to be appropriately empowered by them.

'TUSSLES' AND DESIGNING FOR CHOICE
The notion of 'tussle' in computer science touches on the issue of choice and the role of design in responding to different parties' interests.[21] 'Tussle points' are points in the design of code that implicate conflicting interests. Such conflicts can be technical, legal, social, or economic, and ought to be anticipated by the designer:

> Our position is that the laws of men and the so-called whims of bureaucrats are part of the fabric of society, like it or not. They are some of the building blocks of tussle, and must be accepted as such. We, as technical designers, should not try to deny the reality of the tussle, but instead recognize our power to shape it.[22]

The commercial attractions of computational legalism are in conflict with the goals of legitimacy, and thus they create a 'tussle space': enterprise uses the former to advance its interests – ruleishness and immutability provide predictability; opacity provides protection of commercial secrets and can hide profitable but dubious normativities; immediacy gives feedback and marketable results. There is thus a potential tussle between the interests of the end-user and the enterprise that wishes to channel her behaviour in predictable (and profitable) ways. Digisprudential legitimacy seeks to uphold basic 'constitutional' safeguards against illegitimate regulation of behaviour, but these are by nature absent in the default conditions of computational legalism.

Anticipating points of tussle during the production phase is crucial to avoiding problems during operation. One approach to dealing with tussles is to design for choice, the premise being that the design ought to anticipate and allow for different possibilities: '[r]igid designs will be broken; designs that permit variation will flex under pressure and survive.'[23] Although Clark et al. are concerned mainly with infrastructural design, from a digisprudential perspective we can think of designs that afford spaces that facilitate end-user

---

[20] Ibid. 598. For an early and influential study on this point, see WE Mackay, 'Triggers and barriers to customizing software' in *Proceedings of the SIGCHI Conference on Human Factors in Computing Systems Reaching through Technology – CHI '91* (ACM Press 1991).

[21] DD Clark et al., 'Tussle in cyberspace: Defining tomorrow's Internet' (2005) 13 *IEEE/ACM Transactions on Networking (ToN)* 462.

[22] Ibid. 473.

[23] Ibid. 466.

autonomy (all things being equal – the notional scope for exercising autonomy depends of course on the fundamental purpose of the design). This
accords with the requirement, identified in Chapter 5, that code permit individuals to make choices in order to preserve their capacity for moral action.

Designing for choice also fits the legisprudential principle of alternativity, which as we saw concerns the legitimate use of 'rigid' rules that admit of
no latitude, versus alternatives that incentivise or suggest courses of action.
Leaving the tussle space open to allow for choice thus shifts constitutive
power away from the designer.[24] The principle of alternativity in this context
requires that (1) the implementation of unconfigurable normativity in the
code be more desirable than not, and (2) the use of a strict rule *per se* rather
than some less ruleish mechanism be necessary, for example a suggested
default, or a configurable option. The first speaks to the enterprise's business
model and how this is articulated in code, raising some potentially existential
questions as to the fundamental desirability of a given approach or product.
As Hartzog warns, 'too often industry wants the freedom to experiment on
the public without accepting the responsibility for the harm they cause'.[25]
We might then think of a kind of Hippocratic oath for code – 'first, do no
harm' – leading the responsible designer/enterprise to conclude that the feature or product should not be developed at all.[26] Shifted into the present context, a computational principle of alternativity would assess first whether a
given (dis)affordance/inscription is necessary for the operation of the artefact
and the business model being pursued. If it is not, then *a priori* it should not
be included in the design because it represents an unnecessary and unjustified
limitation of the end-user's freedom.

If that element of the design is necessary, however, the question then
becomes one of the ruleishness of the implementation – how 'wired in' does
the functionality need to be to achieve the designer's goal? Could the code
require the end-user to exercise a choice, or perhaps provide a passive configurable option? Or does the purpose of the code imply the need for 'nudging'/inscription, or even the requirement (wiring in) of one of the possible
options to the exclusion of all others? The latter is the most 'ruleish' form
of technological normativity, while the former approaches are progressively

---

[24] Ibid. 473.
[25] W Hartzog, *Privacy's Blueprint: The Battle to Control the Design of New Technologies* (Harvard University Press 2018) 85.
[26] AD Selbst et al., 'Fairness and abstraction in sociotechnical systems' (Social Science Research Network 2018) SSRN Scholarly Paper ID 3265913, 13–14 <https://papers.ssrn.com/abstract=3265913> last accessed 4 March 2021.

less constraining.[27] As with the legisprudential principle of alternativity, the decision to choose a more 'ruleish' (and therefore less choice-oriented) design approach must be justified because of the correspondingly larger limitation it places on freedom. I will consider this issue further in the discussion below of default choices.

The anticipation of conflicting interests that the concept of tussle implies is connected to the notion of agonism in a democracy,[28] the theory that adversarial debate can be fruitful where it enables contrasting points of view to be ventilated and compromise thereby to be achieved. 'Inviting dissent' in this way, which can be consciously facilitated by design,[29] is ultimately at 'the core of both democracy and the rule of law'.[30] For Hildebrandt, this is reflected in ex ante participatory design processes like constructive technology assessment[31] which aim to achieve a 'settlement' during the design process that takes into account the views of those with a stake in the outcome.[32] I have already suggested that such processes are unlikely to be used in many design contexts, and particularly in small and medium enterprises. As previously noted, however, design for all need not entail design with all.[33] Initiatives like constructive technology assessment seek to legitimise a design by the fact of having involved stakeholders in decisions as to its substantive characteristics – the design is legitimate because those affected by it have in some sense approved it. This is a separate concern from digisprudential legitimacy, since such processes are built around the value of participation, rather than an underlying theory of what provides legitimacy.[34] Recalling the earlier discussion of input and output legitimacy, these approaches follow a 'thick' conception of legitimacy that is based on particulars, rather than a 'thinner' formal conception that is separate from, and prior to, the substantive content of participants' views on the merits of a design. The 'constitutional' concerns

---

[27] Recall the discussion in Chapter 2 of the spectrum of technological normativity.

[28] M Hildebrandt, 'Algorithmic regulation and the rule of law' (2018) 376 *Philosophical Transactions of the Royal Society A* 20170355, 7–8.

[29] See generally C DiSalvo, *Adversarial Design* (MIT Press 2012) and JL Davis, *How Artifacts Afford: The Power and Politics of Everyday Things* (MIT Press 2020) chapter 6.

[30] Hildebrandt, 'Algorithmic regulation and the rule of law' (n 28) 7.

[31] JW Schot, 'Constructive technology assessment and technology dynamics: The case of clean technologies' (1992) 17 *Science, Technology, & Human Values* 36.

[32] Recall the discussion in the previous chapter contrasting input and output assessments of code legitimacy.

[33] A Pols and A Spahn, 'Designing for the values of democracy and justice' in J van den Hoven, PE Vermaas and I van de Poel (eds), *Handbook of Ethics, Values, and Technological Design: Sources, Theory, Values and Application Domains* (Springer 2015) 351.

[34] Ibid. 353.

of digisprudence are sited at an earlier point in the design process than is the question of whether stakeholders have had their views taken into account. The two do not conflict, and a design process can certainly involve both, but if the design is not otherwise digisprudentially legitimate then the fact that a participatory process was used to shape it will not by itself provide legitimacy of the more fundamental kind I propose.

Nevertheless, the preservation of agonistic space can stand as a constitutional principle for code design, along the lines of tussle: by anticipating in advance the points at which tussle is likely to arise in the course of the design's operation, it is possible to avoid imposing one path or outcome for that tussle ahead of time, thus preserving the space for both choice and agonism. This expanded view of designing for choice enjoins the designer consciously to 'retreat' from any impulse to impose a constitutive outcome, thus preserving a space for agonism, for tussle, within the operating geography of the design itself. The domain of the morality of duty (computational legalism; external limitations on freedom) is reduced, and the domain of aspiration ('legality'; individual conceptions of freedom) accordingly expanded. This twist on agonism operates at runtime but is necessarily facilitated by decisions made at design time. 'Agonism' is in this sense a feature of the artefact's operation, rather than of the design process, although of course both may be present (that is, facilitating participation in the design process on the one hand, and the design affording space for agonism during its operation on the other). The extent to which implementation of this extended affordance of choice will be possible or plausible will depend on the intended use of the artefact. The design of a single-function Internet of Things (IoT) device like the Amazon Dash Button, for example, is less likely to allow for agonistic space than is the design of a social network service. This is an example of how different artefacts can and will reflect the digisprudential affordances to differing degrees.

An important practical design mechanism for facilitating tussle spaces is the modularising of an artefact's functionalities in ways that maintain a separation of interests: 'functions that are within a tussle space should be logically separated from functions outside of that space'.[35] This idea connects with the principle of normative density. In terms of the goals of that principle, the code should avoid bundling together code norms that are not conceptually related, forcing the end-user to acquiesce to multiple heterogeneous normativities simultaneously when she might be willing to accept some but would prefer to resist others. This idea is reflected in the GDPR's provisions requiring consent to be a genuine and free choice, requiring separate consents

---

[35] Clark et al. (n 21) 466.

for separate operations, and preventing the bundling of consent along with performance where the former is not necessary for the latter.[36]

When they exhibit computational legalism, the aggregated normativities of a system can lead to exponential negative effects as each of the legalistic characteristics amplifies the impact of the others. Modularisation can isolate discrete elements of normativity, perhaps along the boundaries of specific features or functions, thus enhancing the end-user's ability to accurately comprehend the system's effects by avoiding conflation of what should be conceptually isolated issues. Only the designer has the ability to 'modularise the design along tussle boundaries, so that one tussle does not spill over and distort unrelated issues'.[37] For example, in a smart thermostat, code profiling the end-user implicates a tussle involving different interests (the end-user's data protection rights versus the enterprise conducting its business). The functionality of that code is distinct from functionality intended to control the heating system efficiently, where the relevant interest is the end-user's need for domestic warmth balanced against wasteful energy consumption.[38] Modularising these discrete functionalities enables the end-user to understand them separately and to respond to them in different ways. This highlights the relationship (and tension) between default configurations and the affordance of choice.

DEFAULT CHOICES

Even in the 'offline' world, defaults are all around us – some initial configuration of architecture is an inevitability, which in turn implies the inherent non-neutrality of technologies.[39] We have seen at various points so far how this observation applies even more strongly in the computational context. It is not possible for a designer to leave open to interpretation what the design of the artefact should be in the way that it is possible for the legislator deliberately to leave the meaning of a textual norm somewhat open. Some choice must be made by the designer that constrains the infinite possibilities of the computational *tabula rasa*, and so intervening to ensure those initial decisions are legitimate becomes all the more necessary.

---

[36] GDPR, Arts. 7(2) and 7(4); Recitals 32, 42, and 43.

[37] Clark et al. (n 21) 466.

[38] The latter of course represents all our interests. For a critical discussion of the problems with smart thermostats, see B Krebs, 'IoT reality: Smart devices, dumb defaults' *Krebs on Security* (16 February 2008) <https://krebsonsecurity.com/2016/02/iot-reality-smart-devices-dumb-defaults/> last accessed 4 March 2021.

[39] M Hildebrandt, 'Legal protection by design: Objections and refutations' (2011) 5 *Legisprudence* 223, 238–9.

As Shah and Sandvig note, to rely on default settings is *de facto* to outsource decision-making to designers, shifting the agential emphasis away from both the end-user and the democratic state. It is thus necessary to 'push and prod developers to set default settings that comport with established societal concerns'.[40] If one of those concerns is the legitimacy of behavioural regulation, then the aspects of the code that are made 'chooseable' must in turn accord with that spirit. The number of choices and their quality (that is, what substantive functionality they enable the end-user to configure) are thus important design questions with respect to the scope of autonomy that they provide the end-user, and so too is the way in which these affordances of choice are communicated (signified) to her through the design. The provision of choice for choice's sake does not beget legitimacy if those choices do not facilitate the exercise of true autonomy.

Kesan and Shah identify a spectrum of design mutability, from 'wired-in' functionality that cannot be changed at one end, through default settings that can be changed, and on to the notional 'free choice' of full customisation at the other[41] (but it must be remembered that even this level of configurability can never be completely 'free', because as I noted above the initial commitments of the design by definition circumscribe possibilities, which in turn limits the area within which the end-user can exercise autonomy). The extent to which end-users are aware of the control they have over configuration is a core concern,[42] and is entirely contingent upon the affordance of choice being perceived – it is not enough if the affordance is merely real[43] but unknown (or so complex as in practice to disafford[44]). The authors identify two apparent motivations driving real-world design decisions about setting defaults, namely efficiency and the consideration of novice end-users.[45] They note the vagueness of these goals, particularly with regard to who might be considered a novice, and by whose standards 'efficiency' is to be judged, particularly since

---

[40] RC Shah and C Sandvig, 'Software defaults as de facto regulation: The case of the wireless internet' (2008) 11 *Information, Communication & Society* 25, 42.

[41] Kesan and Shah (n 18) 591 *et seq*. See also LF Cranor and RN Wright, 'Influencing software usage' (1998) arXiv:cs/9809018, 6–7 <http://arxiv.org/abs/cs/9809018> last accessed 4 March 2021.

[42] Kesan and Shah (n 18) 597.

[43] These distinctions were discussed in 'Real and Perceived Affordance' in Section 2.1.

[44] This is a common criticism levied at open source projects, whose configurability gives the end-user great notional power but whose ease-of-use may in practice fail to afford that configurability to those without the necessary expertise. See K Noyes, 'Is Linux really harder to use?' *PCWorld* (2 August 2010) <https://www.pcworld.com/article/202364/is_linux_really_harder_to_use.html> last accessed 4 March 2021.

[45] Kesan and Shah (n 18) 600.

the effect of a default will often impact on 'fuzzy' values that are difficult to calculate in such terms.[46] The latter principle plays a central role in programming practice; we will see below in the discussion of immediacy and the affordance of delay how the goal of increasing or improving 'efficiency' – pervasive among technologists – is not necessarily desirable in every case, even where there is technical scope for achieving it.

In terms of guiding design, Kesan and Shah draw on legal notions of default rules to consider the threshold between what configuration is 'wired in' (immutable) and what is set merely as a default.[47] Where the configuration is 'wired in', it must both notify the end-user and permit a judicial remedy (that is, be contestable). This accords with the affordances of contestability, transparency, and delay. The system ought to provide 'an easy-to-use interface that allows users to configure the software according to their preferences'.[48] This again is of course about the affordances of that interface, which should follow the design and usability conventions end-users are generally familiar with.[49] Added to this, a framework of principles guides designers in setting the initial defaults, the starting point of which is the 'would have wanted' standard. This requires anticipation of what the parties (the enterprise and end-user) would likely have negotiated, had that been a possibility.[50] This principle applies in situations where the setting does not materially affect a fundamental societal concern, such as (they suggest) privacy or online security. To those I might add normative legitimacy, with all the elements described here.

The next requirement is that where there is an information imbalance between designer and end-user, the default must be set to protect the latter, with appropriate information or guidance provided to her should she wish to change it. This is of course inconvenient if the functionality in question is the very purpose of the device. Kesan and Shah discuss the cookie settings in a web browser, arguing that the imbalance of information[51] means the default setting should be to reject them.[52] Should web companies wish them

---

[46] Ibid.

[47] Ibid. 614 *et seq.*

[48] Ibid. 615–16.

[49] Norman calls these 'conventions'. See DA Norman, 'Affordance, conventions, and design' (1999) 6 *interactions* 38, 40 *et seq.*

[50] Kesan and Shah (n 18) 618.

[51] That is, end-users do not readily understand what cookies are and what they are used for. See L Edwards, 'Data protection and e-privacy: From spam and cookies to big data, machine learning and profiling' in L Edwards (ed.), *Law, Policy and the Internet* (Hart 2018) 126 *et seq.*

[52] This is at odds with current practice. See the discussion ibid. and n 134 in Chapter 3 and its accompanying text.

to be enabled, presumably to facilitate the (increasingly discredited) business model of online behavioural advertising, they then must explain to the end-user their purpose and how to enable them[53] (this relates to the affordance of transparency of purpose, discussed below). The idea behind such 'penalty defaults' is that before the end-user can choose the non-default setting, the burden is on the designer to explain its effect. The default is therefore what the party with the greater understanding of the code (the designer or enterprise) would not have wanted, as a delaying mechanism that allows for the end-user to be informed (this is connected with 'friction' and the affordance of delay, discussed below).

The next principle suggested by Kesan and Shah also justifies this 'would not have wanted' standard, based on the economic concept of 'externalities', the broader (potentially negative) effects of the system on third parties. The default setting should reduce externalities or, if the stakes are particularly high, there should be no latitude and the beneficial option should be 'wired in'.[54] An example might be an IoT webcam that is configured by default to stream whatever it captures, with no authentication mechanism enabled by default, or a generic default password such as 'admin'. The negative effects of such designs, especially given the potential pervasiveness of such technology, can be significant.[55] The idea is that although it is convenient for the end-user (and therefore commercially attractive) if the camera starts working immediately, the 'would not have wanted' standard might require that streaming is not enabled by default and that a (strong) password must be set before the device will connect to the network. Anecdotally, this has been the direction of travel in the design of domestic routers, where instead of merely suggesting that end-users change the administration or WiFi authentication passwords/keys, the device is preconfigured with unique and strong options set at the factory.

In terms of design, the cognitive biases mentioned in Chapter 3[56] can strengthen the 'stickiness'[57] of a default setting, militating against the end-user exercising choice; this implies an even greater responsibility to design

---

53 Kesan and Shah (n 18) 621.

54 Ibid. 621–2.

55 For chilling real-world examples of precisely this, see JM Porup, '"Internet of Things" security is hilariously broken and getting worse' *Ars Technica UK* (23 January 2016) <http://arstechnica.co.uk/security/2016/01/how-to-search-the-internet-of-things-for-photos-of-sleeping-babies/> last accessed 4 March 2021.

56 See 'Default Configurations' in Section 3.2.

57 CR Sunstein and RH Thaler, 'Libertarian paternalism is not an oxymoron' (2003) 70 *University of Chicago Law Review* 1159, 1175.

that initial configuration with the appropriate set of interests in mind.[58] Furthermore, the prominence of the setting in an interface can affect end-users' awareness of it, and indeed the designer can explicitly draw attention to defaults that require special attention but do not cross the threshold to merit being 'wired in' (for example the 'would not have wanted' defaults just discussed – making the administration password for a domestic router 'wired in' would be an odd design choice). Attention can be drawn by, for example, alerts requiring the end-user to confirm a choice. She might also be required to make a choice when the device is first used, with no preselected option to influence her decision or option to bypass the configuration request. Such measures can contribute to the beneficial form of delay I discuss below. Importantly, the design of these affordances of choice must take into account 'framing effects',[59] or the way in which wording affects comprehension of one or other of the available options. The design should not promote the enterprise's aim at the expense of digisprudential legitimacy, and of course the use of the adversarial design approaches that we saw in Chapter 2[60] is *de facto* illegitimate.

This analysis of choice *qua* configurability gives added texture to bare suggestions that technological normativity preserve the possibility of choice, and that more choice is *per se* better. The affordances of the artefact ought to reflect the spirit of digisprudential legitimacy at each point of the end-user's 'journey' through the artefact's inscriptions. More choice is not sufficient on its own to legitimate code if it is not the right kind of choice; the design must afford meaningful spaces for the exercise of autonomy and not simply more options. This might raise difficult existential questions as to the desirability of a given artefact or business model, but that of course is precisely the point.

Blockchain Applications
Blockchain applications pose potentially significant problems from the perspective of affording choice. We saw in Chapter 1 how one of their primary attractions is the potential immutability of the code, owing both to how it is stored on the chain and the decentralisation of the network. If the possibility of choice has not been anticipated in advance, the central benefit to blockchains of tamper-resistance becomes a hindrance to its exercise at run-time. To afford choice, then, it is especially necessary to choose carefully in advance how much of the code is ruleish and how much relies on external contingency, including end-user input. This is intimately connected to, and

---

[58] Kesan and Shah (n 18) 633.
[59] Sunstein and Thaler (n 57) 1179–83.
[60] See 'Disaffordance' in Section 2.2.

overlaps with, the issue of immutability, discussed below: the fixity of the code that flows from its storage on, and execution by, a blockchain means that the design of the threshold between wired-in and configurable code is centrally important, particularly given the additional complication of blockchain applications' execution of logic that is automatic and has potentially legally relevant implications.[61]

If blockchain applications are to be used to implement legally relevant operations such as transfers of assets, one approach to ameliorating ruleishness is to reconceive of them as mere 'custodians' of the multi-interpretability of language, and thus to change emphasis on what ought to be implemented computationally. The Ricardian Contract, for example, aims not to automate the purposive elements of a contract-like agreement (the goal of some smart contract maximalists), but rather to maintain the flexibility of textual agreement and to augment it with a limited amount of coded functionality that complements, rather than replaces, the latter.[62] The (natural language) text of the agreement is 'wrapped' in a minimal code semantics that enables basic code-based features such as tamper-resistance and provenance checking, through the use of hashing and public key cryptography. Because the actual text of the agreement retains all the possibilities of multi-interpretive nuance that natural language accommodates,[63] the notional immutability of the agreement can nevertheless be combined with the inherent flexibility of expression. In other words, the execution of the agreement remains 'human'; the contribution of code as a medium is in providing the benefits, ancillary to the substance of the agreement, of immutability and provenance checking. Any exercise of choice, then, takes place outside of the code. The extent to which this is practically useful from the perspective of the technology remains to be seen; limiting the ruleishness of blockchain code to such ancillary benefits in this way might in practice undermine their perceived value in the first place – but the benefit of avoiding a computationally legalistic outcome is evident.

Other approaches that maintain the full(er) instrumental utility of code will require the design to afford the end-user choice at key moments. The

---

[61] KEC Levy, 'Book-smart, not street-smart: Blockchain-based smart contracts and the social workings of law' (2017) 3 *Engaging Science, Technology, and Society* 1, 3.

[62] I Grigg, 'The Ricardian Contract' in *Proceedings of the First IEEE International Workshop on Electronic Contracting* (IEEE 2004). This chimes with Wagner's argument in favour of 'more law and less software'. See RP Wagner, 'On software regulation' (2005) 78 *Southern California Law Review* 457.

[63] M Hildebrandt, 'The adaptive nature of text-driven law' (2021) 1 *Journal of Cross-disciplinary Research in Computational Law* <https://journalcrcl.org/crcl/article/view/2> last accessed 19 April 2021.

artefact's inscriptions then need to be sensitive to the architectural implications of blockchains – their particular brand of technological normativity and *de facto* immutability from the perspective of the end-user. The greater the normative impact of the code's logic (its normative density), the greater the need for choice to be preserved; in practice the implementation of this will vary, involving a mixture of notifications to the end-user, the appropriate selection of oracles, appropriately defined choices, and logic that can deal appropriately with the outcomes. Given the peculiar characteristics of blockchains, whether designers can anticipate all the relevant points where choice is necessary is at the very least questionable. Indeed, these requirements may fundamentally undermine the premise of blockchain applications, particularly those (such as distributed autonomous organisations) predicated on their ability to execute operations with minimal or no human input. The existential question is thus raised again of whether such applications can be legitimate *a priori*.

The Internet of Things

A common characteristic of IoT devices is a minimal or even absent interface. One way of affording choice is to provide better, more sophisticated interfaces, perhaps through the connection of the IoT artefact to another device that itself affords more complex interactions. This could be a smartphone or a television, which in turn facilitates the presentation and signifying of choice affordances to the end-user. This is a difficult balance to strike, because of course many IoT devices are intended to have a minimal number of functions. In the next section I discuss the Amazon Dash Button, which consists of a single button but whose background functionality is extremely complex; in that case the affordance of choice at the point of use is dramatically curtailed, this being central to its *raison d'être* – its only real use is the pressing of a button, but the number of configurable variables that are relevant to the process that is put in train by doing so is significant, as we will see.

(b) Opacity

In the computational context opacity is connected most closely with the Fullerian principles of promulgation and intelligibility, and the legisprudential principles of alternativity (PA) and normative density (PN). In terms of promulgation, Fuller is concerned that citizens should know (or be in a position to find out) the rules by which they are governed, in part as a check against them being disregarded by the authorities administering them (this relates also to his eighth principle, requiring congruence between the declared rule and the official action that flows from it). This of course enables citizens to observe their operation, a prerequisite for contesting it. In order to be valid, the rules should also be intelligible; obscurity and incoherence can make legality difficult or impossible to attain.

Under legisprudence, opacity is targeted by the PA and the PN. Under the former, the inherent opacity of code again imbues the decision to implement a rule with extra normative impact as compared with a less ruleish measure. The inability of the end-user to see the rule she is subject to is emphasised in the computational context, and so its use is subject to a higher threshold of justification. As before, that threshold is lowered when a less 'ruleish' design measure is employed, but at all times the fact of code's opacity must also be kept in mind. This in turn speaks to the PN: the more opaque the code, the more difficult it may be for the end-user to appreciate the aggregate 'density' of technological normativity her behaviour is subject to. The PN expects there to be a proportionate connection between the policy aim and the means by which it is achieved, with threats of sanction at the 'denser' end of the scale and mere suggestions towards the 'lighter' end. In terms of justification, the use of a particular design technique must be justified in the context and in light of the other principles, particularly if there are alternative mechanisms that might have achieved the same end in a more digisprudentially legitimate fashion. We have seen how the geography of code is often taken by the end-user to be a 'natural fact', rather than merely one possibility among infinite others.[64] This opacity of normative impact is particularly strong where the configuration of (dis)affordances and inscriptions strongly guides the end-user's behaviour; the need to legitimate such impositions is all the stronger in such situations.

Digisprudential Affordance: Transparency of Provenance
An important aspect of affording transparency, connected to the affordance of contestability, is that of provenance. This can be problematic when even apparently simple digital systems are a bricolage of multiple components, often from different sources[65] – in many, perhaps most, cases, code artefacts are 'a mix of a Frankenstein and a Matryoshka doll concealing dozens of services'.[66] Designers ought to afford reasonable notice of the sources of the code

---

[64] See the affordance of choice above, and 'Default Configurations' in Section 3.2.

[65] P Swartz, 'White boys' code' in *Division III: Essays in Programs as Literature* (Hampshire College 2007) 34–6; S Gürses and J van Hoboken, 'Privacy after the agile turn' in E Selinger, J Polonetsky and O Tene (eds), *The Cambridge Handbook of Consumer Privacy* (Cambridge University Press 2018); D Oberle et al., 'Engineering compliant software: Advising developers by automating legal reasoning' (2012) 9 *SCRIPTed* 280.

[66] Gürses and van Hoboken (n 65) 584.

in their systems (or at least provide a means to find out[67]), so as to inform and to afford contestability.[68] Recent scrutiny of online behavioural advertising has shown just how large the network of unseen third parties operating in the background can be, including situations where the design of a website's interface might suggest to the end-user that there is only one provider involved.[69] The same is often true of other digital artefacts whose back-end processing relies on a host of services (and third-party code) that the end-user is unlikely to be aware of (I return to the theme of bricolage in code production in Chapter 7). Providing access to this information is a necessary part of facilitating *transparency of provenance*.

Digisprudential Affordance: Transparency of Purpose
The bricolage of code's provenance in turn raises the question of its purposive functionalities. From a legitimation perspective, there is a connection here between what the code is designed to do and the third ('environmental') level of coherence in the legisprudential scheme. According to the latter, a rule is never justified on purely internal legal grounds, but must be supported by some external, non-legal theory that independently justifies its character. In the code context, transparency under this rubric will require information as to the reason for a given piece of functionality, where this is not self-evidently the artefact's *raison d'être* – in other words, unexpected functionality must be justified according to something other than the commercial rationality, internal to the perspective of the designer-cum-legislator, of profit maximisation. We saw above the smart thermometer whose design creates a tussle of interests, between regulating the end-user's domestic heating and profiling her habits for profit, the latter functionality not being something reasonably within the scope of what the end-user would expect from a thermostat. The normativity of such functionality ought to be justified via the affordance of transparency, and where this cannot be done the function should not be included in the design. Another real-world example is the inclusion of a geolocator in a smartphone torch application – transparency ought to be

---

[67] I discuss the contrasting ideas of the 'monitoring citizen' versus the 'well-informed citizen' below.

[68] One method of charting the sources of third-party code involved in a project is known as a 'dependency graph'. See for example 'Exploring the dependencies of a repository' *GitHub Docs* <https://docs.github.com/en/enterprise-server@2.22/github/visualizing-repository-data-with-graphs/exploring-the-dependencies-of-a-repository> last accessed 4 March 2021.

[69] See for example Z Yu et al., 'Tracking the trackers' in *Proceedings of the 25th International Conference on World Wide Web – WWW '16* (ACM Press 2016). The authors of the study found that 95 per cent of websites accessed by its German participants contained potential third-party trackers.

afforded on a similar basis, because determining the end-user's location is by no means a standard function of a torch.[70] The designer must then consider from where this unorthodox function of geolocation is justified, given the affordances commonly expected of torches. This form of transparency might be termed *transparency of purpose*.[71]

With each form of transparency, the designer must not succumb to the transparency fallacy, where essentially any function can be included in the code provided the end-user is given ostensible 'notice and choice'.[72] In that vein, Pols and Spahn suggest the 'monitoring citizen' as a better normative ideal than the 'well-informed citizen' that such practices envisage.[73] While the notion of a fully informed end-user might in principle be desirable, the complexity and pervasiveness of code means it can only ever be a mirage.[74] The 'monitoring citizen', on the other hand, is empowered to find out information when she needs to: '[t]he Monitoring Citizen does not *know* everything that is going on but can *monitor* it successfully and can investigate and contest policy when needed.'[75] This ideal is more plausible than aiming for some notion of 'real' or 'full' transparency, and it provides a guiding principle for design: the aim is to empower the end-user by affording her access to appropriate information about the operation and purposes of the code she is interacting with. One can think here of an analogy with legislative procedure: in addition to the citizen being able to access directly the legislative rule in the statutory document (cf. Fuller's first principle), it is also possible for her to access explanatory notes, impact assessments, Hansard, and other ancillary material in order to glean a deeper understanding of the purpose of a piece of legislation.

---

[70] Hartzog (n 25) 24. See also Federal Trade Commission, 'Android flashlight app developer settles FTC charges it deceived consumers' (Federal Trade Commission, 5 December 2013) <https://www.ftc.gov/news-events/press-releases/2013/12/android-flashlight-app-developer-settles-ftc-charges-it-deceived> last accessed 4 March 2021.

[71] Here we begin to touch the edges of the fields of computer ethics and responsible research and innovation. These lie beyond the legal-philosophical analysis of technological normativity that I am principally concerned with, although the connection is worth exploring further. See for example S Vallor, *Technology and the Virtues: A Philosophical Guide to a Future Worth Wanting* (Oxford University Press 2016); von Schomberg (n 6); L Floridi, *The Ethics of Information* (Oxford University Press 2013).

[72] Hartzog (n 25) 68 *et seq.*

[73] Pols and Spahn (n 33) 348.

[74] Such a goal also has the effect of shifting responsibility away from the enterprise and onto the citizen as *homo economicus*, a neoliberal orthodoxy that digisprudence seeks to counter.

[75] Pols and Spahn (n 33) 348 (emphasis supplied; references omitted).

Digisprudential Affordance: Transparency of Operation

The most obvious mechanism here is transparency in the imposition of normativity, in the form of documenting the use of a design that lies at a particular point on the normativity spectrum or actively informing the end-user of this fact. As we saw above, however, transparency is a contested concept. In the context of machine learning systems, it has been criticised as a means by which engineers can 'whitewash' decisions that are antagonistic to end-users' interests;[76] similar concerns apply in the code-driven context. Transparency as a goal can be framed such that including descriptions of functionality in lengthy terms documents that notionally inform the end-user is legitimate, when in practice it does little to illuminate what is actually going on.[77] The (ideological) belief is that simply providing more information will enable end-users to make informed choices about which products can and cannot fulfil their preferences, thus leading to greater competition and better products by dint of the operation of the market[78] (see the normative distinction between the 'monitoring citizen' and the 'well-informed citizen' just discussed).

Other work argues for solutions that do not involve the end-user directly. For example, the source code that underpins regulatory software systems could be required to be open – viewable – in order that it can be audited by third parties.[79] Proposals of this kind may be plausible for public sector regulators,[80] but as the 'code wars' in the late 1990s to mid-2000s showed, commercial enterprise has been reticent if not actively hostile to the idea of opening up the proprietary code at the core of its products and services.[81] Others have suggested an escrow system, where an artefact's source code is

---

[76] See for example L Edwards and M Veale, 'Slave to the algorithm: Why a right to an explanation is probably not the remedy you are looking for' (2017) 16 *Duke Law & Technology Review* 18.

[77] Hartzog (n 25) chapter 2; M Piekarski and W Wachowski, 'Artefacts as social things: Design-based approach to normativity' (2018) 22 *Techné: Research in Philosophy and Technology* 400, 414–15.

[78] O Ben-Shahar and CE Schneider, 'The failure of mandated disclosure' (2011) *University of Pennsylvania Law Review* 647.

[79] DK Citron, 'Open code governance' (2008) *University of Chicago Legal Forum* 355; L Lessig, *Code: Version 2.0* (Basic Books 2006) chapter 8. Both authors are specifically concerned with abuse by public institutions.

[80] The European Commission, for example, follows such a mandate. See its 'Open Source Software Strategy' (European Commission 2019) <https://ec.europa.eu/info/departments/informatics/open-source-software-strategy_en> last accessed 4 March 2021.

[81] This may be changing, however. See for example E Angelova, 'Microsoft embraces open source' (2018) *Fordham Intellectual Property, Media & Entertainment Law Journal* <http://www.fordhamiplj.org/2018/11/28/microsoft-embraces-open-source/> last accessed 4 March 2021.

held by a trusted third party who can be required to release it by a court if litigation should arise.[82]

Neither of these suggested approaches takes into account the full context and texture of the code's materiality. (Dis)affordance and inscription speak to more than just the bare logic of the code, so while it is true that a great deal can be gleaned from code by studying it (I will discuss some possibilities in Chapter 7), a broader sensitivity to qualitative design concepts is required to fully appreciate its effects in operation, particularly those that impact the end-user. Perhaps more importantly, such approaches are not based on input legitimacy, because they operate as a kind of insurance policy to be invoked after malfeasance has been suspected or detected. Relying on ex post assessment does nothing to avoid the production of illegitimate code in the first place; by the same token, if no issues are detected, the harmful code will simply continue to operate, potentially indefinitely.

The goal of transparency in this context should not, therefore, be limited to the literal openness of source code. As we saw in Chapter 2, design can signify to the end-user what the functionality of the system is and what it allows her to do.[83] What matters is comprehension, not just notification, and so it is incumbent on the designer to ensure as far as reasonably possible that the end-user's mental model of the system matches what it actually does.[84] This model is constructed from various sources, to a greater or lesser extent under the designer's control, including advertisements, press releases, instruction manuals, and of course the artefact's interface itself. Empathy with the end-user also requires acknowledgement from the designer that, with her intimate knowledge of the system's operation, her own conceptual model is likely to differ significantly from the situated (and necessarily less informed) understanding of the end-user.[85]

Similar considerations arise in relation to the legisprudential principle of coherence (PC). In terms of internal coherence (levels 0 and 1), the code should be consistent in its design language (cf. the grammar and basic meaning of words under the PC), and it is the designer's role to ensure the artefact

---

[82] Cf. JL Mezrich, 'Source code escrow: An exercise in futility' (2001) 5 *Marquette Intellectual Property Law Review* 117.

[83] See also Hartzog (n 25) 27.

[84] Ibid. 278; DA Norman, *The Design of Everyday Things* (MIT Press 2013) 26, 31.

[85] LA Suchman, *Human–Machine Reconfigurations: Plans and Situated Actions* (2nd edn, Cambridge University Press 2007) chapter 11; PE Agre, 'Conceptions of the user in computer systems design' in PJ Thomas (ed.), *The Social and Interactional Dimensions of Human–Computer Interfaces* (Cambridge University Press 1995); Norman, *The Design of Everyday Things* (n 84) 31.

is 'understandable and usable'.[86] To avoid misapprehension, end-users should not be confronted with conflicting or inconsistent design. In terms of the first level of coherence, this includes arbitrary changes that can confuse or trick the end-user, especially after she has developed a familiarity with how the code works.

This is *transparency of operation*, or designing in such a way that the end-user can, within reason, understand what the code is doing as it does it. This form of transparency is an ongoing concern, linked with the affordance of oversight, discussed below. Because many systems are frequently updated with features added and removed, it is incumbent on the designer to appropriately communicate such changes where they 'reconfigure' the relationship between end-user and enterprise.[87]

Blockchain Applications

On public blockchains, the code of an application can generally be viewed by anyone. From a transparency perspective this potentially repeats the problem of source code transparency described above – having access to the application's code does not automatically render it intelligible to those likely to be affected by its operation. Various initiatives in the cryptocurrency community seek to ameliorate this problem. For example, the 'Ethereum Natural Specification Format' ('ENSF')[88] is a form of code commentary that allows the designer to descriptively tag the elements of an Ethereum application, from which a natural language explanation of the application's operation can be automatically generated. The result is a commentary of the blockchain application, for example:

> Send 1.125 BTC from the account of ABC to an account
>   accessible only by XYZ[89]

This message is generated from the following tags, immediately preceding the actual code performing the action:

```
/// @notice Send `(valueBTC / 1000).fixed(0,3)` BTC
    from the account of `message.caller.address()` to
    an account accessible only by `to.address()`
```

---

[86] Norman, *The Design of Everyday Things* (n 84) 32.
[87] Gürses and van Hoboken (n 65) 594.
[88] Ethereum Foundation, 'Ethereum Natural Specification Format' in *The Ethereum Wiki* (Ethereum Foundation 2018) <https://github.com/ethereum/wiki/wiki/Ethereum-Natural-Specification-Format> last accessed 4 March 2021.
[89] This and the next example are simplified versions of those found in ibid.

One can see how the elements between the backticks (`) are placeholders for the actual values generated within the application's logic, from which the accessible commentary above can be derived.

This provides a measure of transparency of operation, in that the logic of the blockchain application can theoretically be explained to the end-user. A continuing problem, however, is that such approaches rely on the designer's subjective understanding of the code. For the approach to work she must accurately model, in a combination of natural language and code placeholders, the logic of the application. If she fails to do this, intentionally or mistakenly,[90] the end-user might end up with both an erroneous understanding of the system and a misplaced confidence in that understanding, an outcome which is arguably less desirable than if there were no explanation at all. The result of this is similar to the earlier-noted tendency of legal scholars to focus on the decisions which led to the use of code, rather than the normativity that it actually implements. Descriptions of this sort add an additional layer of interpretation between the end-user and the normativity of the code, increasing the likelihood of errors and misinterpretations on the part of both the designer and the end-user. In this case, the re-emergence of the hermeneutic gap, this time between the commentary-text and the code's instrumentality, is no welcome thing.

Progress might be made by leveraging the programmer of the programmer, in the form of the integrated development environment (IDE) detecting instances during code writing where such tags might be included in the code and to suggest the designer add them. I discuss this further in Chapter 7.

The Internet of Things

Affording transparency in the IoT is a complex challenge for several reasons. IoT devices are often intended to be embedded and pervasive, creating a network of devices that communicate with one another to create 'ambient intelligence' or 'ubiquitous computing'.[91] As a consequence of such devices 'receding' into the background of everyday life, they often have either minimal (or no) interfaces with which the end-user can interact in order to observe what is actually going on. Many IoT devices offer few or even no perceptual affordances, and with such minimal means of communicating their presence

---

[90] As noted above at n 14, even safety-critical applications often have software errors.
[91] M Weiser, 'The computer for the 21st century' (1991) *Scientific American* 94.

and/or purposes to the end-user, the opacity of their normativities is all the more impenetrable. As Matassa and Simeoni warn,

> the existing affordances in connected and technologically augmented objects are becoming unable to immediately communicate to people their actual values and meanings . . . The impossibility of establishing a clear connection between objects and functionalities could become a threat for humans, since they are missing their innate ability to understand what they can do only based on their knowledge and perception of the surrounding context.[92]

This relates to real and perceived affordances, discussed in Chapter 2. The invisibility of IoT devices, and/or their minimal interfaces, means that the communication of even perceived (dis)affordance is already limited, much less the real (dis)affordances embodied in the design. The scope then is all the greater for the end-user to experience dissonance between what she thinks is happening, what her possibilities for action are, and what is actually taking place.[93]

It may be, then, that to achieve legitimacy an IoT device must be designed actively to facilitate understanding on the part of the end-user, even where this is not necessary for the product's purpose to be achieved.[94] The normativity of the artefact should on this account be made apparent to the end-user. IoT devices are hybrids – they combine the up-front physicality of a tangible object with the background processing of (networked) code, the latter being made even less tractable by the absence of an interface.

I mentioned earlier that one means of facilitating intelligibility is via a separate device (a smartphone or television) that provides an interface through which the user can interact with and monitor the IoT device. 'Smart' thermostats and doorbells follow this approach. The degree to which the obscured (dis)affordances/inscriptions embodied in the device are communicated to the end-user will vary according to the complexity of the device's functions. For example, after it is configured, the Amazon Dash Button provides the most minimal of interfaces: a simple adhesive push-button which when pressed reorders the product indicated by a logo on its surface.[95] The apparent

---

[92] A Matassa and R Simeoni, 'Eliciting affordances for smart objects in IoT era' in *Internet of Things: User-Centric IoT* (Springer 2015) 77–8.

[93] Ibid. 78.

[94] As Robertson suggests, designers have a responsibility to facilitate end-user agency, which can only be achieved through the provision of 'resources for awareness'. See T Robertson, 'The public availability of actions and artefacts' (2002) 11 *Computer Supported Cooperative Work (CSCW)* 299.

[95] Amazon, 'Amazon help: Set up your Dash Button' <https://www.amazon.co.uk/gp/help/customer/display.html?ref=amb_link_1?nodeId=201746340> last accessed 4 March 2021.

simplicity of the single-button interface belies the black-boxing of the complex set of operations involved: infrastructurally, there are multiple networking processes (WiFi connection, TCP/IP and HTTPS handshaking, and authentication of the connected Amazon account via the company's API), a financial transaction (communication between Amazon's servers and the provider of the end-user's bank account, usually one or more third-party payment processors), and of course the generating of data deepening Amazon's profile of the end-user's preferences and shopping habits. The gap between the simplicity of the device and what actually goes on demonstrates the dissonance referred to by Matassa and Simeoni, between the purposive end of the code and what it is actually doing. In Fullerian terms, the 'rule' as declared may not be congruent with 'official' action: the Dash Button may well 'reorder dishwasher fluid', but what does this tell us about the layers of activity that pressing the button in fact sets in motion?

(c) Immediacy

The immediacy of code is especially problematic when combined with the contradictory or impossible rules Fuller warns of in his fifth and sixth principles. In the code context, design language can be confusing to the end-user at the level of the interface if it lacks consistency. Impossible rules can guide end-users into situations where there is no logical way out. For example, website cookie notices often give the illusion of providing the choice of whether or not to consent but in reality require acquiescence in order to gain access. Frequent changes to the code can also be problematic – end-users can become accustomed to one way of working with an artefact then find this being changed or reversed by a software update. Depending on the kind of artefact, the scope for such changes can vary; changes to the design of online platforms' interfaces have often disoriented end-users to the point of backlash.[96] Beneath the surface of code, alterations to functionality can also have important effects: the periodic tweaks to Google's search algorithm significantly alter what material is found on the web, with reflexive societal implications.[97]

From a legisprudential perspective, code's immediacy invokes the principle of normative density. The immediate imposition of a given normative

---

[96] For example, one might recall Facebook's move to a 'news feed' layout in the mid-2000s. See J Leyden, 'Users protest over "creepy" Facebook update' *The Register* (7 September 2006) <https://www.theregister.co.uk/2006/09/07/facebook_update_controversy/> last accessed 4 March 2021.

[97] See Moz, 'Google algorithm change history' *Moz* (2018) <https://moz.com/google-algorithm-change> last accessed 4 March 2021.

configuration makes ex ante consideration of its design especially necessary. We saw above in the discussion of opacity how the density of technological normativity is a crucial concern; the immediacy of its application heightens this. This in turn implicates the legisprudential principle of temporality, requiring sensitivity to the moment of the imposition of normativity and ongoing justification to ensure the mechanism for achieving the aim of the norm continues to be appropriate in light of the other principles.

Digisprudential Affordance: Delay

Speed and immediacy of execution are quintessential elements of computational legalism. As we have seen, the design of the artefact reflects an 'intentionality' which reflects some normative conception of how things ought to be done.[98] As Floridi suggests, in the computational era the lack of 'informational friction' contrasts with preceding historical periods where the inherent makeup of the social fabric meant that information could not travel above a certain speed or beyond a certain geographical radius.[99] For him, information privacy is facilitated in part by the 'ontological friction' within a system, which operates to oppose the flow of information and increase the effort required to gain access to it.[100] This chimes with Hildebrandt's arguments to the effect that the affordances of text as a medium are what have resulted in the existence and character of law as we know it.[101] When instantiated in text, the meaning of legal norms is under-determined, but their expressions are nevertheless stable enough to facilitate the understanding and consensus (always contingent and defeasible) that can, through incremental democratic evolution, respond to societal change.[102] The affordances of text as a technology open up spaces for these processes to take place.

---

[98] Recall the discussion of Ihde's comparison of a fountain pen and word processor in 'Code Mediating Action' in Section 2.2.

[99] L Floridi, *The Fourth Revolution: How the Infosphere is Reshaping Human Reality* (Oxford University Press 2014) chapter 5. See also W McGeveran, 'The law of friction' (2013) 2013 *University of Chicago Legal Forum* 15.

[100] Floridi, *The Ethics of Information* (n 71) 231 *et seq.*

[101] M Hildebrandt, *Smart Technologies and the End(s) of Law: Novel Entanglements of Law and Technology* (Edward Elgar Publishing 2015) *passim.* See also WJ Ong, *Orality and Literacy: The Technologizing of the Word* (3rd edn, Routledge 2012); J Goody, *The Logic of Writing and the Organization of Society* (Cambridge University Press 1986); J Goody and I Watt, 'The consequences of literacy' (1963) 5 *Comparative Studies in Society and History* 304.

[102] Hildebrandt, *Smart Technologies* (n 101) chapter 3. I have contrasted Hildebrandt's conception of institutional law as an affordance of text and the printing press with the idea of code's affordances being compatible with the substantive requirements of the law. See L Diver, 'Law as a user: Design, affordance, and the technological mediation of norms' (2018) 15 *SCRIPTed* 4, 30 *et seq.*

Such spaces are in principle susceptible to conscious implementation by the designer. Where the technology is particularly plastic – like code – this requires a conscious and serious commitment, particularly when the presumption amongst technologists is that 'inefficiency' and 'friction' are undesirables that *a priori* operate in opposition to the end-user's aims. Such positions perhaps betray a market-centred rationality that presumes too much about the values the end-user holds, both instrumental and intrinsic, and how these can and ought to be reflected in system design. What matters is identifying the points at which purposely avoiding this instrumental notion of 'efficiency' is necessary for the protection of some broader value.[103] I am therefore not advocating a naïve approach to inefficiency, where designers simply stop optimising their code. This would be arbitrary in any case, since the forms of delay that were retained or introduced would be contingent on both how they arise 'naturally' within a given system and the designer's expertise and conscientiousness in identifying an ameliorating them. It might also be irresponsible, where the lack of optimisation undermines what should be universal goals, such as reducing unnecessary energy consumption. The point, rather, is to identify what matters for a given value, and consciously to implement delays in the code's inscriptions that facilitate respect for that value.

DESIRABLE INEFFICIENCY

In recent work Ohm and Frankle posit the notion of 'desirable inefficiency',[104] where code's efficiency (its ruleishness and its immediacy) is consciously tempered to protect some value that might otherwise be undermined. For them, efficiency in computer science is 'the extent to which [code] minimizes the consumption of time, energy, space, or cost in satisfying a specification of correctness for a given problem'.[105] A desirably inefficient approach is one that sacrifices this goal in service of solving some other problem.

The 'basic problem' is the technical outcome the designer seeks, while the 'enhanced problem' is one requiring 'human judgment, values, or discretion in the definition of success or failure'.[106] Sometimes the latter requires

---

[103] I discuss the normative role of delay in the context of legal practice in L Diver, 'Computational legalism and the affordance of delay in law' (2021) 1 *Journal of Cross-disciplinary Research in Computational Law* <https://journalcrcl.org/crcl/article/view/3> last accessed 19 April 2021. See also C Storni, 'The problem of de-sign as conjuring: Empowerment-in-use and the politics of seams' in *Proceedings of the 13th Participatory Design Conference on Research Papers – PDC '14* (ACM Press 2014).

[104] P Ohm and J Frankle, 'Desirable inefficiency' (2019) 70 *Florida Law Review* 1.

[105] Ibid. 28.

[106] Ibid. 32.

the conscious imposition of 'inefficiency', making space for a human to do something that only a human can. The authors argue in favour of desirable inefficiency as a set of design patterns, part of a call for a 'new interdisciplinary research agenda investigating how values can be embedded into code'.[107] An example is a smartphone's passcode screen, which locks for a progressively longer period when incorrect attempts are registered. Designs like this balance the inconvenience that a forgetful end-user experiences with the security of the device that might otherwise be compromised in the hands of a thief.[108] The technical 'basic problem' is providing the end-user with secure access to her smartphone, while the societal 'enhanced problem' is preventing access to thieves, and in turn the disincentivising of smartphone theft.[109] Blockchain proof-of-work is another example,[110] where what would otherwise be near-instant (storing a transaction's outcome in a database) is made sufficiently 'inefficient' to allow reintroduction of values of trust and 'clock time'.[111] The basic problem is tamper-resistant validation of transactions, while the enhanced problem is their fair validation.[112]

Ohm and Frankle's analysis focuses on the underlying logics of computation, explicitly excluding designs that 'do no more than slow down the operation of a computer to match the speed of human processing systems'.[113] There are myriad circumstances, however, in which the service of 'human processing systems' – that is, humans – is ultimately what matters. Indeed, at the heart of what makes many if not most 'enhanced problems' enhanced will be humans, or human interests. There is therefore value in applying the notion of desirable inefficiency to the design of end-user-facing code, especially where doing so can help to facilitate another human value such as respect for autonomy. Even where greater efficiency is possible from a technical perspective,

---

[107] Ibid. 5.

[108] Ibid. 15. Or indeed the authorities; recall attempts by the US Department of Justice to compel Apple to unlock a phone belonging to a perpetrator of the 2015 San Bernardino shooting. The phone was on the verge of wiping its memory because the passcode had been entered incorrectly numerous times. See B Bailey, 'Apple vs. FBI – what happened?' *Associated Press* (29 March 2016) <https://apnews.com/article/c8469b05ac1b4092b7690d-36f3409a4a> last accessed 4 March 2021.

[109] Ohm and Frankle (n 104) 29–30.

[110] This is the 'mathematical challenge' discussed in 'Blockchain Design' in Section 1.1.

[111] Ohm and Frankle (n 104) 19–22. Proof-of-work is often extremely wasteful of energy, but that is inefficiency of an undesirable kind.

[112] Ibid. 29–30.

[113] Ibid. 35–6. Ohm and Frankle describe humans as 'unpredictable and fiddly devices', apparently akin to other peripherals such as printers and scanners, for whose benefit the computer must limit its intrinsic speed.

in some cases it will be better to opt for a less efficient design where doing so makes it possible to separate points at which the artefact's design implicates diverging or conflicting interests (this is the idea of tussle discussed above).[114] The goal, then, is to frame slowness and 'inefficiency' as potentially beneficial features rather than as tolerated bugs, at least when their conscious inclusion in the code's design can help facilitate respect for some broader normative value.[115]

When framed in terms of (dis)affordances and inscriptions, the concept of desirable inefficiency can be applied fruitfully to end-user-facing code where that inefficiency operates to throttle computational immediacy in service of comprehension and empowerment. Kitchin and Fraser's notion of 'slow computing' puts the human *qua* human centre-stage, consciously reducing 'time compression, fragmentation, densification and stresses' in end-user interactions with code.[116] This notion can be seen in the work of the Slow Research Lab, which aims 'to evoke a quality of being, characterized by critical thinking, deep spaces of reflection, and the unique forms of creative expression that are born of them'.[117] Pols and Spahn connect this outlook with critical theories of technology that view it as a fundamental threat to democracy and justice.[118] From these perspectives, social spheres in which democratic values ought to be given time and space to operate are in danger of being limited by a 'technological rationality that centers on efficiency and strategic manipulation'.[119] Democracy and justice depend on 'communicative' rather than 'strategic' rationality, and thus on the provision of open spaces within which the former can be allowed to happen. The affordance of delay is thus about circumscribing 'technological rationality' (speed, efficiency, certainty) in favour of those spaces.[120] There is a thematic link here to the counterintuitive notion of intentionally fostering ambiguity in a design's affordances, so as not to constrain the end-user's responses to the artefact to only those

---

[114] Clark et al. (n 21) 467.

[115] Cf. Diver, 'Computational legalism and the affordance of delay in law' (n 103).

[116] R Kitchin and A Fraser, *Slow Computing: Why We Need Balanced Digital Lives* (Bristol University Press 2020).

[117] See Slow Research Lab, 'Slow Research Lab' <https://slowlab.net/about> last accessed 4 March 2021.

[118] Pols and Spahn (n 33) 342 *et seq*.

[119] Ibid. 345.

[120] See also Cohen's notion of the exploratory 'play of everyday practice', necessary for the autonomous individual to explore and exploit the space between predictability and contingency. See JE Cohen, *Configuring the Networked Self: Law, Code, and the Play of Everyday Practice* (Yale University Press 2012) chapter 2.

possibilities constituted by the designer.[121] This echoes the postphenome-nological concept of multistability, discussed in Chapter 2,[122] and the cru-cial distinction I have already explored between constitutive and regulative normativity.

FRICTION

Discussions of code friction in the literature generally refer to its opposite, especially in the context of sharing on social networks. As with efficiency, the presumption is often that less is better,[123] when in truth a lack of friction often stands in opposition to the exercises of autonomy exemplified by deliberation and the weighing up of choices and consequences.[124] 'Frictionless sharing' refers to the ease and speed with which the design of social networks afford sharing,[125] for example through the use of metadata standards like Open Graph that provide attention-grabbing previews, or widgets that make shar-ing to social networks from third-party websites so easy as to enable 'viral' posting. This reduction in friction can be taken even further, to the point where everyday events like visiting a shop or going for a run are automatically shared by the code on social media platforms, without the end-user's input.[126] Before these affordances existed, the act of sharing online meant going through various manual steps: copying the URL of the item into an email or instant message, choosing the recipient(s), and composing a note to give the item context. All of this requires thought and conscious decision-making, in contrast to the single-click, one-to-many forms of sharing described above.

Designs that include especially efficient affordances can have unforeseen and undesirable consequences if they are not accompanied by appropriately

---

[121] WW Gaver, J Beaver and S Benford, 'Ambiguity as a resource for design' in *Proceedings of the SIGCHI Conference on Human Factors in Computing Systems* (ACM 2003) <http://doi.acm.org/10.1145/642611.642653> last accessed 4 March 2021. See also M Chalmers and I MacColl, 'Seamful and seamless design in ubiquitous computing' in *Proceedings of Workshop at the Crossroads: The Interaction of HCI and Systems Issues in UbiComp*, vol. 8 (2003).

[122] See also Gaver et al. (n 121) 236–7.

[123] McGeveran (n 99) 51; Ohm and Frankle (n 104) 10–13. Calo also argues in favour of a reduction in friction, which he pits in opposition to the 'facilitation' of the end-user's aims. See R Calo, 'Code, nudge, or notice' (2013) 99 *Iowa Law Review* 773.

[124] Narayanan et al. go so far as to say frictionlessness 'robs' end-users of such opportunities, leading them to follow their 'baser impulses'. See A Narayanan et al., 'Dark patterns: Past, present, and future' (2020) 18 *ACM Queue* 25, 82.

[125] McGeveran (n 99). See also C Reed and A Murray, *Rethinking the Jurisprudence of Cyberspace* (Edward Elgar Publishing 2018) 120.

[126] T Bucher, 'A technicity of attention: How software "makes sense"' (2012) 13 *Culture Machine*.

informative signifiers. A problematic aspect of Facebook's frictionless sharing has been some end-users' misunderstanding of who precisely they are sharing intimate posts with.[127] In that respect, McGeveran connects the idea of friction to design: 'the amount of friction is a complex design choice, which inherently helps some users and burdens others. We cannot avoid making some choice, whether through code or law; there is no "natural" state of online friction.'[128] McGeveran suggests a design principle according to which the ability to share should not be made available before the act itself has taken place. This 'law of friction' states that 'it should not be easier to "share" an action online than to do it'.[129] A similar principle might apply to any computational step that will have normative effect: the end-user should be afforded the opportunity to consider it first. The idea here is to consciously design friction into the appropriate parts of the artefact's inscriptions, so that end-users are given an opportunity to take stock before the code moves on to the next step in its logic.[130] The interface of an artefact is like a keyhole; the breadth and depth of the mass of code steps that are in fact being executed are like the vast bulk of an iceberg hidden beneath surface waters.[131] Whereas text as a normative medium is shallow (even with interpretative flexibility taken into account), code has depth that is simultaneously difficult to observe and difficult to comprehend, on account of its inherent complexity.[132] The challenge then is to design interfaces that afford the appropriate pacing of computation, alongside an appropriate level of technical feedback, in order

---

[127] McGeveran calls this a 'misclosure'. See McGeveran (n 99) 39 *et seq.*, citing KE Caine, 'Supporting privacy by preventing misclosure' in *CHI'09 Extended Abstracts on Human Factors in Computing Systems* (ACM 2009). See also S Sengupta, 'Private posts on Facebook revealed' *The New York Times* (28 January 2013) <https://bits.blogs.nytimes.com/2013/01/18/private-posts-on-facebook-revealed/> last accessed 4 March 2021.

[128] McGeveran (n 99) 53–4.

[129] Ibid. 63. Recent changes to Twitter's interface implement McGeveran's 'law' by asking users whether they would like to read an article before retweeting, the idea being to give less exposure to sensationalist headlines. See C Jee, 'Twitter wants you to read articles before you retweet them' *MIT Technology Review* (11 June 2020) <https://www.technologyreview.com/2020/06/11/1003333/twitter-wants-you-to-read-articles-before-you-retweet-them/> last accessed 4 March 2021.

[130] Ohm and Frankle (n 104) 51–2; McGeveran (n 99).

[131] C Vismann and M Krajewski, 'Computer juridisms' (2007) *Grey Room* 90, 100; MC Marino, 'Critical code studies' (2006) *electronic book review* <https://electronicbookreview.com/essay/critical-code-studies/> last accessed 15 April 2021 13–14.

[132] NK Hayles, 'Print is flat, code is deep: The importance of media-specific analysis' (2004) 25 *Poetics Today* 67.

to facilitate a sufficiently detailed mental model for the end-user that she can make reasonable predictions of what is going to happen next.[133]

HUMAN IN THE LOOP

A primary mechanism for forcing delay into code-mediated processes is the 'human in the loop' ('HitL') principle. A distinction is drawn between those elements of the technical process that can appropriately be executed mindlessly by the machine, and those that have social, ethical, or legal import that must therefore be made by a human, either independently or to ratify the machine's output.[134] The classic application of the HitL principle is in lethal autonomous weapon systems, where a military engagement is automated up to the final decision on whether to strike, which is taken by a human controller.[135] In the policing context, Hartzog et al. suggest a 'conservation principle', requiring inefficiency and indeterminacy to be conserved through retention of human judgement at specific points within the criminal justice process.[136] For them, HitL is a necessary bulwark against the determinism of inflexible code, and they suggest that where one of either surveillance, analysis, or crime detection are automated in code, the (desirable) inefficiency and indeterminacy of the other two should be increased proportionately.[137]

In the context of consumer code, the human in the loop is the end-user herself. In order to facilitate desirable delays in that context, then, interfaces must afford end-users notification and choice at appropriate moments before execution takes place. As discussed above, information about these scenarios should not be front-loaded in terms and conditions documents that are not read, but rather should be delivered piecemeal at appropriate moments in the end-user's journey through the code's inscriptions. This can be achieved by, for example, employing 'just in time' notifications, akin to those provided in

---

[133] Hartzog (n 25) 278. For a related argument for making end-user experiences less simple in certain circumstances, see K Roose, 'Is tech too easy to use?' *The New York Times* (12 December 2018) <https://www.nytimes.com/2018/12/12/technology/tech-friction-frictionless.html> last accessed 4 March 2021.

[134] One must, however, be sensitive to the potential reflexivity of this arrangement. For analysis of this phenomenon (among others) in the 'legal tech' context, see the work of the ERC Advanced Grant research project 'Counting as a Human Being in the Era of Computational Law' (COHUBICOL) <https://www.cohubicol.com> last accessed 4 March 2021, of which I am a member.

[135] N Sharkey, 'Grounds for discrimination: Autonomous robot weapons' (2008) 11 *RUSI Defence Systems* 86.

[136] W Hartzog et al., 'Inefficiently automated law enforcement' (2015) *Michigan State Law Review* 1763.

[137] Ibid. 1778.

the Android operating system for the ad hoc granting or denying of permissions to applications at the moment they request them, instead of in bulk at the moment of installation when the end-user might not foresee the relevant implications.[138] The goal is to granularise permissions and make them contextually relevant, empowering the end-user at the point she can make an informed decision.

HitL is also a necessary element of retaining indeterminacy, the quality of a circumstance not being adequately reflected in the code (or data) that comes to represent it (recall the discussion in Chapter 3 on code's limited ontology being reductive of the world).[139] Whereas code can impose such interpretations, 'underdeterminacy'[140] should be preserved, to allow for responses that are sensitive to the contingent and irreducible texture of the real world. The human who is in the loop has a role in 'completing the narrative' in such scenarios, filling in the contextual gaps which computational representations are incapable of showing sensitivity to but which are nevertheless central to the pursuit of justice or of end-user autonomy.[141] The goal, then, is to ensure that the design affords HitL input at all appropriate points in its inscription, so that the aspirations of freedom and autonomy are not effaced by the 'duty' of wired-in code.

Blockchain Applications
Many of the considerations of ruleishness discussed above also apply to immediacy. Levy notes that '[b]ecause they are based on code', blockchain applications 'can be *immediately and automatically* effectuated, without reliance on manual transfer, or the intervention of institutions like courts.'[142] One of the putative benefits of blockchain applications (promoted in particular by smart contract enthusiasts[143]) is their removal of the perceived inefficiency

---

[138] 'Android developers guide – permissions overview' <https://developer.android.com/guide/topics/permissions/overview> last accessed 4 March 2021. For a recent discussion of *kiaros*, or the notion of 'right-time' in algorithmically mediated systems, see T Bucher, 'The right-time web: Theorizing the kairologic of algorithmic media' (2020) 22 *New Media & Society* 1699.

[139] F Pasquale, 'A rule of persons, not machines: The limits of legal automation' (2019) 87 *George Washington Law Review* 1, 49 *et seq.*

[140] M Hildebrandt, 'Legal and technological normativity: More (and less) than twin sisters' (2008) 12 *Techné: Research in Philosophy and Technology* 169, 177.

[141] Hartzog et al. (n 136) 1785 *et seq.*

[142] Levy (n 61) 2 (emphasis supplied).

[143] Pasquale (n 139) *passim.* For an example, see Mattereum, 'Mattereum Protocol: Turning code into law' (Mattereum Project 2018) <https://www.mattereum.com/upload/iblock/784/mattereum-summary_white_paper.pdf> last accessed 4 March 2021.

of ambiguity and processual costs.[144] This is potentially deeply problematic, especially if the code has been poorly designed. When combined with the immutability of a blockchain, the consequences can be serious indeed. As De Filippi and Wright suggest, '[t]he automated nature of smart contracts, combined with the inability to readily alter their underlying code, could further lead to situations where a faultly [sic] piece of code would repeatedly run, to the detriment of all parties involved.'[145]

There is thus a need for ex ante consideration of the implications of automated and immediate execution: assets or funds could be transferred, goods and services ordered, or a person's legal status altered, all according to the predetermined logic of the blockchain application, without any human intervention or oversight. This will happen near-instantaneously if the conditions in the code are met. As with the affordance of choice, providing delay therefore requires the identification of appropriate moments in which the end-user must be afforded the opportunity to consider the situation before execution of the code continues.[146] Given the impossibility of anticipating every outcome of execution,[147] contingency ought not to be the province of the code, and any attempt so to 'enclose' it is perhaps likely to set up unforeseen and undesirable results. Simultaneously, however, imposing friction in blockchain applications is arguably anathema to their very ethos. This may be necessary for them to be deemed legitimate, however, given their potential exemplification of computational legalism.

The Internet of Things
In the discussion of default choices above I mentioned IoT webcams that have problematic 'out-of-the-box' configurations, such as insecure default administrative passwords.[148] We have seen how end-users often trust designers to know better than they do, and so assume that the default configuration must be the most sensible one. Such configurations are especially problematic in the IoT, because the object itself might be 'plug and play', meaning it starts

---

144 Levy (n 61) 2.
145 P De Filippi and A Wright, *Blockchain and the Law: The Rule of Code* (Harvard University Press 2018) 201.
146 For a wider developmental and environmental angle on 'considering the situation', which takes into account much more than the end-user's immediate interests, see the combined blockchain/IoT project BitBarista: L Pschetz et al., 'Bitbarista: Exploring perceptions of data transactions in the Internet of Things' in *Proceedings of the 2017 CHI Conference on Human Factors in Computing Systems* (ACM 2017).
147 Cf. CD Clack, VA Bakshi and L Braine, 'Smart contract templates: Foundations, design landscape and research directions' (2017) arXiv:1608.00771 [cs], 4.
148 Krebs (n 38).

operating according to its default configuration as soon as it is switched on. This single action may be enough by itself to set off various undesirable path dependencies, for example joining an open wireless network and connecting to a remote server to register its existence. Designing in delay in this context, then, could involve ensuring that IoT devices have all defaults set initially to prevent any functionality that is not immediately and obviously signified by the physical characteristics of the device. This relates back to the 'would not have wanted' standard, discussed above.

In the example of the smart fridge, switching it on for the first time would mean it immediately starts to refrigerate because that is its inherent purpose, but all 'smart' (networked) functionalities would remain disabled until the end-user takes the active step of configuring and enabling them. Building in a delay before the normative code executes can open up space for the other affordances to be facilitated: the end-user can consider the implications of the device's provenance and purpose, giving her a chance to respond to any misgivings she may have before potentially opaque harm is done. If she decides to go ahead, she can then think about which configurable choices best fit her interests. Like the suggestion below regarding a 'floor' of security in the IoT, we can imagine a baseline delay where no normative functionality that is not clearly signified by the physical properties of the artefact can be enabled prior to the end-user taking the active choice to do so, even (and particularly) where this is in opposition to the commercial interests of the manufacturer. In addition to a 'floor' of security, one can therefore imagine an initial 'ceiling' of affordance, extendable only by the conscious choice of the end-user.

(d) Immutability

The problems of code's immutability overlap with those demonstrated by its ruleishness and immediacy. Fuller's principle regarding frequency of change applies, but in the opposite sense: the fact that certain media are resistant to being changed must be borne in mind at design time;[149] the threshold between 'duty' and 'aspiration' must be set in the knowledge that path dependencies might arise that lock end-users into the constraints of a particular design. This relates to the legisprudential principle of temporality, which, as previously mentioned, requires sensitivity to the concreteness of the imposed rule particularly where there is less scope for future alteration, in which case the need for justification is all the stronger. Given the ways in which immutable code crystallises a particular configuration of technological normativity, there is a need both to justify that configuration and to balance it with the affordance

---

[149] Hartzog (n 25) 76–7.

of oversight. There is a connection here too with the principle of coherence, which under its third level requires a broader societal justification for the rule and not just coherence in accordance with the system's internal rationale. From that perspective, the digisprudential strategy of oversight means that a change in the external justification must be capable of being reflected via alteration of the code; a failure to afford this would mean the continued operation of illegitimate code, regardless of its legitimacy at original time of release.

Digisprudential Affordance: Oversight

The manufacturer ought not to release code unless the necessary conditions are in place for them to maintain oversight of it and to correct any (unforeseen) negative consequences. This is similar to the concept of *revocability* in the HCI-Security literature, where the end-user must be afforded the possibility of revoking any permissions she has granted within the system.[150] In this context, the concept of revocability requires that the creator of the code be capable of maintaining some control over it.[151] In this light, maintaining legitimacy requires that the design anticipate ex ante the potential need to make changes ex post. Respect for this principle requires that the design itself permit it; any design that does not is *prima facie* illegitimate.[152]

Consider again the Sony BMG DRM scandal discussed in Chapter 1. The problematic effects of its design were amplified by its storage on an inherently immutable medium, the compact disc. Although the system was ultimately revoked, this was only as a result of the significant public relations impact of the scandal, and that revocation took the form of a laborious, expensive, and wasteful physical recall of more than seven million CDs. Similar issues arise

---

[150] K-P Yee, 'User interaction design for secure systems' in R Deng et al. (eds), *Information and Communications Security* (Springer 2002).

[151] As Winner puts it, 'men release powerful changes into the world with cavalier disregard for consequences', discussing the central theme of Shelley's *Frankenstein; or, the Modern Prometheus*. See L Winner, *Autonomous Technology: Technics-Out-of-Control as a Theme in Political Thought* (2nd edn, MIT Press 1977) 314. For an annotated edition of the latter that illuminates the novel's themes from an engineering perspective, see M Shelley, *Frankenstein: A New Edition for Scientists and Engineers*, ed. E Finn, D Guston and JS Robert (MIT Press 2017).

[152] This goal is echoed in recent EU developments mandating that product designs afford repairability to reduce waste and extend the lifespan of consumer electronics. See for example M Anastasio, 'EU governments support first set of laws for more repairable products' (EEB – The European Environmental Bureau, 13 December 2018) <https://eeb.org/eu-governments-support-first-set-of-laws-for-more-repairable-products/> last accessed 4 March 2021.

in the IoT, where slim margins on inexpensive devices mean the incentive to invest in long-term updates and support is diminished. Code is thus rushed to market with neither the capacity for ex post software updates nor the ongoing commitment to provide bug and security fixes.[153]

From a legitimacy perspective, the design must afford oversight by the designer or enterprise so that any necessary changes to the code can be made. This will involve anticipation of software updates, now a fairly standard feature in modern networked devices.[154] As with elsewhere within the digisprudential framework, the implication is that if the enterprise cannot commit to such standards of oversight then the legitimacy of the design has *de facto* not been demonstrated and its technological normativity is not justified. Similarly, where the design does not permit updates by its very nature (for example due to limited connectivity or processing power) then the scope of wired-in functionality should be to that extent limited to ensure that the unchangeable code will not cause future negative effects. The design must therefore anticipate external change, either by the facilitation of remote updates or by restricting the scope of its normativity from the outset. Where it proves too difficult to anticipate these eventualities, ex post remedial measures of the sort envisaged by Hartzog and Selinger (for example third-party maintenance or insurance) must be put in place. If none of this is possible, the inevitable conclusion is that the design is *a priori* illegitimate.

SUNSETTING AND 'LOBOTOMY SWITCHES'

Discussing the Sony BMG DRM scandal, Halderman and Felten suggest the inclusion of 'sunsetting', a mechanism that renders the system inert after a specified period or date.[155] Depending on the business model being pursued, this might avoid some of the problems of code executing indefinitely, particularly if it is especially difficult to alter it ex post (as with physical CD media). The Sony BMG system could have been designed to execute for only as long as there was commercial benefit in enforcing copyright by means of code. Halderman and Felten suggest a period of three years, during which most of the revenue from disc sales would have been raised. Whether an approach

---

[153] W Hartzog and E Selinger, 'The Internet of Heirlooms and Disposable Things' (2016) 17 *North Carolina Journal of Law & Technology* 581.

[154] In the security context, Hartzog and Selinger suggest a 'minimum expectation of servicing' standard, and a 'floor of data security even for disposable items' (ibid. 597). See also ENISA's recent report on IoT supply chains: 'Guidelines for Securing the Internet of Things' (European Union Agency for Cybersecurity (ENISA) 2020).

[155] JA Halderman and EW Felten, 'Lessons from the Sony CD DRM episode' in *15th USENIX Security Symposium* (USENIX Association 2006) 89.

of this kind is effective depends on the business model – the economics of CD sales have of course changed significantly since the Sony BMG scandal. Nevertheless, the principle is valid: designers ought to consider the medium- and long-term effects of the technological normativity they embody in their systems, and where oversight over such a period is anticipated to be difficult or impossible, sunsetting is a mechanism that can limit the possible effects of the code operating blindly in unforeseen contexts.

Related to sunsetting is what Hartzog calls a 'lobotomy switch', which reduces the system to a set of core functions while disabling any optional affordances (particularly network access).[156] This is the mirror image to the discussion of core affordances above in the section on delay: basic functionality is retained, but optional 'smartness' is disabled. Hartzog gives the example of a child's Internet-enabled doll: once the lobotomy switch is flipped, the doll can still be played with, but its potentially security- and privacy-harming connectivity is disabled. Again, the efficacy of this approach depends on the type of device; if networking is a central aspect of its utility (as for example with the Amazon Dash Button) then disabling it through a lobotomy switch might render the device essentially useless. It is also complicated by questions of who should control the switch, and under what conditions it might be activated. These questions represent a point at which the institutional law might reprise its traditional regulative role.[157]

In any event, the overarching question of legitimacy operates, raising the thorny question of whether the device should have been designed in such a way in the first place. If the manufacturer cannot commit to (1) supporting the device with updates and maintenance for a reasonable period, (2) 'sunsetting' the device (or the relevant parts of its functionality) after a specified period, or (3) retaining sufficient control to permit a 'lobotomy' to be performed should this turn out to be necessary, then the design is not legitimate, because it does not afford the necessary level or quality of oversight.

Blockchain Applications

One of the notional selling points of blockchains is that data stored on them is tamper-resistant.[158] From the perspective of orthodox contract law this is problematic, since the ex ante interpretation formalised in the code of the

---

[156] Hartzog (n 25) 272. Even the simplest networked devices can be zombified as part of a bot net, used for example in distributed deniable of service (DDOS) attacks.

[157] Ibid. 273; B Schneier, 'I've seen the future, and it has a kill switch' *Wired* (26 June 2008) <https://www.wired.com/2008/06/securitymatters-0626/> last accessed 4 March 2021.

[158] De Filippi and Wright (n 145) 35–7.

blockchain application is what will be executed when the relevant conditions arise, regardless of any intervening factors which might otherwise have invited more flexibility.[159] The technical necessity for consensus to be reached in order to make changes, coupled with the inability unilaterally to breach the 'contract', makes these artefacts especially problematic in terms of oversight. Observing the fact of the application's execution may be possible because the output of a blockchain application's execution is generally stored on the underlying chain. This is a different kind of oversight, however. What matters from a digisprudential perspective is ongoing maintainability and revocability, to ensure that the code's normativity can be accounted for; both are undermined by the immutability of a blockchain. If one 'party' to the application's 'contract' changes her mind, or is incapacitated, or the codified norms are otherwise illegal, the code will in principle remain on the blockchain and will execute as stored, regardless of such contingencies.

This goes to the very heart of the kind of ex ante anticipation that digisprudence is concerned with. Designers of blockchain applications must be aware of contingencies well in advance. Because of the immediacy of the code, they must therefore limit the normative scope of the latter to those facts that they can be reasonably certain of. Even if the context of the code's operation entails emergence or complexity, this will not prevent the application from operating unless its code is designed to include some external check of such contingencies.[160] The question must then be faced of whether it is feasible to predetermine all the relevant contingencies that might arise, and whether even those that are foreseen are supported by reliable third-party sources of information. Oracles – third-party sources of contingent data used in the application[161] – might not provide the necessary information at the moment it is needed, or that information might be inaccurate, incomplete, or not in a format the code is equipped to 'understand'. Even where these issues do not arise initially, there is an inherent assumption that the oracle will continue to operate as it did at the time the application was designed, but this may not be the case if the third party alters the oracle's code, or shuts down altogether. Furthermore, in terms of contestability, even where a judicial process might in theory be invoked to attempt to address any conflict that arises, it may be difficult to identify the parties from the application's code in order to demonstrate legal standing to contest or seek decree, because identification

---

[159] K O'Hara, 'Smart contracts – dumb idea' (2017) 21 *IEEE Internet Computing* 97, 98.

[160] RH Weber, '"Rose is a rose is a rose is a rose" – what about code and law?' (2018) 34 *Computer Law & Security Review* 701, 5.

[161] Cardozo Blockchain Project, '"Smart contracts" & legal enforceability' (Benjamin N Cardozo School of Law 2018) 8.

is by means of anonymous public keys rather than names. In any event, even were it possible, such an appeal to judicial process would take place after the code has executed and its negative effects have been felt.

Two factors might ultimately militate against blockchain applications in terms of the affordance of oversight. First, if the designer cannot be sure whether certain crucial facts will obtain at point of execution, she must limit the 'wired-in' elements of the code to exclude these. Difficulties arise in identifying the threshold between what Clack et al. call the 'operational aspects' of the blockchain application, namely those that are automatable, and those that are 'non-operational' and cannot or should not be automated.[162] Too much automation and many or all of the effects of computational legalism are amplified; too little and what remains automated in the blockchain application's logic may be so simplified as to obviate its 'smartness'. This might be a useful limitation, however, rendering the code a 'mechanism'[163] for the execution of a real-world agreement between humans, the latter retaining responsibility for managing any ambiguity.[164] Thus, the social level of agreement (including institutional legal contracting) continues to be the locus of the contingent parts of 'real-world' human arrangements, while the role of the blockchain application is constrained to those limited factors susceptible to reliable and predictable code-based representation and enforcement.[165] This is, in a sense, to flip the 'lobotomy switch' ex ante, limiting the design of the application from the beginning, in the knowledge that it might otherwise harbour too much normative power. Whether or not such a notionally legitimated blockchain application would retain any commercial attractiveness remains to be seen, but exposing business models that rely on illegitimate code would be a price worth paying.

The second factor militating against the use of blockchain applications relates to the code's ability to respond to contingent facts. If the designer is unwilling to forego the 'smartness' of the application in the manner just described, the external contingent facts that it relies upon must be verifiable at the point of execution. This implies the use of oracles that are themselves trustworthy and accurate. This will be problematic from an oversight

---

[162] Clack et al. (n 147) 5.

[163] Felten suggests this term as an alternative to the confusing 'smart contract'. See E Felten, 'Smart contracts: Neither smart nor contracts?' *Freedom to Tinker* (20 February 2017) <https://freedom-to-tinker.com/2017/02/20/smart-contracts-neither-smart-not-contracts/> last accessed 4 March 2021.

[164] De Filippi and Wright (n 145) 199–200; Cardozo Blockchain Project (n 161) 4.

[165] Levy (n 61).

perspective because it devolves the determination of a crucial element of the artefact's logic away from the manufacturer, thus undermining its ability to oversee the operation of its own design. One response to this is to design in a kind of 'meta-contingency', somewhat akin to sunsetting, where the blockchain application will simply lie inert if, at point of execution, it cannot confirm a given fact to the requisite degree of certainty. Of course, any such safety valve must be consciously designed into the logic of the code. Whether the precise set of facts that would come within this bracket can be identified by a designer in advance (rather than by a court ex post, with all the benefits of expert evidence and time to deliberate), and whether they can be provided by an oracle in a form that is susceptible to computational representation, are questions that are themselves contingent on many external conditions being in place (for example a facility providing information that the relevant end-users are still alive and *capax*, or that the property or goods that the application purports to transact with still exist and are in the possession of the relevant party who retains a right of disposal). The complexity and variety of factors that ought to be taken into consideration might mean these standards of oversight cannot be met, which again will call into question the legitimacy of such applications *a priori*.[166]

The Internet of Things

We have already seen in the discussion above some suggestions relating to IoT devices specifically. Because they tend to be low-cost, there are numerous examples where manufacturers have under-invested in the ongoing maintenance of their devices.[167] The resources required to track and fix bugs and to provide infrastructure for delivering updates to the devices can mean that in a febrile market resources are directed instead towards developing new products. Some manufacturers have even resorted to altering legal terms in an attempt to contract out of responsibility for the technological normativity of their designs. For example, after a serious breach of personal data toy manufacturer Vtech simply changed their terms document to shift responsibility onto the end-user, instead of altering the design of their product.[168] Whatever

---

[166] Pasquale (n 139) 24 *et seq*.

[167] L Edwards, D McAuley and L Diver, 'From privacy impact assessment to social impact assessment' in *2016 IEEE Security and Privacy Workshops (SPW)* (IEEE 2016).

[168] L Franceschi-Bicchierai, 'Hacked toy company VTech's TOS now says it's not liable for hacks' (2016) *Motherboard* <http://motherboard.vice.com/read/hacked-toy-company-vtech-tos-now-says-its-not-liable-for-hacks> last accessed 4 March 2021.

the legal (de)merits of this approach, it does nothing to make legitimate the technological normativity of the device.

For IoT devices, then, oversight must be designed into the system itself, including the ability to update its code should this be required in future (which implies a commitment to support such updates). As Hartzog and Selinger suggest,

> [i]magine a system where companies told users how long they think a wired object will last and how long the company will commit to providing security patches. In the event that a company goes bankrupt before then, companies would work quickly to either notify users of its impending shut down or facilitate the [transfer of] responsibility for security patches to a third party.[169]

This might be combined with sunsetting facilities that either warn the end-user that the device has an expected operating life of a specified period or, if the supporting infrastructure becomes unavailable (for example due to insolvency of the manufacturer), that either there will be a third-party support mechanism, or the system will gracefully degrade (sunsetting/the lobotomy switch) or be disabled altogether. What such measures might mean for consumer protection or contract law remains to be seen; of course, as with all the other digisprudential affordances, if the manufacturer of the device cannot commit to producing a design that embodies a sufficient level of foundational legitimacy then the conclusion must always remain open that the design is *a priori* illegitimate and it should not be released.

(e) Pervasiveness

The pervasiveness of code connects with the idea of 'juridification' and the legalistic proliferation of 'ever more refined and rigid systems of formal definitions'.[170] This is an implied problem that the legisprudential principle of normative density aims to reduce, by increasing the level of justification required in proportion to the limitation of freedom (criminal sanction being the 'densest' example). The concept of juridification takes this wider to consider not just the 'density' of a given norm's limitation on freedom, but the aggregate impact on freedom of the proliferation of legal normativity more generally.[171] In the legal sphere, the effects of juridification are limited by both institutional resources and human cognitive capability. Beyond a certain threshold,

---

[169] Hartzog and Selinger (n 153) 597.
[170] JN Shklar, *Legalism* (Harvard University Press 1964) 2.
[171] LC Blichner and A Molander, 'What is juridification?' (Centre for European Studies, University of Oslo 2005) 12 *et seq*.

citizens cannot comprehend the body of norms they are subject to, and there are limited resources for enforcing every applicable norm. There is thus a natural limit to pervasiveness within the legal domain. In the computational realm, however, such limits do not exist (or their threshold is much higher); the number of norms or the aggregate normativity that can be created and enforced by and through code is potentially unlimited, at least within the domain of the artefact. Pervasiveness under computational legalism thus exemplifies these dual aspects of juridification: the density of the individual norms, and complex aggregations of normativity embodied in the inscriptions of both individual and networked collections of devices. We have already seen how technological normativity can have an immediate regulating effect in a way that law cannot (and ought not[172]); whereas traditional legal norms can be directed at whole populations (or even large classes of individual), their text-bound character dramatically limits the real-time imposition of their normative effect. The ways that code differs in this respect, discussed earlier, are made all the stronger when the artefact has widespread adoption – large numbers of individuals can be subject simultaneously to the normative effect of even a single design decision.[173] We can therefore adapt the legisprudential principle of normative density to take account of this collective dimension of code normativity, in terms of both the effects of multiple artefacts and the effects on multiple end-users. When combined with the other digisprudential affordances, the question of aggregate technological normativity becomes extremely salient; pervasiveness takes the other qualitative aspects of computational legalism and adds a quantitative element into the legitimacy equation.

6.4 Conclusion

This chapter has strengthened the relationship between legal-theoretical notions of legitimacy and the practical question of what legitimate code ought to afford (1) the end-user (contestability, choice, transparency, and delay), (2) legal institutions (evidential standards), and (3) code's own creators (oversight). The framework of digisprudential affordances is set out, providing a basis for guiding the design of code towards legitimacy.

---

[172] Here the distinction between 'legal protection by design' and 'legal by design' is crucially important. See M Hildebrandt, *Law for Computer Scientists and Other Folk* (Oxford University Press 2020) 302 *et seq.*

[173] A Huldtgren, 'Design for values in ICT' in J van den Hoven, PE Vermaas and I van de Poel (eds), *Handbook of Ethics, Values, and Technological Design* (Springer 2014) 741.

By discussing their potential application to concrete technologies, I have also tried to begin bridging the divide between legal-theoretical notions of normative legitimacy and their practical, real-world instantiations. The next chapter pushes further in this practical direction, focusing on the code development cycle and how the 'programmer of the programmer' can be employed as a 'constitutional' guide, encouraging the production of legitimate code.

7

Operationalising Digisprudence

> An insurmountable barrier between users and system programmers safe-
> guards the computer's inalterable functions. Beyond this barrier, as in
> Kafka's story, a new barrier appears between the programmer and the pro-
> grammer of the programming language who decides how the basic set of
> elements is to be designed, which rights and properties will be granted to
> whom, and which will be denied.[1]

The previous chapter set out the digisprudential affordances as an adapted
representation of both the legal-theoretical principles of legality and legisprudence, and as normative criteria for code. This penultimate chapter discusses
some practical ways to operationalise some elements of that framework. This
is not an exhaustive survey of coding practices – that would require several
volumes in its own right – but rather my goal is to draw attention to some
points where operationalising the framework is especially important, as well
as to existing approaches that could contribute to digisprudential legitimacy.
There will without question be further avenues for exploration, some of
which I highlight in the next and final chapter.

We have seen that the intent of the framework is to bind the design
of code to underlying 'constitutional' principles, regardless of the artefact's
ultimate commercial purpose. (A corollary being that those principles may
logically prevent certain business models from being pursued.) We saw in
Chapter 1 how this idea of the product designer being herself constrained
by a prior set of 'constitutional' design choices can be conceptualised in the
notion of the *programmer of the programmer* ('PoP').[2] This is an under-studied
area in the legal literature, and part of the contribution here is to strengthen
the practical connection between the PoP and its legal-theoretical analogues.

---

[1] C Vismann and M Krajewski, 'Computer juridisms' (2007) *Grey Room* 90, 101.
[2] Ibid. 100.

7.1 The Programmer of the Programmer

I referred in Chapters 1 and 2 to Vismann and Krajewski's discussion of the 'structural homologies' between computers and law. The vertical model of normative relationships (Figure 1.1 in Chapter 1[3]) hints at the analogy described there: the constitution binds the legislature, which promulgates norms that regulate the citizen, those norms being legitimated by the democratic process and the formal requirements of legality and legisprudential legitimation (including their contestability in court). This is the top-down aspect of the vertical model. By analogy, from a bottom up perspective there is the *programmer of the programmer* ('PoP'), which represents the software, tools, and development practices used by designers. These have the potential to impose 'constitutional' limits within the design environment, binding the product designer's coding activities ex ante. This possibility is particularly relevant to integrated development environments, which are the software applications that lie at the very heart of code production (I discuss these in more detail below). The 'legislative' work of the product designer can thus be constrained according to the (dis)affordances and inscriptions contained in that design environment, which, if defined according to the digisprudential perspective, can in turn mean that the normativities embodied in an artefact's code are legitimate from the outset.

The product designer is thus herself rendered a 'user', because despite the vast freedom she enjoys in defining her code's normativity, she is nevertheless constrained by prior design decisions made by notional PoPs and embodied in the tools of her trade: hardware, programming languages, and the software tools used to write new code. The parallel runs down to the fundamental level of the computer's architecture, where Vismann and Krajewski characterise the chip as a 'sovereign' and Intel (one of the world's largest processor manufacturers) as a 'legislator', by dint of the power they wield over the design of the internal rules, or 'instruction sets', of the processor.[4] This is the apotheosis of the PoP metaphor; the ultimate technical constitution lies in the low-level instructions defined physically in the very silicon of the chip. For Vismann and Krajewski, the PoP

> maintains the ultimate power because he or she, as the constructor of the
> programming language itself, defines what the 'normal' programmer, as a

---

[3] See 'Normative Relationships in Code and Law' in Section 1.4.

[4] Vismann and Krajewski (n 1) 96–7. See also FA Kittler, 'Protected mode' in J Johnston (ed.), *Literature, Media, Information Systems: Essays*, trans. S Harris (Psychology Press 1997) 162, suggesting that our conceptions of power should come not from analysing society but from examining chip architectures.

user, will be able to do. Both types of programmers establish the conditions of using the computer, and, as such, they behave like lawmakers or, rather, *code*-makers.[5]

One can appreciate the implications of this 'meta-architecture', and how it mediates the work of the product designer. We can therefore conceive of the PoP not as an individual person or enterprise, but as the conditions of possibility that govern what the product designer can possibly do. The latter is situated within an assemblage of programming languages, a community with standardised practices and design patterns, and pre-existing libraries of code, all of which are to some extent constitutive of her work before she writes even a single line of her own code.

Viewed from this broader perspective, the PoP is a deeply normative force, operating at a 'constitutional' level within the design process. And, again, just as with production code itself, nothing is given; the conditions represented by the PoP are all to some extent contingent on design choices, which can themselves be guided through the support of certain values.

(a) From Primary and Secondary Rules to Primary and Secondary (Dis)affordances

Thinking normatively about the role of the PoP, we can consider how to leverage it to impose elements of the 'constitutional' framework of digisprudence on product designers working later in the production process. The idea is to push for 'legitimacy by design, by design', through the structuring, guiding, and restraining of product design practices according to the requirements and aims of digisprudence. This should be aimed for whatever the substantive purpose of the code being produced and whatever the underlying business model being pursued.

One might think of this in terms of Hart's primary and secondary rules. As we saw previously, primary rules are those that require a substantive behaviour (or forbearance) on the part of the addressee.[6] Secondary rules are those that define the conditions under which the primary rules can be created, changed, and adjudicated.[7] Secondary rules are thus ex ante and 'constitutional', defining how to create primary rules and the proper form that they should take.

The primary rules find their analogue in the (dis)affordances and inscriptions embodied in the design of the artefact, constraining and enabling the

---

[5] Vismann and Krajewski (n 1) 100 (emphasis supplied).
[6] HLA Hart, *The Concept of Law* (2nd edn, Clarendon Press 1994) 91–3.
[7] Ibid. 95–6.

Table 7.1 Hartian–legisprudential–digisprudential homologies

Hartian Norm	Legisprudential Locus	Digisprudential Actor
Secondary rule	Constitution binds the rule-maker	PoP implements primary digisprudential (dis)affordances/inscriptions in design environment
Primary rule	Legislature creates rules of conduct, subject to legisprudential legitimation	Product designer creates technological normativity, subject to constraining (legitimating) secondary (dis)affordances/inscriptions in the design environment
–	Citizen is subject to legitimated text-based legal normativity	End-user is subject to legitimated technological normativity

behaviour of the end-user (this was the focus of Part I of the book). In the digisprudential context, we can envisage including in the design process secondary rules that constrain what primary (dis)affordances and inscriptions the designer may build into her product's code. This analysis suggests certain homologies between Hart's thesis, the legisprudential hierarchy, and digisprudence, which are set out in Table 7.1. The concept in the central column of a hierarchy of regulative force building up from a base 'constitutive' foundation maps onto the legisprudential model of legitimation discussed in Chapter 3.[8]

In terms of operationalisation, where the legislature is constrained by secondary rules and the legisprudential principles in traditional law-making, we can imagine in the design sphere the 'legislature' of the design process (including on a concrete technical level the integrated development environment, discussed below) being similarly constrained by secondary rules which guide what primary (dis)affordances and inscriptions can possibly be created there.

Assessing the embodiment of some of the secondary digisprudential affordances will involve qualitative judgements, for example whether a given delay is sufficient to enable comprehension, or the extent to which oversight is afforded. In addition to such qualitative questions, however, we can also envisage 'secondary' (dis)affordances/inscriptions, built into the very design environment itself, which guide the work of the 'designer-legislator' in her creation of primary (dis)affordances/inscriptions. The product designer thus becomes another regulatee, this time at the hand of the PoP. Substantive 'primary' (dis)affordances and inscriptions are aimed at the end-user, while the constitutional 'secondary'

---

[8] See 'Legalism According to Legisprudence' in Section 3.1.

(dis)affordances and inscriptions are aimed at the product designer. The latter operate to produce legitimate instances of the former.

In the following sections I discuss elements of the software development process that are appropriate targets for this kind of 'meta-normativity'. Development practice is a multifaceted and ever-evolving thing, so as suggested above the intention is not to set out a hard and fast roadmap for digisprudence. The topics selected here are, however, representative of the levels of the process at which the greatest impact is likely to be made in terms of legitimation, and are chosen in light of the need to take into account long-term trends in code production. I first consider the agile development process, then the software applications (integrated development environments) used to write code, followed by the interpretative affordances of code, facilitated by commentary, programming languages, and visual modelling.

7.2 Agile Development

A welcome shift in focus towards the production of code is beginning to emerge amongst legal scholars. An example is Gürses and van Hoboken's discussion of the 'agile' development methodology, which they describe as a 'paradigmatic transformation in the production of digital functionality'.[9] Although their primary focus is privacy and the production of platforms rather than individual artefacts, they acknowledge the 'wider societal implications of the agile turn',[10] and as we saw in Chapter 5 their concern about production is equally applicable to the more fundamental question of legitimacy.

According to the Agile Manifesto, agile development processes are characterised by a focus on end-users, continuous development and testing, collaboration, and response to change.[11] This approach contrasts with the 'waterfall' paradigm, dominant between the 1970s and 1990s,[12] which is built around discrete, sequential stages that have limited recursion and feedback between them.[13] The waterfall model is thus brittle: whereas the focus of the agile model is on producing modularised, working code as early as possible, with feedback being integrated as it is gathered throughout the

---

[9] S Gürses and J van Hoboken, 'Privacy after the agile turn' in E Selinger, J Polonetsky and O Tene (eds), *The Cambridge Handbook of Consumer Privacy* (Cambridge University Press 2018) 579.

[10] Ibid. 580.

[11] Beck K et al., 'Manifesto for agile software development' (2001) <https://agilemanifesto.org/> last accessed 4 March 2021.

[12] WW Royce, 'Managing the development of large software systems' in *Proceedings of IEEE WESCON* (Los Angeles 1970). See also Gürses and van Hoboken (n 9) 582.

[13] DA Norman, *The Design of Everyday Things* (MIT Press 2013) 234–5.

process,[14] the waterfall model relies on 'rigorously regimented practices, extensive documentation and detailed planning and management'.[15] Agile processes are cyclical and responsive, while waterfall processes move between predetermined phases that are less flexible vis-à-vis contingencies and feedback. By nature, agile processes also accelerate the code development process because kinks and problems tend to be identified and fixed 'on-the-fly', rather than waiting until later testing phases when more significant problems might be expensive and time-consuming to fix (and might therefore be quietly ignored).[16]

This idea of incremental cycles responsive to changing requirements fits well with a notion of a process involving continual assessment of legitimacy.[17] In that vein, the technology ethics thinktank doteveryone suggests augmenting agile cycles with anticipatory assessments of the potential consequences of design choices to enable the mitigation of problems during the design process.[18] This chimes with the idea of continually assessing code functionality according to whether and how it reflects the digisprudential affordances. As with Wintgens's plotting of proposed legislative norms that we saw in Chapter 6, an element of code functionality can be assessed according to its embodiment and balancing of the affordances. Taking a digisprudential 'stance' can continually adjust the design throughout cycles of agile development, refining it towards greater legitimacy. This is important, since design processes are often long and complex and cannot be neatly compartmentalised as in the waterfall model. The common enjoinder that 'by design' of whatever form (legitimacy, privacy, or legal compliance more generally) take place during the 'early stages of the process' is thus insufficient;[19] the proper

---

[14] T Hoeren and S Pinelli, 'Agile programming – introduction and current legal challenges' (2018) 34 *Computer Law & Security Review* 1131, 1132.

[15] Gürses and van Hoboken (n 9) 582.

[16] See for example 'The Lean Startup | Methodology' <http://theleanstartup.com/principles> last accessed 4 March 2021, promoting a cyclical 'build–measure–learn' approach to code development. See also E Luger and M Golembewski, 'Towards fostering compliance by design; drawing designers into the regulatory frame' in M Taddeo and L Floridi (eds), *The Responsibilities of Online Service Providers* (Springer 2017) 296.

[17] For a practical discussion making this point in relation to Privacy by Design, see AC García et al., 'PRIPARE privacy- and security-by-design methodology handbook' (EU FP7 2015) 103 *et seq.*

[18] S Brown, 'An agile approach to designing for the consequences of technology' *doteveryone* (13 February 2019) <https://medium.com/doteveryone/an-agile-approach-to-designing-for-the-consequences-of-technology-18a229de763b> last accessed 4 March 2021.

[19] L Diver and B Schafer, 'Opening the black box: Petri nets and privacy by design' (2017) 31 *International Review of Law, Computers & Technology* 68, 76; Gürses and van Hoboken (n 9) 592. On the inadequacy of a 'checklist' approach to privacy by design, see S Gürses,

embodiment of the value-based affordances I have described requires continual assessment and reassessment throughout the process, which the cyclical agile methodology can help facilitate.

7.3 Integrated Development Environments

Returning to the discussion above of primary and secondary (dis)affordances and inscriptions, one place in which this concept might be implemented in a technically robust way is the integrated development environment (IDE). In contemporary development the text of code is written in an IDE, which compiles it into object code executable by the machine.[20] This fundamental function has over time been augmented by further features designed 'to assist the software lifecycle process'.[21] They do this in myriad ways (too many to fully canvass here), but some important points to note are that applications for writing code vary in complexity and sophistication, from those that are simple text editors requiring additional software (a compiler) to produce executable code, to more powerful suites that include compilers, debuggers, build automation tools, version control, tools for highlighting syntax and auto-completing code statements, et cetera. Most IDEs can detect problems in source code, including syntax errors identified according to the requirements of the programming language being used, naming mistakes (incorrect variable or method names), logically impossible statements, and other incorrect programming 'grammar' that will cause errors fatal to execution. More sophisticated IDEs auto-complete formulaic expressions in the relevant programming language, and will keep track of a project's structure, suggesting relevant connections between code modules as the designer is working (this is termed 'intelligent code completion'). It is also possible to suggest points at which the code might be documented, or explanatory comments added (see the next section),[22] to enable other developers to interpret and understand what the code is designed to do. We saw in Chapter 3 the importance of being able to interpret a code-based rule; this is one means by which transparency could be implemented within the IDE, the software requiring the designer to include explanatory comments.

C Troncoso and C Diaz, 'Engineering privacy by design' (2011) 14 *Computers, Privacy & Data Protection*.

[20] In practice development tool chains often separate the IDE from the compiler.

[21] A Abran et al., *Guide to the Software Engineering Body of Knowledge (SWEBOK)* (IEEE Computer Society and Angela Burgess 2004) 10–11.

[22] In modern sophisticated IDEs this kind of functionality is included for documenting traditional code. See for example Microsoft, 'XML documentation (Visual C++)' (Microsoft 2016) <https://docs.microsoft.com/en-us/cpp/ide/xml-documentation-visual-cpp> last accessed 4 March 2021.

One can appreciate from this extremely brief survey of IDE functionality how the particular features of the software being used to produce code – its affordances – play a central role in structuring how the product designer does her job.[23] As an element of the PoP, the IDE structures and even dictates the scope of action of the product designer. The (secondary) affordances of the IDE might therefore be designed to discourage or prevent not only logical or aesthetic infelicities in the product designer's code – as the features just described already do – but also the writing of code that fails to meet digisprudential standards.

Some initiatives already exist that augment the purely practical or logical aspects of the programming assistance that IDEs provide. One example is the use of machine learning to provide code completion suggestions that are derived from the code of existing, third-party projects. Here the 'wisdom of the crowd', embodied in the code of those projects, constitutes a dataset from which the algorithm provides 'predictions' that go beyond the static syntax-derived suggestions provided by traditional intelligent code completion.[24] Microsoft's Intellicode system, for example, uses as training data the open source code from popular projects on the company's GitHub platform. When enabled, the code recommendations in Microsoft's Visual Studio IDE[25] are thus based in part on real-world projects, which will inevitably include aesthetic and value-based code design choices.

This phenomenon can be looked at as both a risk and an opportunity; the intention behind Intellicode is of course to encourage 'best practice' in the production of new code, the assumption being that the most popular projects on GitHub represent such practice by dint of their prominence. It is of course questionable whether popularity is the appropriate measure for the quality of code, assuming a quantitative measure is even possible where the medium has so much inherent normative power. The risk, then, is that systems like Intellicode in fact perpetuate bad practice, reflexively setting in train path-dependent 'habits of mind'[26] in the designers who rely on its computationally legalistic suggestions.

---

[23] RB Kline and A Seffah, 'Evaluation of integrated software development environments: Challenges and results from three empirical studies' (2005) 63 *International Journal of Human-Computer Studies* 607.

[24] M Bruch et al., 'IDE 2.0: Collective intelligence in software development' in *Proceedings of the FSE/SDP Workshop on Future of Software Engineering Research – FoSER '10* (ACM Press 2010).

[25] Microsoft, 'Visual Studio IntelliCode' (Microsoft 2018) <https://visualstudio.microsoft.com/services/intellicode/> last accessed 4 March 2021.

[26] P Graham, 'Beating the averages' (2003) <http://www.paulgraham.com/avg.html> last accessed 4 March 2021; J Weizenbaum, *Computer Power and Human Reason: From Judgment to Calculation* (Freeman 1976) 102–4.

A more desirable possibility is that digisprudentially legitimate code might have a positive effect on such data-driven code completion systems. Code that embodies the sorts of legitimacy-creating practices I am discussing might, if promulgated widely, come to be reflected in the suggestions provided by systems like Intellicode, in turn contributing to a greater standardisation of these concepts at the level of source code.

(a) Code Verification versus Legal Proof: Justice being Seen to be Done

The importance of transparency and contestability has led to increased interest in formal methods that not only guarantee a certain outcome in the code, but also allow relevant parties to see the 'why' of the code's behaviour.

From that perspective, the goal is to verify in advance that a system will operate according to a predefined set of characteristics (this is of course the core of code's ruleishness). Although this is an important development from the perspective of legal compliance, it is not necessarily sufficient to afford true contestability (recall the distinction made in Chapter 1 between compliance by design and legitimacy[27]). Legal proof and formal verification of code may have similarities, but there are also crucial differences. In practice, a legal proof contains not just the empirical evidence and legal sources necessary to construct a valid syllogism,[28] but also evidence of procedural propriety as a concern separate from the validity of the syllogism's conclusion. In other words, the code may be compliant, but in order for legitimate contestability properly to be afforded, it must provide evidence of 'due process' in order for the matter to be proven according to the relevant legal standard.[29] Merely 'doing justice' is insufficient; due process requires evidence of the procedure that was followed; justice must not simply be done, it must be seen to be done. Apprehending the right person in a criminal case is only one part of the equation; if their confession is obtained without legal representation then it is *de facto* illegitimate, regardless of any truth it might contain. Due process under the law thus takes what might have happened to be as important as what actually happened. Evidence of this proof must be communicable in a specific way; legitimacy of the legal process requires a form of evidential transparency that goes beyond merely telling the 'whole truth' in a given instance; it requires that this truth be demonstrated to external observers (including

---

[27] See 'Why Not "Compliance by Design"?' in Section 1.4.

[28] On which, see N MacCormick, *Rhetoric and the Rule of Law: A Theory of Legal Reasoning* (Oxford University Press 2005) chapter 3.

[29] For a salient analysis in the US context, see DK Citron, 'Technological due process' (2008) 85 *Washington University Law Review* 1249.

the courts) in a form that is intelligible to them. In institutional law this is of course achieved by means of a public trial.

Affording true contestability, then, requires enabling the end-user to detect code conditions that are susceptible to contest (transparency of operation, discussed in the previous chapter). Crucially, however, it can also be interpreted as requiring the demonstration of how the code was developed in the first place.[30] In a sense, documenting the design process (particularly the outcomes of agile cycles discussed above) will in itself provide this, but it is also feasible to integrate a measure of this kind of 'due process' into the IDE by bridging the gap between human comprehension and machinic execution, guided by the goal of ensuring legally relevant intelligibility.

7.4 Code and Natural Language

At the level of its source, code is a bi-directional text: it is both a set of instructions for the computer to perform, and a document for the human interpreter that explains what the machine will do upon execution. This central characteristic of code as simultaneously performative and documentary separates it from most other types of text, in degree if not category[31] (legal texts are of course also performative, albeit within the constraints of a text-based normative order). On the one hand, we can think of what code affords the end-user at the interaction level, described in Chapter 2.[32] But on the other, we can also think of what code affords, and to whom, when it is looked at as a text. The digisprudential affordances are not concerned only with this first level of communication, namely what will ultimately be afforded to the end-user in operation; they also, necessarily, require the code-as-text to afford certain things. The production of 'interactive' code, or 'architecture', is by definition dependent on the writing of code's text, and so some engagement with that text is necessary to gain a holistic sense of what the code does and does not do, and what it does and does not afford.

In code of any real complexity, the documentary function of the medium is crucial for understanding what the system does or is intended to do. This is particularly true where more than one designer is involved in its creation: the ability to understand what a programmer 'meant' by choosing one particular

---

[30] TJ Bench-Capon and FP Coenen, 'Isomorphism and legal knowledge based systems' (1992) 1 *Artificial Intelligence and Law* 65, 70–1.

[31] P Swartz, 'How do programs mean?' in *Division III: Essays in Programs as Literature* (Hampshire College 2007); I Arns, 'Code as performative speech act' (2005) 4 *Artnodes*.

[32] Lessig's 'code as law' analysis is focused primarily on this level. See L Lessig, *Code: Version 2.0* (Basic Books 2006) *passim*.

approach rather than a reasonable alternative can be crucial to a successful implementation, even within a small team (and all the more across continents and potentially significant stretches of time, where third-party open source code is being used).

The documentary function of code has two basic aspects. The first comes in the form of *ad hoc* comments included alongside the executable code. These are ignored by the machine, but can explain to the human reader what that part of the code is intended to do, why the designer chose this particular approach, or for example that some element of code is a temporary 'hack'[33] that works ostensibly but will need future revision. These comments are like notes in the margin of a book; they are intended for a human reader and can include however much detail the designer wishes, without this in any way affecting the nature or execution of the code statements they appear alongside. Providing commentary in this way is a powerful means of explicating what code does, although a corollary of its *ad hoc* nature is that the designer might fail to provide it, or might mischaracterise what the code in fact does because of misunderstanding or the desire to obfuscate.[34] It is possible to some extent to bridge the 'isomorphic gap' between natural language commentary and executable statement; I will discuss some potential approaches below but for now we turn to the second aspect of code's documentary function, which flows from the programming language itself.

(a) The Interpretative Affordances of Programming Languages

While *ad hoc* comments need not have any isomorphism with the code they accompany, it is also possible for the code to speak for itself, through the programming language in which it is written and the structures and functions that constitute its 'grammar'. Whether or not these will afford intelligibility will vary according to the language: on the one hand, some languages aim as far as possible to promote human understanding over computer 'cognition' (I discuss these below), while many so-called esoteric languages are explicitly designed to be as difficult to understand as possible, despite being, from the

---

[33] P Swartz, 'The hack as form' in *Division III: Essays in Programs as Literature* (Hampshire College 2007).

[34] The intelligibility of comments can facilitate differing ends: at the centre of the 'climategate' controversy were comments in climate modelling code that appeared to suggest to non-experts (specifically James Delingpole) that the code had been written intentionally to produce false data in support of the consensus on anthropogenic climate change. In this case, a little knowledge was a dangerous thing. For a full account, see MC Marino, *Critical Code Studies* (MIT Press 2020) chapter 4.

perspective of the machine, every bit as intelligible as their human-friendly counterparts.[35]

Programming languages that are designed for intelligibility will communicate their meaning more clearly and thus afford a wider notion of transparency at the level of the text,[36] which can have positive reflexive effects during production that would be a valuable addition to the forms of operational transparency previously described. By using a more intelligible programming language, the designer is in effect anticipating the affordance of contestation, and particularly its evidential dimension. In this way, the PoP plays a role in this aspect of digisprudential legitimacy through the design of the language.

Programming languages, as tools that are themselves designed by the PoP, have interesting properties as compared with human languages. Whereas the grammar of a natural language is an ever-changing crystallisation of its use in practice,[37] for programming languages this arrangement is almost entirely upended.[38] As participants in the hermeneutic development of a natural language we all to some degree contribute to the evolution of its grammar; the same cannot be said for the designer in respect of the language in which she is writing her code. There, the 'speaker' of the language is entirely constrained by the syntax imposed ex ante by the PoP; she has no input into the specification of its rules. Furthermore, a given statement in code is entirely ineffectual if it fails to meet the precise requirements of that predetermined grammar – there can be no ex post reinterpretation to make up for infelicities of expression.[39] In that case, the code will simply not execute. (Any reader who has programmed will know all too well the experience of staring hopelessly at lines of code that will simply not execute, unable to identify precisely where the error lies.)

---

[35] An example of such an esoteric language, whose name sums up this ethos perfectly, is Brainfuck. For an interesting discussion of the aesthetic qualities of such languages, see M Mateas and N Montfort, 'A box, darkly: Obfuscation, weird languages, and code aesthetics' in *Proceedings of the 6th Digital Arts and Culture Conference* (IT University of Copenhagen 2005).

[36] P Swartz, 'A tower of languages' in *Division III: Essays in Programs as Literature* (Hampshire College 2007) 118–19.

[37] P Ricoeur, *Interpretation Theory: Discourse and the Surplus of Meaning* (TCU Press 1976) chapter 1.

[38] WJ Ong, *Orality and Literacy: The Technologizing of the Word* (3rd edn, Routledge 2012) 7.

[39] Swartz, 'How do programs mean?' (n 31) 81–4.

(b) The Linguistic Relativity of Programming Languages

The 'grammar' and design conventions of a programming language are particularly responsible for framing the solution to a given problem.[40] Nearly all modern languages are Turing complete, meaning they can perform the same set of atomic calculations, regardless of the higher-level abstractions they include to make them easier for designers to use in practice. Despite this, some languages are designed for, or are especially appropriate for solving, particular kinds of problem.[41] This is down to the amount and forms of abstraction they include, for example predetermined functions that achieve particular computational goals in a single black-boxed step that does not require further bespoke coding by the designer. These 'off-the-shelf' functions are integrated into the core grammar of the language, somewhat akin to idioms in natural language that 'formalise' particular meanings in a single phrase that those familiar with the language can understand.

Setting aside for a moment the factors that make a particular programming language more fashionable at a given point in history, the choice to use one language over another can in principle be tied to the usefulness of the abstractions it provides, and how these 'fit' the designer's understanding of the problem at hand.[42] Of course, the question of what constitutes the 'best' solution will be contested, but my argument is that any answer should include the goal of mitigating computational legalism.[43] Programming languages are, as Graham puts it, 'not just technologies, but habits of mind'.[44] These habits

---

[40] Marino (n 34) 144.

[41] Ibid. 124–5. This often results in (heated) debates about the relative merits of languages, an example being the rivalry in the statistics/machine learning world between proponents of R and Python.

[42] See Graham's discussion of the 'power' of different programming languages (n 26). The W3C recommends the use of the 'least powerful language' suitable for a given task. See W3C, 'The rule of least power' (W3C 2006) <https://www.w3.org/2001/tag/doc/least-Power.html> last accessed 4 March 2021. This latter suggestion reflects the ethos behind designing for modularity along 'tussle lines', recommended in DD Clark et al., 'Tussle in cyberspace: Defining tomorrow's Internet' (2005) 13 *IEEE/ACM Transactions on Networking (ToN)* 462 and discussed in detail in the previous chapter.

[43] This is far from the norm. Amongst programmers, the 'best' solution (assuming it works, *ceteris paribus*) is usually the 'most efficient'. I argued against this framing in the previous chapter's discussion of the affordance of delay. For a discussion relating to legal technologies, see L Diver, 'Computational legalism and the affordance of delay in law' (2021) 1 *Journal of Cross-disciplinary Research in Computational Law* <https://journalcrcl.org/crcl/article/view/3> last accessed 19 April 2021.

[44] Graham (n 26). See also Swartz, 'A tower of languages' (n 36).

develop over time, based in part on the kinds of problem being solved. Given that a designer will usually become 'fluent' in only a handful of languages, she will begin to see the problems she is charged with solving through the lens of those languages, with the affordances of their syntax, functions, and data structures coming to frame the solutions she conceives.[45]

This representational idea relates to the notion of linguistic relativity, the theory that the language we use mediates our situatedness within empirical reality.[46] Much like a native tongue, the language we are most familiar with frames our experience; the available vocabulary and grammatical structures form a lens through which our worlds are constructed, culture shaping language and vice versa.[47]

Whatever the merits of the theory of linguistic relativity in the context of linguistics, from a pragmatic perspective it is no stretch to claim that programming languages structure how designers approach the problems they are tasked with solving.[48] The ultimate design of a given code's ontology will be affected to whatever degree by the data structures the programming language 'naturally' accommodates (for example arrays, data frames, matrices), while the rules that process the system's inputs and outputs will be affected by the grammar and functions that the language provides in the first instance. An inexperienced or unconfident programmer will avoid tackling complex functionality that the language does not accommodate by default, which in turn will affect her approach to building her application.

Chen's discussion of linguistic relativity in programming languages is instructive here. For him, once the practice of writing code has begun, the 'boilerplate and design patterns' of a given programming language are internalised as 'unconscious and automatic idioms', ready to be 'regurgitated on demand'.[49] In a study of the standard 'split, apply, combine' task in data science, Chen illuminates linguistic relativity as between the R, MATLAB, APL, and Julia languages (the latter of which he helped design). Depending on the language, the higher-order functions that were immediately available to the programmer varied, such that in some languages the tools for solving the problem were very much more 'ready-to-hand' than in others in which the

---

[45] For an early study confirming this tendency, see RL Wexelblat, 'The consequences of one's first programming language' (1981) 11 *Software: Practice and Experience* 733.

[46] BL Whorf, 'Science and linguistics' in JB Carroll (ed.), *Language, Thought, and Reality: Selected Writings of Benjamin Lee Whorf* (28th edn, MIT Press 2007).

[47] E Sapir, 'The status of linguistics as a science' (1929) *Language* 207.

[48] Swartz, 'A tower of languages' (n 36) 105 *et seq*.

[49] J Chen, 'Linguistic relativity and programming languages' (2018) arXiv:1808.03916 [cs, stat], 2 <http://arxiv.org/abs/1808.03916> last accessed 4 March 2021.

problem required sustained attention and the coding of a bespoke solution. Thus, where some languages have relatively constrained data structures and prefigured 'habits', others are more flexible in their generative possibilities. The designer is necessarily situated within a set of habitual and community practices that surround the language and its associated libraries and tools, and thus will to a greater or lesser degree be guided in her understanding of the solution to the programming challenge she is faced with.[50]

In the end, then, the programming language wields significant power over the product designer, framing her actions from the outset.[51] From the perspective of digisprudence, the design of the language ought to reflect values of legitimacy, facilitating their embodiment in the code written using them. Proposals already exist for such explicitly value-driven programming languages, in the sense that the values are clearly and intentionally embodied in their design, rather than passively or unthinkingly represented. These proposals have been aimed for example at representing feminist perspectives[52] or the particularities of non-Western cultures, as in 'ethnoprogramming'.[53] An example of the latter is قلب ('heart'), a language that poses a vivid challenge to the Anglo-centricity of contemporary programming languages, the vast majority of which use English verbs and nouns.[54]

(c) Describing Code Isomorphically

Returning to code's bi-directionality, approaches exist that intertwine the documentary and performative roles of the text. A prominent, early example

---

[50] Ibid. 8. See also C Thompson, *Coders: Who They Are, What They Think and How They Are Changing Our World* (Pan Macmillan 2019) chapter 1.

[51] Weizenbaum (n 26) 102–3.

[52] Cf. Schlesinger's proposals for a feminist programming language. See A Schlesinger, 'Feminism and programming languages' *HASTAC* (26 November 2013) <https://www.hastac.org/blogs/ari-schlesinger/2013/11/26/feminism-and-programming-languages> last accessed 4 March 2021. For a perspective on how masculinity has structured the practices of science and software production, see T Estrin, 'Women's studies and computer science: Their intersection' (1996) 18 *IEEE Annals of the History of Computing* 43; P Swartz, 'White boys' code' in *Division III: Essays in Programs as Literature* (Hampshire College 2007) 32 *et seq.*

[53] O Laiti, 'The ethnoprogramming model' in *Proceedings of the 16th Koli Calling International Conference on Computing Education Research* (Association for Computing Machinery 2016). Laiti's work stems from the broader concept of *ethnocomputing*, which aims to challenge the positivism dominant in (Western) computer science. See M Tedre et al., 'Ethnocomputing: ICT in cultural and social context' (2006) 49 *Communications of the ACM* 126.

[54] R Nasser, *Nasser/---* (Github 2020) <https://github.com/nasser/---> last accessed 4 March 2021. On English as the *lingua franca* of programming, see NK Hayles, 'Print is flat, code is deep: The importance of media-specific analysis' (2004) 25 *Poetics Today* 67, 79; Marino (n 34) 151 *et seq.*

is Knuth's Literate Programming paradigm and its WEB language, which tightly weave together executable code and commentary in a single file, from which both isomorphic documentation and the executable code can be generated.[55] A more recent incarnation is the Jupyter Notebook, a self-contained 'document' that allows the designer to combine executable code with 'interactive widgets, plots, narrative text, equations, images, and video'.[56] These approaches are motivated by the notion that programming ought to serve human ways of thinking, rather than imposing computational structures upon the latter. This means, at least notionally, that culture can shape the code (mediated by the language) rather than the converse, which in turn shines a normative light on the linguistic relativity of those languages. We see this aim reflected throughout the history of programming in the design of business-oriented languages such as COBOL and its ancestor FLOW-MATIC,[57] as well as languages like LOGO, which aims to reflect the programmer's embodied perception,[58] and Inform 7, which uses entirely natural language sentences for its executable expressions.[59] The ends of a given language are expressed in its vocabulary and grammar; these might conceivably reflect the aim of legitimacy and legitimation. And even if the underlying language still facilitates the building of legalistic structures (as invariably it will, if it is Turing complete), the IDE might provide hints or even mandates that encourage new forms of 'best practice' that can avoid them.

Behaviour-Driven Development

Beyond the programming language itself, Behaviour-Driven Development (BDD) is an approach that focuses on the point of practical implementation, bridging the isomorphism gap between *ad hoc* comments and what the code in fact will do. Like the Petri net visual model discussed below, BDD facilitates isomorphism between code and a representation that is intelligible to non-technologists, in this case a natural-language textual description. BDD's originator North describes it as an 'outside-in' methodology, starting from a set of desired outcomes and evolving towards the code features that

---

[55] DE Knuth, 'Literate programming' (1984) 27 *The Computer Journal* 97.

[56] 'What is the Jupyter Notebook?' (27 March 2019) <https://jupyter-notebook.readthedocs. io/en/latest/examples/Notebook/What%20is%20the%20Jupyter%20Notebook.html> last accessed 4 March 2021.

[57] Marino (n 34) chapter 5.

[58] See for example S Papert, 'Different visions of LOGO' (1985) 2 *Computers in the Schools* 3. See also Estrin (n 52) 45. The notion of the PoP shaping the designer's perception shaping the end-user's perception is clear.

[59] 'About' *Inform 7* <http://inform7.com/about> last accessed 4 March 2021.

implement them.[60] Although usually aimed at bridging the domains of business requirements and code development, the quasi-isomorphism of BDD means it can operate as a post hoc evidentiary mechanism as much as a means of developing ex ante design specifications.

BDD uses natural language[61] templates for defining features the code is required to implement. These are combined with IDE tools that generate both the framework of code statements from those specifications and the 'unit tests', or granular checks of the output of discrete sections of code, that verify that they behave as expected. Code features are defined using natural language, making them intelligible for evidentiary purposes (and indeed feasibly for end-users). Here is an example specification of a shopping basket in an online application:

```
Feature: Online shop basket
  In order to buy products
  As a customer
  I need to be able to put interesting products into a
    basket
Rules:
  Delivery for basket under £10 is £3
Scenario: Buying a single product under £10
  Given there is a "Product X", which costs £5
  When I add the "Product X" to the basket
  Then I should have 1 product in the basket
  And the overall basket price should be £8[62]
```

The IDE parses the keywords in the template (feature, in order to, as a, I need to, rules, scenario, given, when, and then) and generates the necessary code functions. These have a specificity that encourages the

---

[60] Dan North & Associates, 'What's in a story?' (Dan North & Associates, 11 February 2007) <https://dannorth.net/whats-in-a-story/> last accessed 4 March 2021. This mirrors the concept of 'bottom-up' programming, which, like agile development cycles, is about 'following the path of the program [system] as it develops'. See Swartz, 'White boys' code' (n 52) 36.

[61] Known as a 'ubiquitous language', or a 'business readable domain specific language'. See M Fowler, 'Business readable domain specific language' *martinfowler.com* (15 December 2008) <https://martinfowler.com/bliki/BusinessReadableDSL.html> last accessed 4 March 2021.

[62] This and the next example are adapted from 'Behat documentation' *Behat* <http://docs.behat.org/en/latest/quick_start.html> last accessed 4 March 2021. Behat is a set of tools for implementing BDD in the PHP programming language.

designer to write modular code, which in turn facilitates more cyclical testing and verification. For example:

```
/**
 * @Given there is a(n) :arg1, which costs £:arg2
 */
public function thereIsAWhichCostsPounds($arg1, $arg2) {
   [the implementing code goes here]
}
```

One can see how the function name ('`thereIsAWhichCostsPounds`') has been automatically generated from the natural language '`Given`' line in the feature description. Within the curly braces – { and } – the designer writes the code that corresponds to that precise element of functionality, and nothing more (the automated inclusion of only two *arguments* `$arg1` and `$arg2` – values passed into the function for processing – limits the scope of what this function can feasibly be written to perform). This discreteness of functionality is ideal for granular testing and for achieving the aim of modularity discussed in the previous chapter. The goal of BDD, then, is to achieve 'living documentation', both intelligible to non-developers and simultaneously isomorphic with the underlying instrumentality of the code.

Interpreting Code as a Visual Model

If BDD is concerned with textual isomorphic descriptions of code, the Petri net is one approach to visual description. Dating from 1962,[63] the Petri net is a standardised formal modelling approach for representing arbitrary processes in terms of 'states' and the 'transitions' between them. Petri nets have been applied in many domains, not least in the modelling of legal provisions and processes.[64] The nets are commonly used in the early stages of the design of code to visually map the changing states of the system over time. Despite their graphical appearance and apparent simplicity, the temporal flow of a Petri

---

[63] CA Petri, *Kommunikation Mit Automaten* (PhD thesis, University of Bonn 1962) <http://epub.sub.uni-hamburg.de/informatik/volltexte/2011/160/> last accessed 4 March 2021.

[64] J Freiheit et al., 'Lexecute: Visualisation and representation of legal procedures' (2006) 3 *Digital Evidence & Electronic Signature Law Review* 19; JA Meldman, 'A Petri-net representation of civil procedure' (1977) 19 *Idea* 123; JA Meldman and AW Holt, 'Petri nets and legal systems' (1971) 12 *Jurimetrics Journal* 65. More recent work has used Petri nets to model normative relationships in law, with a view to aligning norms with technical implementation in the way outlined below. See for example G Sileno, A Boer and T van Engers, 'Towards a representational model of social affordances from an institutional perspective' in *Proceedings of the Workshop Computational Social Science and Social Computer Science: Two Sides of the Same Coin* (Institute of Advanced Studies, University of Surrey 2014).

net can be both easily simulated and formally verified. This means it can be mathematically proven whether or not the system enters a given state, and the conditions under which this takes place.[65] Petri nets in a sense facilitate the 'live documentation' of the system, describing the functionality of the code in a way that is both intelligible to non-technologists but that is also isomorphic with the concrete behaviour of the code.[66] Existing research has demonstrated the automated generation of Petri nets from object-oriented source code[67] as well as (contrariwise) the automated generation of code from Petri models of intended functionality.[68] The validation and certification affordances of Petri nets through formal proofs and reachability analysis[69] mean we can be sure of isomorphism between the code and the net, thus making the graphical representation a potentially valuable evidential tool for making intelligible the concrete behaviour of the code.[70]

The states and transitions in the model are represented by circles and rectangles, respectively. These are connected with arcs (arrows) that represent the flow of the process, which at any given moment is represented by the distribution of 'tokens' across the model's states. These four basic elements (states, transitions, arcs, and tokens) are the essence of all Petri nets (Figure 7.1).

A state containing a token (a dot) currently 'holds'. Multiple states can lead to, or from, a given transition, and they can hold simultaneously. When a transition fires, all the states leading to it will lose x tokens, and all the states leading from it will gain y tokens, where x and y correspond to the numerical weightings alongside each of the relevant arcs (the default being one). A transition can only fire – and will always fire – where the number of tokens in its preceding state(s) is greater than or equal to the weighting of the relevant arc. This is demonstrated in Figure 7.2, where the transitions T_1 and T_2 are

---

[65] Both viewed of course from within the limits of the system's ontology – but that indeed is precisely the point; to be able to contest that ontology and to argue why it is limited in ways that are unlawful.

[66] B Lin, 'Software synthesis of process-based concurrent programs' in *Proceedings of the 35th Annual Design Automation Conference* (ACM 1998); SM Shatz and WK Cheng, 'A Petri net framework for automated static analysis of Ada tasking behavior' (1988) 8 *Journal of Systems and Software* 343.

[67] Lin (n 66); Shatz and Cheng (n 66).

[68] KH Mortensen, 'Automatic code generation method based on coloured Petri net models applied on an access control system' in M Nielsen and D Simpson (eds), *Application and Theory of Petri Nets* (Springer 2000).

[69] Diver and Schafer (n 19) 82–3.

[70] K Salimifard and M Wright, 'Petri net-based modelling of workflow systems: An overview' (2001) 134 *European Journal of Operational Research* 664, 667. This can be contrasted with other software modelling tools that are not necessarily isomorphic, for example entity-relationship diagrams.

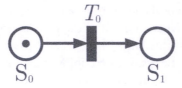

Figure 7.1 A basic Petri net

competing, with T_2 'winning' because the two states leading to it have the requisite number of tokens to trigger that transition.

This allows for control over the flow of the net, as tokens are distributed across the net according to the outcomes of prior transitions. This limited semantics enables complex processes to be simplified into graphical representations without losing formal validity.[71]

Mechanistic elements of complex processes can be abstracted into 'subnets' and then subsequently into transitions, thus mirroring the fundamental concept of abstraction in object-oriented programming.[72] Recursive abstraction of this kind allows for the modelling of even very complex systems, whilst simultaneously enabling the interpreter to drill down into the particulars of the code's logic as required. It can be appreciated how these representations might be useful from an evidential perspective, should the code ultimately be contested in court.

I have demonstrated the normative complexity that can be represented by Petri nets in prior work with Burkhard Schafer.[73] For example, the net in Figure 7.3 shows a model of Article 8 of the Data Protection Directive, precursor to the GDPR, which concerns the processing of special categories of data.

In principle, such a model of a legal provision could be interfaced with an abstracted model of a code system, providing a way of communicating between the states generated, and required, by each, as illustrated in Figure 7.4.

As one can appreciate from this simplified example, in order for the code to traverse between states S_0 and S_4, it must first pass the test in the legal

---

[71] For a more detailed discussion of Petri nets' application in the legal domain, see Diver and Schafer (n 19). For a theoretical background, see either Petri's doctoral thesis (Petri (n 63)) or T Murata, 'Petri nets: Properties, analysis and applications' (1989) 77 *Proceedings of the IEEE* 541.

[72] Bench-Capon and Coenen (n 30) 72.

[73] Diver and Schafer (n 19) 77 *et seq*.

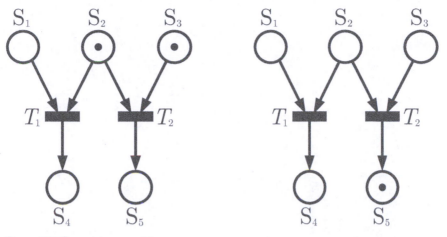

Figure 7.2 Competing transitions

net (left), which is itself contingent on an input from a sub-element of the software net. The idea is that the legal net will permit the code to 'continue' (that is, reach state S_4) only if there is some other condition in place that demonstrates the existence of a legally required state. The discussion of the model above in the original article envisages a registration form that collects sensitive personal data (in that case, the end-user's ethnic origin). This fact was represented by S_2, which when set thus communicates to the legal net that a special category of data was being processed, which in turn means one of the Article 8(2) exceptions must apply for processing to be lawful.[74]

Of course, these latter examples concern compliance with the substantive law; in other words, they are about 'compliance by design'. Nevertheless, the very existence of the model as a form of documentation demonstrates the second aspect of contestability I have been discussing. Whether or not the formal verification of the model results in compliance by design (indeed, legal compliance may not be the aim), the model itself affords contestability by providing intelligible evidence of how the code operates. One can appreciate the flexibility and abstraction of this kind of approach, and its ability to model and communicate in a single representation more than one aspect of the code.

---

[74] For a more in-depth discussion, see ibid. 79 *et seq*. For a more sophisticated example of this kind of approach, see Sileno et al. (n 64).

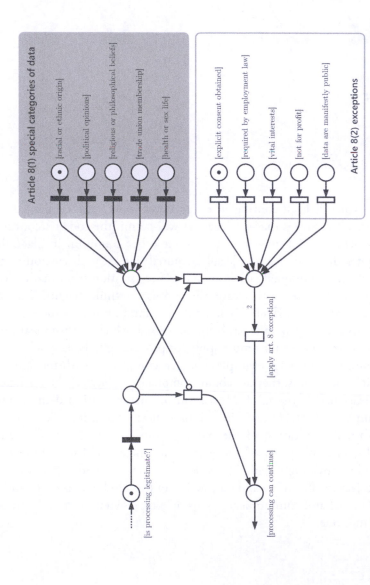

Figure 7.3 A Petri net model of Article 8 of the Data Protection Directive

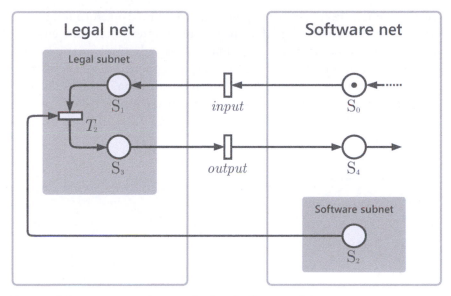

Figure 7.4 Communication between legal and software models

7.5 Conclusion

The goal of this chapter has been to highlight various aspects of the practical implementation of digisprudence, rather than to canvass all possible ways of achieving legitimacy. Especially relevant is the 'constitutional' role of the PoP, as embodied in code development paradigms, programming languages themselves, and the software environments in which code is invariably produced, known as integrated development environments (IDEs). Neither programming languages nor IDEs are in any sense 'found'; they are themselves the product of many design decisions that have normative weight which, to a greater or lesser degree, filter through to the code that is produced with(in) them. There is thus a parallel between constitutional and parliamentary law-making on the one hand, and the programmer of the programmer – represented *inter alia* in the affordances of the integrated development environment – and the product designer on the other. By considering what the (secondary) affordances of the design environment are and ought to be, we can imagine binding the creator of the (primary) technological normativity embodied in the finished product.

The approaches described above (and others that achieve similar ends) can only ever be a part of a broader commitment to legitimate design. At best they address only some aspects of the digisprudential scheme, concerned as they are primarily with formal contestability rather than the qualitative aspects of design described in Chapter 2. It would be dangerous to assume that the approaches of the kind described in this chapter would on their own exhaust the duty to legitimise code as a normative order. Fashions and technologies change of course; the discussion above has pointed to some classes of approach that can have a bearing on the operationalisation of digisprudence, without becoming so granular as to be left behind as coding practices evolve.

8

Rebooting Code as Law:
Conclusions and Next Steps

> When technologies are always influencing human actions, we had better try
> to give this influence a desirable form.[1]

Code is not law, but as this book has shown, that fact must not deter lawyers
from taking an active interest in how it shapes and constitutes the behaviour
and actions of citizens in a democracy. We critique the form taken by the legal
rules that govern our lives, and we should do the same with code rules – especially since they are used increasingly as instruments to sidestep the supposed
'inefficiency' of text-based law that at its best respects, protects, and even
makes possible our autonomy as citizens. This should be of concern to anyone
interested in preserving the rule of law.

This cross-disciplinary study has brought together the practical question
of how code regulates with a legal-theoretical view of what constitutes legitimate regulation. Part I of the book sets out a descriptive analysis of code as
a normative concern, from the perspectives of both design and legal theory,
framing the problems so identified using the concept of *computational legalism*. In Part II, I discuss in greater depth the existing literature on what constitutes legitimate regulation, again from a legal-theoretical perspective (how
legal rules are made, or designed), and in terms of the existing discussions of
code by legal scholars. What becomes clear from the discussion in Chapter 5
is the lack of sustained attention on the ex ante nature of code, and thus
the need to engage seriously with the practices of its production. Part III
of the book – a synthesis of the first two parts – proposes a way forward
from computational legalism, the central position being that the methods of
ameliorating legalism in the legal realm ought to be applied in other normative domains, including – with appropriate modification – 'code as law'. The
result is the framework of *digisprudential affordances* set out in Chapter 6,

---

[1] P-P Verbeek, 'Materializing morality: Design ethics and technological mediation' (2006) 31
Science, Technology, & Human Values 361, 370.

which are grounded in practical reality first through their application to real technologies, and second through an analysis, in Chapter 7, of some of the processes and tools of real-world code production.

Ultimately, digisprudence is about taking code seriously as a regulator on its own terms, but without giving ground to what we ought to expect of a legitimate exercise of regulative power in a democracy. Unlike most existing treatment of code in the legal literature, built as much of it is on the Lessigian framework, I have treated code not as an abstract medium or 'regulatory modality', but as a mechanism that is embodied in very real, very particular artefacts whose design affects individuals and communities in concrete ways at identifiable moments in time. The specific configuration of (dis)affordance experienced by a particular individual in her use of an artefact is where regulative force is actually 'applied', and so our analysis of code must in the end include the relations that these artefacts have with those whose behaviour and actions they enable, constrain, and indeed constitute.

Given this focus on relationality, the goal in this book has been to suggest a set of affordances – relational as they by definition are – that when present legitimise the code at a 'constitutional' level, prior to considerations of its commercial purposes or whether or not it complies with the specific requirements of substantive law. The digisprudential affordances therefore serve as a guide for the production of legitimate code; where it fails to provide those affordances to the relevant parties – the user, and the court – then it ought to be deemed illegitimate. Saying so is not something we should be coy about doing, given what is at stake.

I will conclude in this final chapter by reiterating the relevance of digisprudence to contemporary technologically mediated life, before highlighting some of the exciting avenues for future research that have emerged in the course of this work.

8.1 The Contemporary Relevance of Digisprudence

I highlighted in Chapter 1 the tension between law as the paradigmatic normative order on the one hand, and code as an alternative order on the other. This speaks to fundamental questions of law and of normativity – what it is for an a-legal order to arise in parallel with (or even to supplant) democratically legitimated law, particularly when that alternative order is commercially motivated and benefits from the 'legalistic' characteristics of ruleishness, opacity, immediacy, immutability, and pervasiveness. When we fail to enquire as to the processes through which private code-based normativity is created and imposed, the result is a situation that is deeply problematic on two fronts, each of which compounds the other: we have technical rules which are by their very nature opaque and instrumental, created through commercial processes that lack democratic incentives, ratification, and oversight. The implications are profound, particularly given the ever-increasing role of code in ordering our social, political, and economic lives.

It is clear from the literature that this is a fundamental but under-studied problem. While the regulation of code by law is a topic that has generated a significant literature across many contexts, it has mostly failed to account adequately for the myriad ways in which designers impose normativity *in practice*, often outside of any awareness or cognisance of the substantive law which they should be applying to and through their practices. Related to this is the common assumption that more law will result in better code. I have argued that the translation of legal text into code – assuming the designer is aware of the text in the first place – is problematic, and so there are inevitable gaps between what the law expects and what the code actually does.[2] Appealing for more law will undoubtedly help close some of these gaps, but it is unlikely to solve the problem at a foundational level, not least because ever-more complex and precise sets of textual rules undermine rather than encourage compliance.[3] In the absence of a more computationally friendly form of legislation (I discuss this below), designers need to be guided in their creation of code that is not necessarily 'legal' *per se* but whose design embodies constitutional protections that can minimise the possibility of substantive illegality and can facilitate judicial action should such illegality be found.

As we saw in Chapter 5, the legal literature focused specifically on normative criteria for code is very small indeed, and while a few legal scholars have argued for greater engagement with the disciplines this book discusses, there is sometimes, ironically, an element of legalism in the unwillingness to look outside the boundaries and the conceptual lenses of the legal discipline in order to engage with what lies beyond.[4] This is unfortunate, because it is not possible fully to understand the alternative normative order of code by observing it through only a legal lens, far less is it possible to think pragmatically about how to tackle the real problems, discussed in this book, that it raises. By stepping outside of one's discipline, temporarily adopting the horizons of the domains against which it rubs or upon which it relies, we can gain new insights into how successfully and unsuccessfully it interfaces with

---

[2] L Diver, 'Law as a user: Design, affordance, and the technological mediation of norms' (2018) 15 *SCRIPTed* 4.

[3] C Reed, 'How to make bad law: Lessons from cyberspace' (2010) 73 *The Modern Law Review* 903, 904 *et seq*.; JN Shklar, *Legalism* (Harvard University Press 1964) 2.

[4] Cf. S Gutwirth, P De Hert and L De Sutter, 'The trouble with technology regulation: Why Lessig's "optimal mix" will not work' in R Brownsword and K Yeung (eds), *Regulating Technologies: Legal Futures, Regulatory Frames and Technological Fixes* (Hart 2008).

its environment. Such insights can be transformative when eventually we step 'back inside'.

8.2 Next Steps?

Various avenues for future research came to light while researching the thesis on which this book is based. Here is a brief survey of the most pressing concerns, particularly given the increasing appetite for outsourcing to code what has until recently been the domain of institutional law.

(a) The Future of Compliance by Design

Digisprudence is consciously focused on code as a normative order parallel to law, but within this focus lies the seed of an obvious question: how might the parallel orders be brought more closely together in the future? As code is increasingly the medium upon which other parts of social, political, and commercial life are built, it seems reasonable to assume that it will become the target of more and more positive law. However, laws that fail properly to be embodied in the code that they target tacitly undermine law-making as an expression of the democratic will. This is the problem I referred to early in Chapter 6, where the belief in the validity of the rule that animates the use of code transfers into a belief that the resulting code is itself also valid. The limits that this belief places on our knowledge of what is actually happening might come to have significant negative effects as code continues to proliferate deeper into the fabric of society.

Continuing in the legisprudential spirit, then, we might consider how legislators could better couch the terms of legal norms such that they are more susceptible to application in the design environment, and particularly in terms of affordances. The field of legal informatics is concerned with the question of translation from law to computational representations, but much of the work there does not engage the practices of norm creation themselves, continuing instead to view legislation as a passive source of textual rules to be grappled with by various external computational processes.[5] Although approaches to legal formalism have existed for decades, these seem to have had little impact on legislative practice. This may be changing with the emergence of 'Rules as Code', an umbrella term for a variety of emerging initiatives

---

[5] See for example P Lippe, DM Katz and D Jackson, 'Legal by design: A new paradigm for handling complexity in banking regulation and elsewhere in law' (2014) 93 *Oregon Law Review* 833; D Oberle et al., 'Engineering compliant software: Advising developers by automating legal reasoning' (2012) 9 *SCRIPTed* 280; DM Katz, 'Quantitative legal prediction – or – how I learned to stop worrying and start preparing for the data driven future of the legal services industry' (2012) 62 *Emory Law Journal* 909.

whose goal is for legislation to be drafted from the outset in machine-readable formats. Those working in this area have differing views on the ultimate purpose and value of this.[6] At the conservative end of the scale, some seek merely to add underlying 'semantic' structure to the text of legislative documents in order to improve various ancillary computational processes such as classification, searching, and archiving. Such an approach does not alter the instrument's textual nature, but merely its representation to the machine,[7] which in turn benefits drafting through the ability to, for example, keep track of provisions across versions of the document. More sophisticated are suggestions involving drafting the text of a legislative instrument alongside an equivalent computational representation that can be 'executed' to check for logical anomalies or lacunae, the goal being to assist parliamentary drafters in producing more logically coherent legislation.[8] Lastly, some seek to have legislative norms expressed directly in executable code that can be integrated directly into artefacts that implement policy on behalf of the state (as in tax calculators or benefit entitlement decisions) or whose commercial designers seek to make compliant with legislative requirements.[9] This is of course the mirror image of digisprudence: the creation of code-friendly institutional law, as opposed to the creation of 'legality-friendly' code. This is an emerging area, and while some of its goals are clearly valuable (there is no obvious downside to the semantic structuring of a legislative document or the elimination of logically impossible conditions between rules), others may have unforeseen reflexive effects on the nature of law built around accessible, natural language text. This is true even of rules as code approaches that are not concerned with creating the mythical 'robot judge'.

In any event, such a focus on positive law elides the relational stance I have been advocating. In that respect, I am not aware of any analysis of

---

[6] For a sober overview, see M Waddington, 'Machine-consumable legislation: A legislative drafter's perspective – human v artificial intelligence' (2019) *The Loophole – Journal of Commonwealth Association of Legislative Counsel* 21.

[7] Using, for example, the Akoma Ntoso XML standard.

[8] This is the goal of 'better rules' initiatives. See for example New Zealand Government, 'Better rules for government – discovery report' (New Zealand Government 2018) <https://www.digital.govt.nz/dmsdocument/95-better-rules-for-government-discovery-report> last accessed 4 March 2021. Interestingly, this goal is echoed in Meldman's use of a Petri net to model US federal civil procedure, where a lacuna that was hidden in the natural language came 'right to the surface' in the model. See JA Meldman, 'A Petri-net representation of civil procedure' (1977) 19 *Idea* 123, 145.

[9] Waddington (n 6) 24 *et seq*. For a real-world application currently under active development, see D Merigoux and L Huttner, 'Catala: Moving towards the future of legal expert systems' (INRIA 2020) <https://hal.inria.fr/hal-02936606> last accessed 4 March 2021.

how the substantive content of laws might be couched in the language of affordance, rendering them more capable of direct implementation by producers of code. Hildebrandt, for example, mentions 'detecting, configuring or designing affordances that are compatible with specific legal norms',[10] but does not discuss the opposite notion of couching laws in terms compatible with affordance theory. From a digisprudential perspective, the norm that is in fact embodied in the artefactual design is the norm that ultimately matters, and so the articulation of textual norms ought as far as possible to facilitate the most isomorphic code possible.[11]

We have seen how the concepts of (dis)affordance and inscription are simultaneously both concrete and technology-agnostic, because of their relational focus; the digisprudential affordances are specific enough to identify the presence or absence of defined capabilities, but abstract enough to apply across a wide spectrum of technologies. This might suggest affordance theory as a good candidate for expressing a range of substantive legal requirements in terms that lie closer to the actual practices of those expected to comply with them. The expressive texture of such an approach might be enhanced by recent work couching affordances in deontological terms appropriate for legal articulation,[12] the classification of affordances according to their cognitive, physical, sensory, and functional characteristics,[13] or even the various relationships of technological mediation that, as we saw in Chapter 2, structure our realities.[14]

(b) Design and Private Law

Another avenue for research is the relationship between design and private contracting (recall the discussion in Chapter 1 of the normative relationships in code and law). The observation that online contracting is a form of non-state legal ordering is not new,[15] but some of the observations about design

---

[10] M Hildebrandt, *Smart Technologies and the End(s) of Law: Novel Entanglements of Law and Technology* (Edward Elgar Publishing 2015) 218.

[11] I raised the problem of code's mediation of textual norms in Diver (n 2) 39–40.

[12] JL Davis and JB Chouinard, 'Theorizing affordances: From request to refuse' (2017) *Bulletin of Science, Technology & Society* 241. See also JL Davis, *How Artifacts Afford: The Power and Politics of Everyday Things* (MIT Press 2020).

[13] R Hartson, 'Cognitive, physical, sensory, and functional affordances in interaction design' (2003) 22 *Behaviour & Information Technology* 315.

[14] D Ihde, *Technology and the Lifeworld: From Garden to Earth* (Indiana University Press 1990) chapter 5.

[15] See for example L Belli and J Venturini, 'Private ordering and the rise of terms of service as cyber-regulation' (2016) *Internet Policy Review* 5; W Schulz and K Dankert, '"Governance by things" as a challenge to regulation by law' (2016) 5 *Internet Policy Review* <https://doi.

have implications that require further exploration. Building on the discourse around 'clickwrap' licensing in the 2000s, Hartzog moots the idea of design elements being considered as contractual terms *per se*.[16] This explicitly intertwines design practice with legal practice, and is something that design theory might helpfully inform. Although Hartzog does not employ those theories, their role is implicit in his analysis when he argues that specific features of design (such as Facebook's privacy settings, structured by the affordances of its interface) ought to be deemed part of the contract between the end-user and a website's operator.[17]

As with unfair contract terms, we can imagine (dis)affordances that are illegitimate terms of such a design-based contract. More recently Hartzog discusses 'promissory design', or 'the implicit (and sometimes even explicit) promises embedded in and expressed through design'.[18] He questions the disparity between liability arising from textual contract terms and the lack of accountability for promises expressed via design. Given the interface of the website is frequently the only medium by which end-users communicate with online providers, their expression of preferences through the configuration of website settings (that is, by configuring its affordances) ought to constitute a form of agreement. From the perspective of code's production, the provision of a setting in an interface perhaps ought to imply a legal duty on the provider to ensure the background code operates in accordance with (a reasonable interpretation of) the technical state the setting purports to create. The role that design plays in end-users' understanding of the products they use suggests the potential to explore further the role that design plays in foundational legal concepts of negotiation, consensus, and performance. This in turn will require jurisdiction-specific analyses, and the application of design theory to the perennial question of code versus jurisdiction.

(c) 'Legitimacy Impact Assessment'

A growing area of research activity, particularly in the fields of privacy and data protection,[19] is impact assessment. Impact assessments aim to provide

---

org/10.14763/2016.2.409> last accessed 19 April 2021; MJ Radin, 'Regulation by contract, regulation by machine' (2004) 160 *Journal of Institutional and Theoretical Economics (JITE)* 142.

[16] W Hartzog, 'Website design as contract' (2010) 60 *American University Law Review* 1635.

[17] Ibid. 1650 *et seq*.

[18] W Hartzog, *Privacy's Blueprint: The Battle to Control the Design of New Technologies* (Harvard University Press 2018) 169 *et seq*.

[19] The latter is required by Art. 35 of the GDPR under certain circumstances, including for new technologies.

'a systematic process for evaluating the potential effects of privacy of a project, initiative, or proposed system or scheme' and to assist in 'finding ways to mitigate or avoid any adverse effects'.[20] The European Commission has published guidance on their use for the Internet of Things,[21] and they are a common feature of government procurement processes.[22] As Clarke observes, one interpretation of why impact assessments have emerged in recent years is as a reaction to the 'increasingly privacy-invasive actions of governments and corporations' in the late twentieth century.[23] Because of these actions, 'people want to know about organisations' activities, and want to exercise control over their excesses', with the privacy impact assessment demonstrating a 'ceding by large organisations of some of the substantial power that they exercise over citizens'.[24] There is of course an appreciable overlap here with the ethos of digisprudence. Key to privacy impact assessment processes is their focus on a single project or initiative, their anticipatory (ex ante) nature, their wide scope in considering forms of privacy and the actors whose interests might be affected, their desire to identify both problems and solutions, and their focus on organisational engagement.

The notion of impact assessment is not limited to privacy. In previous co-authored work I have considered the notion of a 'social impact assessment',[25] taking into account not just data protection, but factors such as security, transparency, sustainability, resilience, and interoperability.[26] There might be scope here for a kind of 'legitimacy impact assessment', developed by adapting existing impact assessment methodologies towards a focus on legitimacy. This research might also consider the inter-relationship between digisprudence

[20] D Wright, 'Should privacy impact assessments be mandatory?' (2011) 54 *Communications of the ACM* 121, 123. See also D Kloza et al., 'Data protection impact assessments in the European Union. Complementing the new legal framework towards a more robust protection of individuals' (DPIA Lab 2017).

[21] European Commission, 'Privacy and Data Protection Impact Assessment Framework for RFID Applications' (European Commission 2011) <https://ec.europa.eu/digital-single-market/en/news/privacy-and-data-protection-impact-assessment-framework-rfid-applications> last accessed 4 March 2021.

[22] L Edwards, D McAuley and L Diver, 'From privacy impact assessment to social impact assessment' in *2016 IEEE Security and Privacy Workshops (SPW)* (IEEE 2016) 54.

[23] R Clarke, 'Privacy impact assessment: Its origins and development' (2009) 25 *Computer Law & Security Review* 123, 124.

[24] Ibid.

[25] Edwards et al. (n 22).

[26] Ibid. 56–7.

and substantive initiatives that guide the production of code already mentioned, for example data protection by design, mandated by the GDPR, value-sensitive design,[27] and participatory design.[28] The appropriate interplay between the baseline constitutional requirements of digisprudence and the higher-level substantive outputs of such approaches is a potentially fruitful direction for future research.

8.3 Concluding Thoughts

The theory I have presented in this book builds on existing work in legal and design theory, seeking to build a bridge between the two worlds whilst maintaining focus on what ought to be an issue of fundamental importance in any democracy: commercial enterprises regulating and constituting the behaviour of citizens. Power is undoubtedly shifting away from the public legislator onto private actors who have pervasive control over the digital products and infrastructures that permeate contemporary life, whose exercise of that power need not be valid for it nevertheless to be exercised. Code can supplant law as the dominant normative enterprise, its processes of creation both hidden by veils of legal and technical inscrutability and guided by neoliberal ideas of unfettered 'innovation'.

As I suggested in the opening chapter, the legal academy has been somewhat reticent to move beyond or to evolve Lessig's seminal work on 'code as law'. Perhaps in line with the nature of the profession, lawyers often retain a kind of external perspective, talking simply of 'regulating', often without much appreciation for what this actually means in practical terms or reflection on whether the promulgation of more textual rules is the best way to address the elephant in the room, namely the question of whether and under what conditions the constituting, by code, of citizens' behaviour and action can in a democratic state be said to be legitimate.

Rather than each discipline sniping at the other from the outside, I have tried in each case to adopt an internal perspective that is necessary both to acknowledge the commitments of each domain, and for achieving a pragmatic synthesis of these into a starting point for practical application. There

---

[27] M Flanagan, DC Howe and H Nissenbaum, 'Embodying values in technology: Theory and practice' in J van den Hoven and J Weckert (eds), *Information Technology and Moral Philosophy* (Cambridge University Press 2008); B Friedman, 'Value-sensitive design' (1996) 3 *interactions* 16.

[28] Verbeek (n 1); J Schot and A Rip, 'The past and future of constructive technology assessment' (1997) 54 *Technological Forecasting and Social Change* 251.

is still much to be done of course, but the essential point is this: code must always afford citizens ways of resisting its heteronomy, both individually at point of execution, and ex post via the courts who, as the arbiter of last resort in a democracy, must themselves be able to exercise their function as guardians of the rule of law.

Bibliography

'About' *Inform 7* <http://inform7.com/about> last accessed 4 March 2021.

Abran A et al., *Guide to the Software Engineering Body of Knowledge (SWEBOK)* (IEEE Computer Society and Angela Burgess 2004).

Agre PE, 'From high tech to human tech: Empowerment, measurement, and social studies of computing' (1994) 3 *Computer Supported Cooperative Work (CSCW)* 167.

Agre PE, 'Conceptions of the user in computer systems design' in Thomas PJ (ed.), *The Social and Interactional Dimensions of Human–Computer Interfaces* (Cambridge University Press 1995).

Agre PE, *Computation and Human Experience* (Cambridge University Press 1997).

Akrich M, 'The de-scription of technical objects' in Bijker WE and Law J (eds), *Shaping Technology/Building Society: Studies in Sociotechnical Change* (MIT Press 1992).

Amazon, 'Amazon help: Set up your Dash Button' <https://www.amazon.co.uk/gp/help/customer/display.html/ref=amb_link_1?nodeId=201746340> last accessed 4 March 2021.

Anastasio M, 'EU governments support first set of laws for more repairable products' (EEB – The European Environmental Bureau, 13 December 2018) <https://eeb.org/eu-governments-support-first-set-of-laws-for-more-repairable-products/> last accessed 4 March 2021.

'Android developers guide – permissions overview' <https://developer.android.com/guide/topics/permissions/overview> last accessed 4 March 2021.

Angelova E, 'Microsoft embraces open source' (2018) *Fordham Intellectual Property, Media & Entertainment Law Journal* <http://www.fordhamiplj.org/2018/11/28/microsoft-embraces-open-source/> last accessed 4 March 2021.

Angwin J et al., 'Machine bias' *ProPublica* (23 May 2016) <https://www.propublica.org/article/machine-bias-risk-assessments-in-criminal-sentencing> last accessed 4 March 2021.

Arns I, 'Code as performative speech act' (2005) 4 *Artnodes* <https://doi.org/10.7238/a.v0i4.727> last accessed 19 April 2021.

Asscher L, '"Code" as law: Using Fuller to assess code rules' in Dommering E and Asscher L (eds), *Coding Regulation: Essays on the Normative Role of Information Technology* (TMC Asser Press 2006).

Association for Computing Machinery, 'ACM Code of Ethics and Professional Conduct' (2018) <https://www.acm.org/about-acm/acm-code-of-ethics-and-professional-conduct> last accessed 4 March 2021.

Austin J, *The Province of Jurisprudence Determined*, ed. WE Rumble (Cambridge University Press 1995).

Austin JL, *How to Do Things with Words* (Oxford University Press 1962).

Bailey B, 'Apple vs. FBI – what happened?' *Associated Press* (29 March 2016) <https://apnews.com/article/c8469b05ac1b4092b7690d36f3409a4a> last accessed 4 March 2021.

Bamberger KA, 'Technologies of compliance: Risk and regulation in a digital age' (2010) 88 *Texas Law Review* 669.

Bańkowski Z, 'Don't think about it: Legalism and legality' in Karlsson MM, Páll Jónsson Ó and Brynjarsdóttir EM (eds), *Rechtstheorie: Zeitschrift für Logik, Methodenlehre, Kybernetik und Soziologie des Rechts* (Duncker & Humblot 1993).

Bańkowski Z, 'Bringing the outside in: The ethical life of legal institutions' in Gizbert-Studnicki T and Stelmach J (eds), *Law and Legal Cultures in the 21st Century* (Wolters Kluwer 2007).

Bańkowski Z and MacCormick N, 'Legality without legalism' in Krawietz W et al. (eds), *The Reasonable as Rational? On Legal Argumentation and Justification; Festschrift for Aulis Aarnio* (Duncker & Humblot 2000).

Bańkowski Z and Schafer B, 'Double-click justice: Legalism in the computer age' (2007) 1 *Legisprudence* 31.

Barlow JP, 'A declaration of the independence of cyberspace' (1996) <https://www.eff.org/cyberspace-independence> last accessed 4 March 2021.

Barthes R, 'The death of the author' in Heath S (ed.), *Image – Music – Text* (Fontana 1977).

Bartoletti M and Pompianu L, 'An empirical analysis of smart contracts: Platforms, applications, and design patterns' (2017) arXiv preprint arXiv:1703.06322 <https://arxiv.org/abs/1703.06322> last accessed 4 March 2021.

Bates & Ors v Post Office Ltd (No 6: Horizon Issues) [2019] EWHC (QB) 3408.

Bayamlıoğlu E, 'On the possibility of normative contestation of automated data-driven decisions' in Baraliuc I et al. (eds), *Being Profiled: Cogitas Ergo Sum – 10 Years of Profiling the European Citizen* (Amsterdam University Press 2018).

Bayamlıoğlu E and Leenes R, 'The "rule of law" implications of data-driven decision-making: A techno-regulatory perspective' (2018) *Law, Innovation and Technology* 1.

BBC News, 'Sony slated over anti-piracy CD' *BBC News* (3 November 2005) <http://news.bbc.co.uk/1/hi/technology/4400148.stm> last accessed 4 March 2021.

BBC News, 'UK's internet use surges to new highs in lockdown' *BBC News* (24 June 2020) <https://www.bbc.com/news/technology-53149268> last accessed 4 March 2021.

Beck K et al., 'Manifesto for agile software development' (2001) <https://agilemanifesto.org/> last accessed 4 March 2021.

'Behat documentation' *Behat* <http://docs.behat.org/en/latest/quick_start.html> last accessed 4 March 2021.

Belli L and Venturini J, 'Private ordering and the rise of terms of service as cyber-regulation' (2016) *Internet Policy Review* 5.

Bench-Capon TJ and Coenen FP, 'Isomorphism and legal knowledge based systems' (1992) 1 *Artificial Intelligence and Law* 65.

Ben-Shahar O and Schneider CE, 'The failure of mandated disclosure' (2011) *University of Pennsylvania Law Review* 647.

Binns R, 'Analogies and disanalogies between machine-driven and human-driven legal judgement' (2021) 1 *Journal of Cross-disciplinary Research in Computational Law* <https://journalcrcl.org/crcl/article/view/5> last accessed 19 April 2021.

Black J, 'Critical reflections on regulation' (2002) 27 *Australian Journal of Legal Philosophy* 1.

Blichner LC and Molander A, 'What is juridification?' (Centre for European Studies, University of Oslo 2005).

Booth R, 'Facebook reveals news feed experiment to control emotions' *The Guardian* (29 June 2014) <https://www.theguardian.com/technology/2014/jun/29/facebook-users-emotions-news-feeds> last accessed 4 March 2021.

Bowker GC and Star SL, *Sorting Things Out: Classification and Its Consequences* (MIT Press 2000).

Boyle J, 'Foucault in cyberspace: Surveillance, sovereignty, and hardwired censors' (1997) 66 *University of Cincinnati Law Review* 177.

Bratton BH, *The Stack: On Software and Sovereignty* (MIT Press 2016).

Brodkin J, 'EU fines Microsoft €561 million for not giving users a browser choice' *Ars Technica* (6 March 2013) <https://arstechnica.com/tech-policy/2013/03/eu-fines-microsoft-e561-million-for-not-giving-users-a-browser-choice/> last accessed 4 March 2021.

Brown S, 'An agile approach to designing for the consequences of technology' *doteveryone* (13 February 2019) <https://medium.com/doteveryone/an-agile-approach-to-designing-for-the-consequences-of-technology-18a229de763b> last accessed 4 March 2021.

Brownsword R, 'What the world needs now: Techno-regulation, human rights and human dignity' in Brownsword R (ed.), *Global Governance and the Quest for Justice*, vol. 4 (Hart 2004).

Brownsword R, 'Code, control, and choice: Why east is east and west is west' (2005) 25 *Legal Studies* 1.

Brownsword R, 'Lost in translation: Legality, regulatory margins, and technological management' (2011) 26 *Berkeley Technology Law Journal* 1321.

Brownsword R, 'In the year 2061: From law to technological management' (2015) 7 *Law, Innovation and Technology* 1.

Brownsword R, 'Technological management and the rule of law' (2016) 8 *Law, Innovation and Technology* 100.

Bruch M et al., 'IDE 2.0: Collective intelligence in software development' in *Proceedings of the FSE/SDP Workshop on Future of Software Engineering Research – FoSER '10* (ACM Press 2010).

Bucher T, 'A technicity of attention: How software "makes sense"' (2012) 13 *Culture Machine*.

Bucher T, 'The right-time web: Theorizing the kairologic of algorithmic media' (2020) 22 *New Media & Society* 1699.

Buolamwini J and Gebru T, 'Gender shades: Intersectional accuracy disparities in commercial gender classification' (2018) 81 *Proceedings of Machine Learning Research* 1.

Burrell J, 'How the machine "thinks": Understanding opacity in machine learning algorithms' (2016) 3 *Big Data & Society*.

Buterin V, 'DAOs, DACs, DAs and more: An incomplete terminology guide' *Ethereum Foundation Blog* (6 May 2014) <https://blog.ethereum.org/2014/05/

06/daos-dacs-das-and-more-an-incomplete-terminology-guide/> last accessed 4 March 2021.

Buterin V, 'On public and private blockchains' *Ethereum Foundation Blog* (7 August 2015) <https://blog.ethereum.org/2015/08/07/on-public-and-private-blockchains/> last accessed 4 March 2021.

Caine KE, 'Supporting privacy by preventing misclosure' in *CHI'09 Extended Abstracts on Human Factors in Computing Systems* (ACM 2009).

Calo R, 'Code, nudge, or notice' (2013) 99 *Iowa Law Review* 773.

Campbell CM, 'Legal thought and juristic values' (1974) 1 *British Journal of Law and Society* 13.

Cardozo Blockchain Project, '"Smart contracts" & legal enforceability' (Benjamin N Cardozo School of Law 2018).

Center for Humane Technology, 'The problem' (Center for Humane Technology) <http://humanetech.com/problem/> last accessed 4 March 2021.

Chalmers M and MacColl I, 'Seamful and seamless design in ubiquitous computing' in *Proceedings of Workshop at the Crossroads: The Interaction of HCI and Systems Issues in UbiComp*, vol. 8 (2003).

Chen J, 'Linguistic relativity and programming languages' (2018) arXiv:1808.03916 [cs, stat] <http://arxiv.org/abs/1808.03916> last accessed 4 March 2021.

Citron DK, 'Open code governance' (2008) *University of Chicago Legal Forum* 355.

Citron DK, 'Technological due process' (2008) 85 *Washington University Law Review* 1249.

Clack CD, Bakshi VA and Braine L, 'Smart contract templates: Foundations, design landscape and research directions' (2017) arXiv:1608.00771 [cs].

Clark DD et al., 'Tussle in cyberspace: Defining tomorrow's Internet' (2005) 13 *IEEE/ACM Transactions on Networking (ToN)* 462.

Clarke R, 'Privacy impact assessment: Its origins and development' (2009) 25 *Computer Law & Security Review* 123.

Cohen JE, *Configuring the Networked Self: Law, Code, and the Play of Everyday Practice* (Yale University Press 2012).

Cohen JE, 'The regulatory state in the information age' (2016) 17 *Theoretical Inquiries in Law* 369.

Consumer Council of Norway (Forbrukerrådet), 'Deceived by design: How tech companies use dark patterns to discourage us from exercising our rights to privacy' (Consumer Council of Norway (Forbrukerrådet) 2018) <https://fil.forbrukerradet.no/wp-content/uploads/2018/06/2018-06-27-deceived-by-design-final.pdf> last accessed 4 March 2021.

Conti G and Sobiesk E, 'Malicious interface design: Exploiting the user' in *Proceedings of the 19th International Conference on the World Wide Web* (ACM Press 2010).

Coronavirus (Scotland) (No. 2) Act 2020.

Costanza-Chock S, *Design Justice: Community-Led Practices to Build the Worlds We Need* (MIT Press 2020).

Cranor LF and Wright RN, 'Influencing software usage' (1998) arXiv:cs/9809018 <http://arxiv.org/abs/cs/9809018> last accessed 4 March 2021.

Dan North & Associates, 'What's in a story?' (Dan North & Associates, 11 February 2007) <https://dannorth.net/whats-in-a-story/> last accessed 4 March 2021.

Davis JL, *How Artifacts Afford: The Power and Politics of Everyday Things* (MIT Press 2020).

Davis JL and Chouinard JB, 'Theorizing affordances: From request to refuse' (2017) *Bulletin of Science, Technology & Society* 241.

De Filippi P and Wright A, *Blockchain and the Law: The Rule of Code* (Harvard University Press 2018).

de Vries K and van Dijk N, 'A bump in the road. Ruling out law from technology' in Hildebrandt M and Gaakeer J (eds), *Human Law and Computer Law: Comparative Perspectives* (Springer 2013).

DiSalvo C, *Adversarial Design* (MIT Press 2012).

Diver L, 'Law as a user: Design, affordance, and the technological mediation of norms' (2018) 15 *SCRIPTed* 4.

Diver L, 'Computational legalism and the affordance of delay in law' (2021) 1 *Journal of Cross-disciplinary Research in Computational Law* <https://journalcrcl.org/crcl/article/view/3> last accessed 19 April 2021.

Diver L and Schafer B, 'Opening the black box: Petri nets and privacy by design' (2017) 31 *International Review of Law, Computers & Technology* 68.

Dizon MAC, 'From regulating technologies to governing society: Towards a plural, social and interactive conception of law' in Morgan HM and Morris R (eds), *Moving Forward: Tradition and Transformation* (Cambridge Scholars Publishing 2011).

Dworkin R, *Law's Empire* (Belknap Press 1986).

Edinburgh & Dalkeith Railway Company v Wauchope (1842) 1 Bell 278.

Edwards L, 'Data protection and e-privacy: From spam and cookies to big data, machine learning and profiling' in Edwards L (ed.), *Law, Policy and the Internet* (Hart 2018).

Edwards L, McAuley D and Diver L, 'From privacy impact assessment to social impact assessment' in *2016 IEEE Security and Privacy Workshops (SPW)* (IEEE 2016).

Edwards L and Veale M, 'Slave to the algorithm: Why a right to an explanation is probably not the remedy you are looking for' (2017) 16 *Duke Law & Technology Review* 18.

Endicott T, 'Law is necessarily vague' (2001) 7 *Legal Theory* 379.

Estrin T, 'Women's studies and computer science: Their intersection' (1996) 18 *IEEE Annals of the History of Computing* 43.

Ethereum Foundation, 'Ethereum Natural Specification Format' in *The Ethereum Wiki* (Ethereum Foundation 2018) <https://github.com/ethereum/wiki/wiki/Ethereum-Natural-Specification-Format> last accessed 4 March 2021.

Ethereum Foundation, 'Ethereum white paper' (Ethereum Foundation, 22 August 2018) <https://ethereum.org/whitepaper> last accessed 4 March 2021.

European Commission, 'Privacy and Data Protection Impact Assessment Framework for RFID Applications' (European Commission 2011) <https://ec.europa.eu/digital-single-market/en/news/privacy-and-data-protection-impact-assessment-framework-rfid-applications> last accessed 4 March 2021.

European Commission, 'Open Source Software Strategy' (European Commission 2019) <https://ec.europa.eu/info/departments/informatics/open-source-software-strategy_en> last accessed 4 March 2021.

European Commission, 'Proposal for a Regulation on a European approach for Artificial Intelligence' (European Commission, 2021) <https://digital-strategy.

ec.europa.eu/en/library/proposal-regulation-european-approach-artificial-intelligence> last accessed 23 April 2021.

European Commission, 'Shaping Europe's digital future' (European Commission) <https://digital-strategy.ec.europa.eu/en> last accessed 23 April 2021.

European Union Agency for Cybersecurity (ENISA), 'Guidelines for Securing the Internet of Things' (European Union Agency for Cybersecurity (ENISA) 2020).

'Exploring the dependencies of a repository' *GitHub Docs* <https://docs.github.com/en/enterprise-server@2.22/github/visualizing-repository-data-with-graphs/exploring-the-dependencies-of-a-repository> last accessed 4 March 2021.

Faraj S and Azad B, 'The materiality of technology: An affordance perspective' in Leonardi PM, Nardi BA and Kallinikos J (eds), *Materiality and Organizing: Social Interaction in a Technological World* (Oxford University Press 2012).

Federal Trade Commission, 'Android flashlight app developer settles FTC charges it deceived consumers' (Federal Trade Commission, 5 December 2013) <https://www.ftc.gov/news-events/press-releases/2013/12/android-flashlight-app-developer-settles-ftc-charges-it-deceived> last accessed 4 March 2021.

Federal Trade Commission, 'Internet of Things: Privacy and security in a connected world' (Federal Trade Commission 2015).

Felten E, 'Smart contracts: Neither smart nor contracts?' *Freedom to Tinker* (20 February 2017) <https://freedom-to-tinker.com/2017/02/20/smart-contracts-neither-smart-not-contracts/> last accessed 4 March 2021.

Flanagan M, Howe DC and Nissenbaum H, 'Embodying values in technology: Theory and practice' in van den Hoven J and Weckert J (eds), *Information Technology and Moral Philosophy* (Cambridge University Press 2008).

Flores F et al., 'Computer systems and the design of organizational interaction' (1988) 6 *ACM Transactions on Information Systems (TOIS)* 153.

Floridi L, *The Ethics of Information* (Oxford University Press 2013).

Floridi L, *The Fourth Revolution: How the Infosphere is Reshaping Human Reality* (Oxford University Press 2014).

Floridi L, 'Soft ethics, the governance of the digital and the General Data Protection Regulation' (2018) 376 *Philosophical Transactions of the Royal Society A* 20180081.

Fogg BJ, *Persuasive Technology: Using Computers to Change What We Think and Do* (Morgan Kaufmann Publishers 2003).

Forbes Technology Council, '14 predictions for the future of smart home technology' *Forbes* (12 January 2018) <https://www.forbes.com/sites/forbestechcouncil/2018/01/12/14-predictions-for-the-future-of-smart-home-technology/> last accessed 4 March 2021.

Fowler M, 'Business readable domain specific language' *martinfowler.com* (15 December 2008) <https://martinfowler.com/bliki/BusinessReadableDSL.html> last accessed 4 March 2021.

Franceschi-Bicchierai L, 'Hacked toy company VTech's TOS now says it's not liable for hacks' (2016) *Motherboard* <http://motherboard.vice.com/read/hacked-toy-company-vtech-tos-now-says-its-not-liable-for-hacks> last accessed 4 March 2021.

Freiheit J et al., 'Lexecute: Visualisation and representation of legal procedures' (2006) 3 *Digital Evidence & Electronic Signature Law Review* 19.

Friedman B, 'Value-sensitive design' (1996) 3 *interactions* 16.

Friedman B and Hendry D, 'The envisioning cards: A toolkit for catalyzing human-istic and technical imaginations' in *Proceedings of the SIGCHI Conference on Human Factors in Computing Systems* (ACM 2012).

Fuller LL, 'Positivism and fidelity to law: A reply to Professor Hart' (1958) 71 *Harvard Law Review* 630.

Fuller LL, *The Morality of Law* (Yale University Press 1977).

Gadamer H-G, *Truth and Method*, trans. J Weinsheimer and DG Marshall (Bloomsbury 2013).

García AC et al., 'PRIPARE privacy- and security-by-design methodology handbook' (EU FP7 2015).

Gardner J, 'Legal positivism: 5½ myths' in *Law as a Leap of Faith: Essays on Law in General* (Oxford University Press 2012).

Gartner, 'Gartner's 2016 Hype Cycle for Emerging Technologies identifies three key trends that organizations must track to gain competitive advantage' *Gartner* (16 August 2016) <https://www.gartner.com/en/newsroom/press-releases/2016-08-16-gartners-2016-hype-cycle-for-emerging-technologies-identifies-three-key-trends-that-organizations-must-track-to-gain-competitive-advantage> last accessed 4 March 2021.

Gavaghan C, 'Lex machina: Techno-regulatory mechanisms and rules by design' (2017) 15 *Otago Law Review* 123.

Gaver WW, Beaver J and Benford S, 'Ambiguity as a resource for design' in *Proceedings of the SIGCHI Conference on Human Factors in Computing Systems* (ACM 2003) <http://doi.acm.org/10.1145/642611.642653> last accessed 4 March 2021.

Geoghegan P, *Democracy for Sale: Dark Money and Dirty Politics* (Head of Zeus 2020).

Gibson JJ, *The Ecological Approach to Visual Perception* (classic edn, Psychology Press 2015).

Goldoni M, 'The politics of code as law: Toward input reasons' in Reichel J and Lind AS (eds), *Freedom of Expression, the Internet and Democracy* (Brill 2015).

Goldsmith JL and Wu T, *Who Controls the Internet?: Illusions of a Borderless World* (Oxford University Press 2006).

Golumbia D, *The Politics of Bitcoin: Software as Right-Wing Extremism* (University of Minnesota Press 2016).

Goody J, *The Logic of Writing and the Organization of Society* (Cambridge University Press 1986).

Goody J and Watt I, 'The consequences of literacy' (1963) 5 *Comparative Studies in Society and History* 304.

Governatori G and Sadiq S, 'The journey to business process compliance' in Cardoso J and van der Aalst W (eds), *Handbook of Research on Business Process Modeling* (IGI Global 2009).

Graham P, 'Beating the averages' (2003) <http://www.paulgraham.com/avg.html> last accessed 4 March 2021.

Grassl P et al., 'Dark and bright patterns in cookie consent requests' (PsyArXiv 2020) preprint <https://osf.io/gqs5h> last accessed 4 March 2021.

Grigg I, 'The Ricardian Contract' in *Proceedings of the First IEEE International Workshop on Electronic Contracting* (IEEE 2004).

Grimmelmann J, 'Regulation by software' (2005) 114 *The Yale Law Journal* 1719.

Gürses S, Troncoso C and Diaz C, 'Engineering privacy by design' (2011) 14 *Computers, Privacy & Data Protection*.

Gürses S and van Hoboken J, 'Privacy after the agile turn' in Selinger E, Polonetsky J and Tene O (eds), *The Cambridge Handbook of Consumer Privacy* (Cambridge University Press 2018).

Gutwirth S, De Hert P and De Sutter L, 'The trouble with technology regulation: Why Lessig's "optimal mix" will not work' in Brownsword R and Yeung K (eds), *Regulating Technologies: Legal Futures, Regulatory Frames and Technological Fixes* (Hart 2008).

Halderman JA and Felten EW, 'Lessons from the Sony CD DRM episode' in *15th USENIX Security Symposium* (USENIX Association 2006).

Hart HLA, 'Positivism and the separation of law and morals' (1958) 71 *Harvard Law Review* 593.

Hart HLA, *The Concept of Law* (2nd edn, Clarendon Press 1994).

Hartson R, 'Cognitive, physical, sensory, and functional affordances in interaction design' (2003) 22 *Behaviour & Information Technology* 315.

Hartzog W, 'Website design as contract' (2010) 60 *American University Law Review* 1635.

Hartzog W, *Privacy's Blueprint: The Battle to Control the Design of New Technologies* (Harvard University Press 2018).

Hartzog W, 'Inefficiently automated law enforcement' (2015) *Michigan State Law Review* 1763.

Hartzog W and Selinger E, 'The Internet of Heirlooms and Disposable Things' (2016) 17 *North Carolina Journal of Law & Technology* 581.

Harvey D, *A Brief History of Neoliberalism* (Oxford University Press 2005).

Hayles NK, 'Print is flat, code is deep: The importance of media-specific analysis' (2004) 25 *Poetics Today* 67.

Heidegger M, *Being and Time*, trans. J Macquarrie and E Robinson (Blackwell 1962).

Heras-Escribano M, *The Philosophy of Affordances* (Springer 2019).

Hicks A, 'The role of usability, power dynamics, and incentives in dispute resolutions around computer evidence' *Bentham's Gaze* (23 June 2020) <https://www.benthamsgaze.org/2020/06/23/the-role-of-usability-power-dynamics-and-incentives-in-dispute-resolutions-around-computer-evidence/> last accessed 4 March 2021.

Hicks A and Murdoch SJ, 'Transparency enhancing technologies to make security protocols work for humans' in Anderson J et al. (eds), *Security Protocols XXVII*, vol. 12287 (Springer 2020).

Hildebrandt M, 'Legal and technological normativity: More (and less) than twin sisters' (2008) 12 *Techné: Research in Philosophy and Technology* 169.

Hildebrandt M, 'A vision of ambient law' in Brownsword R and Yeung K (eds), *Regulating Technologies: Legal Futures, Regulatory Frames and Technological Fixes* (Hart 2008).

Hildebrandt M, 'Legal protection by design: Objections and refutations' (2011) 5 *Legisprudence* 223.

Hildebrandt M, 'Radbruch's Rechtsstaat and Schmitt's legal order: Legalism, legality, and the institution of law' (2015) 2 *Critical Analysis of Law* 42.

Hildebrandt M, *Smart Technologies and the End(s) of Law: Novel Entanglements of Law and Technology* (Edward Elgar Publishing 2015).

Hildebrandt M, 'Law as an affordance: The devil is in the vanishing point(s)' (2017) 4 *Critical Analysis of Law* 116.

Hildebrandt M, 'Algorithmic regulation and the rule of law' (2018) 376 *Philosophical Transactions of the Royal Society A* 20170355.

Hildebrandt M, 'Code-driven law: Freezing the future and scaling the past' in Deakin SF and Markou C (eds), *Is Law Computable? Critical Perspectives on Law and Artificial Intelligence* (Hart 2020).

Hildebrandt M, *Law for Computer Scientists and Other Folk* (Oxford University Press 2020).

Hildebrandt M, 'The adaptive nature of text-driven law' (2021) 1 *Journal of Cross-disciplinary Research in Computational Law* <https://journalcrcl.org/crcl/article/view/2> last accessed 19 April 2021.

Hildebrandt M and Koops B-J, 'The challenges of ambient law and legal protection in the profiling era' (2010) 73 *The Modern Law Review* 428.

Hoeren T and Pinelli S, 'Agile programming – introduction and current legal challenges' (2018) 34 *Computer Law & Security Review* 1131.

Hoffmann-Riem W, 'Legal technology/computational law: Preconditions, opportunities and risks' (2021) 1 *Journal of Cross-disciplinary Research in Computational Law* <https://journalcrcl.org/crcl/article/view/7> last accessed 19 April 2021.

Huldtgren A, 'Design for values in ICT' in van den Hoven J, Vermaas PE and van de Poel I (eds), *Handbook of Ethics, Values, and Technological Design* (Springer 2014).

IDC Media Center, 'The growth in connected IoT devices is expected to generate 79.4ZB of data in 2025, according to a new IDC forecast' *IDC Media Center* (18 June 2019) <https://www.businesswire.com/news/home/20190618005012/en/Growth-Connected-IoT-Devices-Expected-Generate-79.4ZB> last accessed 4 March 2021.

Ihde D, *Technology and the Lifeworld: From Garden to Earth* (Indiana University Press 1990).

Ihde D, 'The designer fallacy and technological imagination' in *Ironic Technics* (Automatic Press/VIP 2008).

Ihde D, *Ironic Technics* (Automatic Press/VIP 2008).

Ihde D, *Postphenomenology and Technoscience: The Peking University Lectures* (SUNY Press 2009).

Information Commissioner's Office, 'Investigation into the use of data analytics in political campaigns – investigation update' (Information Commissioner's Office 2018).

'Internet of Shit (@internetofshit)' *Twitter* <https://twitter.com/internetofshit> last accessed 4 March 2021.

Introna LD, 'Hermeneutics and meaning-making in information systems' in Galliers RD and Currie WL (eds), *The Oxford Handbook of Management Information Systems: Critical Perspectives and New Directions* (Oxford University Press 2011).

Jee C, 'Twitter wants you to read articles before you retweet them' *MIT Technology Review* (11 June 2020) <https://www.technologyreview.com/2020/06/11/1003333/twitter-wants-you-to-read-articles-before-you-retweet-them/> last accessed 4 March 2021.

Johnson DR and Post DG, 'Law and borders – the rise of law in cyberspace' (1995) 48 *Stanford Law Review* 1367.

Kaminska I, 'Growing scepticism challenges the blockchain hype' *Financial Times* (20 June 2017) <https://www.ft.com/content/b5b1a5f2-5030-11e7-bfb8-997009366969> last accessed 4 March 2021.

Katz DM, 'Quantitative legal prediction – or – how I Learned to stop worrying and start preparing for the data driven future of the legal services industry' (2012) 62 *Emory Law Journal* 909.

Kerr I, 'The devil is in the defaults' (2017) 4 *Critical Analysis of Law* 91.

Kesan JP and Shah RC, 'Setting software defaults: Perspectives from law, computer science and behavioral economics' (2006) 82 *Notre Dame Law Review* 583.

Kiran AH and Verbeek P-P, 'Trusting our selves to technology' (2010) 23 *Knowledge, Technology & Policy* 409.

Kitchin R and Fraser A, *Slow Computing: Why We Need Balanced Digital Lives* (Bristol University Press 2020).

Kittler FA, 'Protected mode' in Johnston J (ed.) *Literature, Media, Information Systems: Essays*, trans. S Harris (Psychology Press 1997).

Kline RB and Seffah A, 'Evaluation of integrated software development environments: Challenges and results from three empirical studies' (2005) 63 *International Journal of Human-Computer Studies* 607.

Kloza D et al., 'Data protection impact assessments in the European Union. Complementing the new legal framework towards a more robust protection of individuals' (DPIA Lab 2017).

Knuth DE, 'Literate programming' (1984) 27 *The Computer Journal* 97.

Koops B-J, 'Criteria for normative technology: The acceptability of "code as law" in light of democratic and constitutional values' in Brownsword R and Yeung K (eds), *Regulating Technologies: Legal Futures, Regulatory Frames and Technological Fixes* (Hart 2008).

Krajewski M, 'Against the power of algorithms closing, literate programming, and source code critique' (2019) 23 *Law Text Culture* 119.

Kranzberg M, 'Technology and history: "Kranzberg's Laws"' (1986) 27 *Technology and Culture* 544.

Krebs B, 'IoT reality: Smart devices, dumb defaults' *Krebs on Security* (16 February 2008) <https://krebsonsecurity.com/2016/02/iot-reality-smart-devices-dumb-defaults/> last accessed 4 March 2021.

Ladkin PB, 'Robustness of software' (2020) 17 *Digital Evidence and Electronic Signature Law Review* 15.

Ladkin PB et al., 'The Law Commission presumption concerning the dependability of computer evidence' (2020) 17 *Digital Evidence and Electronic Signature Law Review* 1.

Laiti O, 'The ethnoprogramming model' in *Proceedings of the 16th Koli Calling International Conference on Computing Education Research* (Association for Computing Machinery 2016).

Latour B, 'Where are the missing masses? The sociology of a few mundane artifacts' in Bijker WE and Law J (eds), *Shaping Technology/Building Society: Studies in Sociotechnical Change* (MIT Press 1992).

Latour B, 'The Berlin key or how to do words with things' in Graves-Brown P (ed.), *Matter, Materiality and Modern Culture* (Routledge 2000).

Latour B, *The Making of Law: An Ethnography of the Conseil d'Etat* (rev. edn, Polity 2009).

Latour B, 'Biography of an inquiry: On a book about modes of existence' (2013) 43 *Social Studies of Science* 287.

Latour B, *An Inquiry into Modes of Existence: An Anthropology of the Moderns* (Harvard University Press 2013).

Law Commission, 'Evidence in criminal proceedings: Hearsay and related topics' (Law Commission 1997) LC245.

Leawoods H, 'Gustav Radbruch: An extraordinary legal philosopher' 2 *Journal of Law and Policy* 28.

Leenes R, 'Framing techno-regulation: An exploration of state and non-state regulation by technology' (2011) 5 *Legisprudence* 143.

Leenes R and Koops B-J, '"Code" and privacy or how technology is slowly eroding privacy' in Dommering E and Asscher L (eds), *Coding Regulation: Essays on the Normative Role of Information Technology* (TMC Asser Press 2006).

Leiner BM et al., 'Brief history of the Internet' (Internet Society 1997) <https://www.internetsociety.org/internet/history-internet/brief-history-internet/> last accessed 4 March 2021.

Lessig L, 'The zones of cyberspace' (1995) 48 *Stanford Law Review* 1403.

Lessig L, *Code: Version 2.0* (Basic Books 2006).

Le Sueur A, 'Robot government: Automated decision-making and its implications for Parliament' in Horne A and Le Sueur A (eds), *Parliament: Legislation and Accountability* (Hart 2016).

Levy KEC, 'Book-smart, not street-smart: Blockchain-based smart contracts and the social workings of law' (2017) 3 *Engaging Science, Technology, and Society* 1.

Leyden J, 'Users protest over "creepy" Facebook update' *The Register* (7 September 2006) <https://www.theregister.co.uk/2006/09/07/facebook_update_controversy/> last accessed 4 March 2021.

Lin B, 'Software synthesis of process-based concurrent programs' in *Proceedings of the 35th Annual Design Automation Conference* (ACM 1998).

Lippe P, Katz DM and Jackson D, 'Legal by design: A new paradigm for handling complexity in banking regulation and elsewhere in law' (2014) 93 *Oregon Law Review* 833.

Livermore MA and Rockmore DN (eds), *Law as Data: Computation, Text, and the Future of Legal Analysis* (SFI Press 2019).

Lockton D, 'Architectures of control in product design' (2006) *Engineering Designer: The Journal of the Institution of Engineering Designers* 28.

Lockton D, 'Disaffordances and engineering obedience' *Architectures* (22 October 2006) <http://architectures.danlockton.co.uk/2006/10/22/disaffordances-and-engineering-obedience/> last accessed 4 March 2021.

London Economics, *Study on the Economic Benefits of Privacy-Enhancing Technologies (PETs)* (London Economics 2010).

Longford G, 'Pedagogies of digital citizenship and the politics of code' (2005) 9 *Techné: Research in Philosophy and Technology* 68.

Luger E and Golembewski M, 'Towards fostering compliance by design; drawing designers into the regulatory frame' in Taddeo M and Floridi L (eds), *The Responsibilities of Online Service Providers* (Springer 2017).

Luhmann N, *Law as a Social System*, ed. F Kastner et al., trans. KA Ziegert (Oxford University Press 2004).

Luhmann N, 'Self-organization and autopoiesis' in Clarke B et al. (eds), *Emergence and Embodiment: New Essays on Second-Order Systems Theory* (Duke University Press 2009).

MacCormick N, 'The ethics of legalism' (1989) 2 *Ratio Juris* 184.

MacCormick N, 'Reconstruction after deconstruction: A response to CLS' (1990) 10 *Oxford Journal of Legal Studies* 539.

MacCormick N, *Legal Reasoning and Legal Theory* (Oxford University Press 1994).

MacCormick N, *Rhetoric and the Rule of Law: A Theory of Legal Reasoning* (Oxford University Press 2005).

MacCormick N, *Institutions of Law: An Essay in Legal Theory* (Oxford University Press 2007).

McGeveran W, 'The law of friction' (2013) 2013 *University of Chicago Legal Forum* 15.

Mackay WE, 'Triggers and barriers to customizing software' in *Proceedings of the SIGCHI Conference on Human Factors in Computing Systems Reaching through Technology – CHI '91* (ACM Press 1991).

McQuillan D, 'Data science as machinic neoplatonism' (2018) 31 *Philosophy & Technology* 253.

Maier JR and Fadel GM, 'Affordance-based methods for design' in *Proceedings of DETC* (The American Society of Mechanical Engineers 2003).

Marino MC, 'Critical code studies' (2006) *electronic book review* <https://electronic-bookreview.com/essay/critical-code-studies/> last accessed 15 April 2021.

Marino MC, *Critical Code Studies* (MIT Press 2020).

Marshall P, 'The harm that judges do – misunderstanding computer evidence: Mr Castleton's story' (2020) 17 *Digital Evidence and Electronic Signature Law Review* 25.

Matassa A and Simeoni R, 'Eliciting affordances for smart objects in IoT era' in *Internet of Things: User-Centric IoT* (Springer 2015).

Mateas M and Montfort N, 'A box, darkly: Obfuscation, weird languages, and code aesthetics' in *Proceedings of the 6th Digital Arts and Culture Conference* (IT University of Copenhagen 2005).

Mattereum, 'Mattereum Protocol: Turning code into law' (Mattereum Project 2018) <https://www.mattereum.com/upload/iblock/784/mattereum-summary_white_paper.pdf> last accessed 4 March 2021.

Mayer-Schönberger V, 'Demystifying Lessig' (2008) *Wisconsin Law Review* 713.

Meldman JA, 'A Petri-net representation of civil procedure' (1977) 19 *Idea* 123.

Meldman JA and Holt AW, 'Petri nets and legal systems' (1971) 12 *Jurimetrics Journal* 65.

'Meltdown and Spectre' (2018) <https://meltdownattack.com/> last accessed 4 March 2021.

Merigoux D and Huttner L, 'Catala: Moving towards the future of legal expert systems' (INRIA 2020) <https://hal.inria.fr/hal-02936606> last accessed 4 March 2021.

Mezrich JL, 'Source code escrow: An exercise in futility' (2001) 5 *Marquette Intellectual Property Law Review* 117.

Microsoft, 'Visual Studio IntelliCode' (Microsoft 2018) <https://visualstudio.microsoft.com/services/intellicode/> last accessed 4 March 2021.

Microsoft, 'XML Documentation (Visual C++)' (Microsoft 2016) <https://docs.microsoft.com/en-us/cpp/ide/xml-documentation-visual-cpp> last accessed 4 March 2021.

Mohr R and Contini F, 'Reassembling the legal: "The wonders of modern science" in court-related proceedings' (2011) 20 *Griffith Law Review* 994.

Mortensen KH, 'Automatic code generation method based on coloured Petri net models applied on an access control system' in Nielsen M and Simpson D (eds), *Application and Theory of Petri Nets* (Springer 2000).

Moz, 'Google algorithm change history' *Moz* (2018) <https://moz.com/google-algorithm-change> last accessed 4 March 2021.

Mulligan DK and Perzanowski A, 'The magnificence of the disaster: Reconstructing the Sony BMG rootkit incident' (2007) 22 *Berkeley Technology Law Journal* 1157.

Murata T, 'Petri nets: Properties, analysis and applications' (1989) 77 *Proceedings of the IEEE* 541.

Murray A, 'Looking back at the law of the horse: Why cyberlaw and the rule of law are important' (2013) 10 *SCRIPTed* 310.

Nagy P and Neff G, 'Imagined affordance: Reconstructing a keyword for communication theory' (2015) 1 *Social Media + Society* 3.

Nakamoto S, 'Bitcoin: A peer-to-peer electronic cash system' (2008) <https://bitcoin.org/bitcoin.pdf> last accessed 15 April 2021.

Narayanan A et al., 'Dark patterns: Past, present, and future' (2020) 18 *ACM Queue* 25.

Nasser R, *Nasser/---* (GitHub 2020) <https://github.com/nasser/---> last accessed 4 March 2021.

Nemitz P, 'Constitutional democracy and technology in the age of artificial intelligence' (2018) 376 *Philosophical Transactions of the Royal Society A* 20180089.

New Zealand Government, 'Better rules for government – discovery report' (New Zealand Government 2018) <https://www.digital.govt.nz/dmsdocument/95-better-rules-for-government-discovery-report> last accessed 4 March 2021.

Noble SU, *Algorithms of Oppression: How Search Engines Reinforce Racism* (New York University Press 2018).

Norman DA, 'Affordance, conventions, and design' (1999) 6 *interactions* 38.

Norman DA, *The Design of Everyday Things* (MIT Press 2013).

Noyes K, 'Is Linux really harder to use?' *PCWorld* (2 August 2010) <https://www.pcworld.com/article/202364/is_linux_really_harder_to_use.html> last accessed 4 March 2021.

Oberle D et al., 'Engineering compliant software: Advising developers by automating legal reasoning' (2012) 9 *SCRIPTed* 280.

O'Hara K, 'Smart contracts – dumb idea' (2017) 21 *IEEE Internet Computing* 97.

O'Hara K and Hildebrandt M, 'Between the editors' in Hildebrandt M and O'Hara K (eds), *Life and the Law in the Era of Data-Driven Agency* (Edward Elgar Publishing 2020).

Ohm P and Frankle J, 'Desirable inefficiency' (2019) 70 *Florida Law Review* 1.

Olejnik L, 'Am I logged in or not? GDPR case study on the example of Chrome browser change' <http://blog.lukaszolejnik.com/am-i-logged-in-or-not-gdpr-case-study-on-the-example-of-chrome-browser-change/> last accessed 4 March 2021.

O'Neil C, *Weapons of Math Destruction: How Big Data Increases Inequality and Threatens Democracy* (Crown 2016).

Ong WJ, *Orality and Literacy: The Technologizing of the Word* (3rd edn, Routledge 2012).

Papadopoulos G et al., 'Statistics on small and medium-sized enterprises' (European Commission 2018) <https://ec.europa.eu/eurostat/statistics-explained/index.php/Statistics_on_small_and_medium-sized_enterprises> last accessed 4 March 2021.

Papert S, 'Different visions of LOGO' (1985) 2 *Computers in the Schools* 3.

Parkin S, 'Has dopamine got us hooked on tech?' *The Observer* (4 March 2018) <https://www.theguardian.com/technology/2018/mar/04/has-dopamine-got-us-hooked-on-tech-facebook-apps-addiction> last accessed 4 March 2021.

Pasquale F, *The Black Box Society: The Secret Algorithms that Control Money and Information* (Harvard University Press 2015).

Pasquale F, 'A rule of persons, not machines: The limits of legal automation' (2019) 87 *George Washington Law Review* 1.

Peachey K, 'Postmasters' huge step towards quashing convictions' *BBC News* (2 October 2020) <https://www.bbc.com/news/business-54384427> last accessed 4 March 2021.

Perez J, 'XYO game-changer: We've executed a smart contract with a drone!' *Medium* (21 November 2018) <https://medium.com/xyonetwork/xyo-game-changer-weve-executed-a-smart-contract-with-a-drone-4deb414af67b> last accessed 4 March 2021.

Petri CA, *Kommunikation Mit Automaten* (PhD thesis, University of Bonn 1962) <http://epub.sub.uni-hamburg.de/informatik/volltexte/2011/160/> last accessed 4 March 2021.

Philipps L and Sartor G, 'Introduction: From legal theories to neural networks and fuzzy reasoning' (1999) 7 *Artificial Intelligence and Law* 115.

Piekarski M and Wachowski W, 'Artefacts as social things: Design-based approach to normativity' (2018) 22 *Techné: Research in Philosophy and Technology* 400.

Pilkington M, 'Blockchain technology: Principles and applications' in Olleros FX and Zhegu M (eds), *Research Handbook on Digital Transformations* (Edward Elgar Publishing 2016).

Pols A and Spahn A, 'Designing for the values of democracy and justice' in van den Hoven J, Vermaas PE and van de Poel I (eds), *Handbook of Ethics, Values, and Technological Design: Sources, Theory, Values and Application Domains* (Springer 2015).

Porup JM, '"Internet of Things" security is hilariously broken and getting worse' *Ars Technica UK* (23 January 2016) <http://arstechnica.co.uk/security/2016/01/how-to-search-the-internet-of-things-for-photos-of-sleeping-babies/> last accessed 4 March 2021.

Pschetz L et al., 'Bitbarista: Exploring perceptions of data transactions in the Internet of Things' in *Proceedings of the 2017 CHI Conference on Human Factors in Computing Systems* (ACM 2017).

Radbruch G, 'Legal philosophy' in Wilk K (ed.), *The Legal Philosophies of Lask, Radbruch, and Dabin* (Harvard University Press 1950).

Radin MJ, 'Regulation by contract, regulation by machine' (2004) 160 *Journal of Institutional and Theoretical Economics (JITE)* 142.

Raz J, 'The rule of law and its virtue' in *The Authority of Law: Essays on Law and Morality* (Oxford University Press 1979).

Reed C, 'How to make bad law: Lessons from cyberspace' (2010) 73 *The Modern Law Review* 903.

Reed C and Murray A, *Rethinking the Jurisprudence of Cyberspace* (Edward Elgar Publishing 2018).

Regulation on the protection of natural persons with regard to the processing of personal data and on the free movement of such data, and repealing Directive 85/46/EC (General Data Protection Regulation) 2016.

Reidenberg JR, 'Lex informatica: The formulation of information policy rules through technology' (1997) 76 *Texas Law Review* 553.

Ribeiro MT, Singh S and Guestrin C, '"Why should I trust you?": Explaining the predictions of any classifier' (2016) arXiv:1602.04938 [cs, stat] <http://arxiv.org/abs/1602.04938> last accessed 4 March 2021.

Ricoeur P, *Interpretation Theory: Discourse and the Surplus of Meaning* (TCU Press 1976).

Robertson T, 'The public availability of actions and artefacts' (2002) 11 *Computer Supported Cooperative Work (CSCW)* 299.

Roose K, 'Is tech too easy to use?' *The New York Times* (12 December 2018) <https://www.nytimes.com/2018/12/12/technology/tech-friction-frictionless.html> last accessed 4 March 2021.

Royce WW, 'Managing the development of large software systems' in *Proceedings of IEEE WESCON* (Los Angeles 1970).

Russinovich M, 'More on Sony: Dangerous decloaking patch, EULAs and phoning home' <https://techcommunity.microsoft.com/t5/windows-blog-archive/more-on-sony-dangerous-decloaking-patch-eulas-and-phoning-home/ba-p/723452> last accessed 4 March 2021.

S.1084 – 116th Congress (2019–2020): Deceptive Experiences To Online Users Reduction (DETOUR) Act (4 September 2019) <https://www.congress.gov/bill/116th-congress/senate-bill/1084> last accessed 4 March 2021.

Salimifard K and Wright M, 'Petri net-based modelling of workflow systems: An overview' (2001) 134 *European Journal of Operational Research* 664.

Sapir E, 'The status of linguistics as a science' (1929) *Language* 207.

Scharpf F, *Governing in Europe: Effective and Democratic?* (Oxford University Press 1999).

Schlesinger A, 'Feminism and programming languages' *HASTAC* (26 November 2013) <https://www.hastac.org/blogs/ari-schlesinger/2013/11/26/feminism-and-programming-languages> last accessed 4 March 2021.

Schmidt A, 'Radbruch in cyberspace: About law-system quality and ICT innovation' (2009) 3 *Masaryk University Journal of Law and Technology* 195.

Schneier B, 'I've seen the future, and it has a kill switch' *Wired* (26 June 2008) <https://www.wired.com/2008/06/securitymatters-0626/> last accessed 4 March 2021.

Schot J and Rip A, 'The past and future of constructive technology assessment' (1997) 54 *Technological Forecasting and Social Change* 251.

Schot JW, 'Constructive technology assessment and technology dynamics: The case of clean technologies' (1992) 17 *Science, Technology, & Human Values* 36.

Schulz W and Dankert K, '"Governance by things" as a challenge to regulation by law' (2016) 5 *Internet Policy Review* <https://doi.org/10.14763/2016.2.409> last accessed 19 April 2021.

Scott C, 'Regulation in the age of governance: The rise of the post-regulatory state' in Jordana J and Levi-Faur D (eds), *The Politics of Regulation: Institutions and Regulatory Reforms for the Age of Governance* (Edward Elgar Publishing 2004).

Searle JR, *The Construction of Social Reality* (Free Press 1995).

Selbst AD et al., 'Fairness and abstraction in sociotechnical systems' (Social Science Research Network 2018) SSRN Scholarly Paper ID 3265913 <https://papers.ssrn.com/abstract=3265913> last accessed 4 March 2021.

Sengupta S, 'Private posts on Facebook revealed' *The New York Times* (28 January 2013) <https://bits.blogs.nytimes.com/2013/01/18/private-posts-on-facebook-revealed/> last accessed 4 March 2021.

Shah RC and Sandvig C, 'Software defaults as de facto regulation: The case of the wireless Internet' (2008) 11 *Information, Communication & Society* 25.

Share Lab, 'Immaterial labour and data harvesting' *Share Lab* (21 August 2016) <https://labs.rs/en/facebook-algorithmic-factory-immaterial-labour-and-data-harvesting/> last accessed 4 March 2021.

Sharkey N, 'Grounds for discrimination: Autonomous robot weapons' (2008) 11 *RUSI Defence Systems* 86.

Shatz SM and Cheng WK, 'A Petri net framework for automated static analysis of Ada tasking behavior' (1988) 8 *Journal of Systems and Software* 343.

Shay LA et al., 'Confronting automated law enforcement' in Calo R, Froomkin A and Kerr I (eds), *Robot Law* (Edward Elgar Publishing 2016).

Shay LA et al., 'Do robots dream of electric laws? An experiment in the law as algorithm' in Calo R, Froomkin A and Kerr I (eds), *Robot Law* (Edward Elgar Publishing 2016).

Shelley M, *Frankenstein: A New Edition for Scientists and Engineers*, ed. E Finn, D Guston and JS Robert (MIT Press 2017).

Shklar JN, *Legalism* (Harvard University Press 1964).

Shoikhedbrod I, *Revisiting Marx's Critique of Liberalism: Rethinking Justice, Legality and Rights* (Springer 2019).

Sileno G, Boer A and van Engers T, 'Towards a representational model of social affordances from an institutional perspective' in *Proceedings of the Workshop Computational Social Science and Social Computer Science: Two Sides of the Same Coin* (Institute of Advanced Studies, University of Surrey 2014).

Slow Research Lab, 'Slow Research Lab' <https://slowlab.net/about> last accessed 4 March 2021.

Smith A, *The Theory of Moral Sentiments* (2nd edn, Millar 1761).

Smith DJ, 'Changing situations and changing people' in von Hirsch A, Garland D and Wakefield A (eds), *Ethical and Social Perspectives on Situational Crime Prevention* (Bloomsbury Publishing 2004).

Stack Overflow, 'Developer survey 2020' *Stack Overflow* <https://insights.stackover-flow.com/survey/2020/> last accessed 4 March 2021.

Stahl BC et al., 'From computer ethics to responsible research and innovation in ICT' (2014) 51 *Information & Management* 810.

Storni C, 'The problem of de-sign as conjuring: Empowerment-in-use and the politics of seams' in *Proceedings of the 13th Participatory Design Conference on Research Papers – PDC '14* (ACM Press 2014).

Suchman LA, *Human–Machine Reconfigurations: Plans and Situated Actions* (2nd edn, Cambridge University Press 2007).

Sunstein CR and Thaler RH, 'Libertarian paternalism is not an oxymoron' (2003) 70 *University of Chicago Law Review* 1159.

Surden H, 'Values embedded in legal artificial intelligence' (University of Colorado Legal Studies Research Papers 2017).

Swartz P, 'The hack as form' in *Division III: Essays in Programs as Literature* (Hampshire College 2007).

Swartz P, 'How do programs mean?' in *Division III: Essays in Programs as Literature* (Hampshire College 2007).

Swartz P, 'A tower of languages' in *Division III: Essays in Programs as Literature* (Hampshire College 2007).

Swartz P, 'White boys' code' in *Division III: Essays in Programs as Literature* (Hampshire College 2007).

Swierstra T and Waelbers K, 'Designing a good life: A matrix for the technological mediation of morality' (2012) 18 *Science and Engineering Ethics* 157.

Tasioulas J, 'The rule of law' in Tasioulas J (ed.), *The Cambridge Companion to the Philosophy of Law* (Cambridge University Press 2019).

Tedre M et al., 'Ethnocomputing: ICT in cultural and social context' (2006) 49 *Communications of the ACM* 126.

'The Lean Startup | Methodology' <http://theleanstartup.com/principles> last accessed 4 March 2021.

Thompson C, *Coders: Who They Are, What They Think and How They Are Changing Our World* (Pan Macmillan 2019).

Tien L, 'Architectural regulation and the evolution of social norms' (2004) 7 *Yale Journal of Law & Technology* 1.

Tillman K, 'How many Internet connections are in the world? Right. Now' *Cisco Blogs* (29 July 2013) <https://blogs.cisco.com/news/cisco-connections-counter> last accessed 4 March 2021.

Twentyman J, 'IoT drives progress towards low-power technology' *Financial Times* (8 January 2018) <https://www.ft.com/content/f2b4de5a-d8ee-11e7-9504-59efdb70e12f> last accessed 4 March 2021.

Utz C et al., '(Un)Informed consent: Studying GDPR consent notices in the field' in *Proceedings of the 2019 ACM SIGSAC Conference on Computer and Communications Security* (ACM 2019).

Vallor S, *Technology and the Virtues: A Philosophical Guide to a Future Worth Wanting* (Oxford University Press 2016).

Van den Berg B and Leenes RE, 'Abort, retry, fail: Scoping techno-regulation and other techno-effects' in Hildebrandt M and Gaakeer J (eds), *Human Law and Computer Law: Comparative Perspectives* (Springer 2013).

Verbeek P-P, *What Things Do: Philosophical Reflections on Technology, Agency, and Design* (Penn State Press 2005).

Verbeek P-P, 'Materializing morality: Design ethics and technological mediation' (2006) 31 *Science, Technology, & Human Values* 361.

Vismann C and Krajewski M, 'Computer juridisms' (2007) *Grey Room* 90.

von Schomberg R, 'A vision of responsible research and innovation' in Owen R, Bessant J and Heintz M (eds), *Responsible Innovation* (John Wiley & Sons 2013).

W3C, 'The rule of least power' (W3C 2006) <https://www.w3.org/2001/tag/doc/leastPower.html> last accessed 4 March 2021.

Waddington M, 'Machine-consumable legislation: A legislative drafter's perspective – human v artificial intelligence' (2019) *The Loophole – Journal of Commonwealth Association of Legislative Counsel* 21.

Wagner RP, 'On software regulation' (2005) 78 *Southern California Law Review* 457.

Waldron J, 'The core of the case against judicial review' (2006) 115 *Yale Law Journal* 1346.

Waldron J, 'The concept and the rule of law' (2008) 43 *Georgia Law Review* 1.

Waldron J, 'Can there be a democratic jurisprudence?' (2009) 58 *Emory Law Journal* 675.

Waldron J, 'The rule of law and the importance of procedure' (2011) 50 *Nomos* 3.

Waldron J, 'How law protects dignity' (2012) 71 *The Cambridge Law Journal* 200.

Weber RH, '"Rose is a rose is a rose is a rose" – what about code and law?' (2018) 34 *Computer Law & Security Review* 701.

Weinberger O, 'The norm as thought and as reality' in MacCormick N and Weinberger O, *An Institutional Theory of Law: New Approaches to Legal Positivism* (Springer 1986).

Weiser M, 'The computer for the 21st century' (1991) *Scientific American* 94.

Weizenbaum J, *Computer Power and Human Reason: From Judgment to Calculation* (Freeman 1976).

Wexelblat RL, 'The consequences of one's first programming language' (1981) 11 *Software: Practice and Experience* 733.

'What is the Jupyter Notebook?' (27 March 2019) <https://jupyter-notebook. readthedocs.io/en/latest/examples/Notebook/What%20is%20the%20 Jupyter%20Notebook.html> last accessed 4 March 2021.

Whorf BL, 'Science and linguistics' in Carroll JB (ed.), *Language, Thought, and Reality: Selected Writings of Benjamin Lee Whorf* (28th edn, MIT Press 2007).

Williams J, *Stand Out of Our Light: Freedom and Resistance in the Attention Economy* (Cambridge University Press 2018).

Winch P, *The Idea of a Social Science and Its Relation to Philosophy* (Routledge & Kegan Paul; Humanities Press 1990).

Winner L, *Autonomous Technology: Technics-Out-of-Control as a Theme in Political Thought* (2nd edn, MIT Press 1977).

Winner L, 'Do artifacts have politics?' (1980) *Daedalus* 121.

Wintgens L, 'Legislation as an object of study of legal theory: Legisprudence' in *Legisprudence: A New Theoretical Approach to Legislation* (Hart 2002).

Wintgens L, *Legisprudence: A New Theoretical Approach to Legislation* (Hart 2002).

Wintgens L, 'Rationality in legislation – legal theory as legisprudence: An introduction' in *Legisprudence: A New Theoretical Approach to Legislation* (Hart 2002).

Wintgens L, 'Legisprudence as a new theory of legislation' (2006) 19 *Ratio Juris* 1.

Wintgens L, *Legisprudence: Practical Reason in Legislation* (Routledge 2012).

Wintgens L, 'The rational legislator revisited. Bounded rationality and legisprudence' in *The Rationality and Justification of Legislation* (Springer 2013).

Wittgenstein L, *Philosophical Investigations*, trans. GEM Anscombe (Blackwell 1968).

Wittkower DE, 'Principles of anti-discriminatory design' *2016 IEEE International Symposium on Ethics in Engineering, Science and Technology (ETHICS)* (IEEE 2016).

Wright A and De Filippi P, 'Decentralized blockchain technology and the rise of lex cryptographia' (Social Science Research Network 2015) SSRN Scholarly